The Age of
Sensation

By Herbert Hendin

Suicide and Scandinavia
Psychoanalysis and Social Research
Black Suicide

The Age of Sensation

Herbert Hendin

W · W · NORTON & COMPANY · INC · New York

First Edition

Library of Congress Cataloging in Publication Data

Hendin, Herbert.
    The age of sensation.

    Bibliography: p.
    1. Adolescent psychology. I. Title.
BF724.H43   155.5   75–19103
ISBN 0–393–01122–4

Published simultaneously in Canada
by George J. McLeod Limited, Toronto

Printed in the United States of America

1   2   3   4   5   6   7   8   9

For Jo, Neil, and Erik

Contents

Preface

AT A TIME when our culture is forced by its own turmoil to examine itself as seldom before, it seems clear that we need a basis for determining what effects our changing society is having on us, for seeing how it affects the way we live with each other, how it is forming and transforming us, and what we like or dislike about what we are and what we are becoming. Young people reflect social change most radically because they are partly its products. Through the lives, fantasies, dreams, and adaptive richness of college students in dealing with reality, I believe it is possible to identify what is changing in our culture and in all of us. I began this study in the political unrest of the late sixties, continued it through the crises over drugs and into the present so-called new materialism of students in an attempt to develop a psychosocial picture of what young people are like and why.

What is changing in young people has far deeper significance than any outward shifts in behavior. One can note the shift from concern for revolution to concern for careers, one can document statistically the dramatic rise in the suicide rate among the young over the past twenty years or the fact that increasing numbers of male students are seeking help for impotence. These are social facts. They do not tell us the inner feelings about life, sex, and work that are producing distress. Social facts are empty numbers unless translated into psychosocial facts that reflect the dynamism of life, the emotion behind the act, the cause for the statistic.

Culture is a two-way street, a flow between individuals and institutions, single minds and collective forces. What is often most interesting about a culture lies in the very tension between inner and outer experience. Psychoanalytic interviewing provides a method for developing the facts of inner life, the ways in which the culture is acting on the individual in the deepest recesses of consciousness. A question-and-answer technique even when conducted by a psychologically trained observer and even when the subject does not consciously wish to conceal information is of limited value because it usually reflects what the subject wants to feel, thinks he feels, or thinks he is expected to feel. In a psychoanalytic interview using free associations, unconscious reactions, dreams, and fantasies, the subject reveals his actual feelings often unawares. Yet psychoanalysis has shied away from utilizing the wonderful tool left by Freud for the study of contemporary society.

Part of the difficulty stemmed from the fact that Freud himself did not utilize psychoanalysis for that purpose. Naturally concerned with establishing the validity of his early psychosexual observations, to establish their universality he utilized fragments from other cultures. No attempt was made to provide perspective on how the differing adaptations of different cultures might have influenced not merely psychosexual development but the entire personality structure of the people of that culture.

Roheim's productive, imaginative, and influential studies of primitive cultures, rooted in the same approach, saw social institutions as projections of some stage of libidinal development at which the culture had been arrested. Eventually Heinz Hartmann incisively criticized this approach when he wrote, "Institutions that characterize a social system have often been interpreted solely as the direct expression of the unconscious and conscious desires of people living in that system, as if reality were not more than a wish fulfillment." But Hartmann's criticism led to another oversimplification. He went on to say that what was missing was an account of "the ways in which individuals are affected by institutions, and the ways in which they manage—or do not manage—to conform." Making this the crucial missing link reflects the view that culture and society are simply what the individual has to adjust to. They remain externals. There is in this interpretation no sense of the way in which society shapes the individual's perception of reality or contributes to anyone's total personality structure.

Erich Fromm's work provided a necessary and valuable statement of the impact of society on personality. Fromm described, for example, the "social character" needed under modern capitalism and then drew useful parallels between capitalistic practice and contemporary character attitudes such as the "exploitative orientation," and "the marketing orientation." Fromm was not interested in how society produces social character and undertook no psychodynamic exploration of the avenues along which the members of society learn, experience, and integrate what is expected of them. Since such experiences are as significant as any desired end, by ignoring the study of the individual, by neglecting psychodynamic integration, Fromm left idle the one remarkable tool the analyst has which the sociologist does not have.

Erik Erikson's work can be seen as an attempt to connect the inner and outer person in a vision of psychosocial man. He helped move psychoanalytic theory away from a purely instinctual psychology and into a much fuller conception of cognitive stages of ego development. But Erikson avoids dealing with those social forces in contemporary society that make it impossible for people to fulfill his developmental plan. In dealing with social institutions Erikson substitutes for Freud's stages of libidinal development his own schedule of ego development so that his approach has some of the same limitations as Roheim's. He attributed, for example, the greatness of the Sioux as warriors to the Sioux practice of beating children to teach them nursing behavior without biting, and of strapping them to cradle boards when they became enraged. According to Erikson, "the necessity of suppressing the biting rage contributed to the tribe's always ready ferocity in that this was stored up, channelized and diverted toward prey and enemy." The hypothesis is dubious since such practices could as well produce numbed, depressed, and passive people and something else is likely to have maintained the Sioux warrior tradition. In any case there is simply no way to connect such childhood experiences of the Sioux with the behavior of the adult tribe without psychodynamic evidence.

Erikson, however, has been wonderfully and beautifully skillful in using psychoanalytic studies of great men like Martin Luther to illuminate their life and times. He has stimulated an interest in psychohistory which often substitutes for a concern with the great man, a concentration on a significant event. Robert Lifton's work with the survivors of the Hiroshima bomb is a brilliant and moving study of the impact of the bomb on Japanese life. But a broader approach than the great man or the shared experience of a major event is required to study the multifaceted American society of today.

Abram Kardiner's work offers a potential approach. His studies of primitive cultures were the first to identify fully the unique contribution that psychoanalysis can make to an understanding of adaptive man. Certainly his work had a sense of the two-way flow between the individual and society and recognized the ways different societies could affect the formation of the "basic personality" of those living in them. Kardiner meaningfully interpreted religion and folklore not simply as projections of instinctual and ego stages of development but as representative and projective of the conflicts and preoccupations that a particular society generates in its individuals.

Kardiner's approach, however, contained unresolved methodological problems. In it the psychodynamic study of the individual is secondary to the formulation of a basic personality that can be hypothesized on the basis of social institutions. Kardiner used whatever case histories were available to him to confirm formulations he had made in advance. Partly this greater reliance on the inferred as opposed to the empirical derived from the fact that Kardiner himself was not doing the interviewing on which his studies were based. His studies of the Marquesan and the Tanalan cultures had no individual histories; the case studies for his work on the Alorese were obtained by the anthropologist Cora Du Bois through an interpreter. Such procedures can work with cultures so vastly different from ours but is of little aid in distinguishing between Western cultures or subcultures. Kardiner continued this approach in his study with Lionel Ovesey of racial oppression in this culture. Here the conclusions are presented by Kardiner first and Ovesey's excellent case histories are used primarily as documentation.

Apart from the predictable effects of such grossly observable practices as the institutionalized maternal neglect of children among the Alorese or the institutionalized racial discrimination in our culture, one does not really know the subtly operative social institutions in a culture except from the study of the individual. Sexual attitudes are not what a culture preaches or even practices, but what people feel about what they do or do not do.

The word *institution*, which suggests something external, fixed, and given, is itself misleading in a rapidly changing society. The social forces that help shape our lives are the operative feelings, values, and expectations that are so widely shared they come to define the condition of our being.

What I have attempted in the pages that follow is an open-ended psychoanalytic study of college youth in America. I have tried to identify the flow between young Americans and their society, to show how cultural forces are operating in the individual to make him what he is and how he is in turn reshaping his society. I hoped in doing it to get at the texture of emotional life in America through the psychodynamic study of actual lives. What was crucial was studying in depth a sufficient number of people to establish the dominant characterological traits and the operative social pressures influencing them.

The value of the psychoanalytic approach in social research is particularly evident with people who are not patients. In the pages that follow appear the lives of students who were not patients, but who were selected at random from the college population. In a series of interviews these students reveal the psychodynamic forces that actually shaped their lives.

People who seek help are not so different from those who do not become patients. Nevertheless, there is a prejudice that those who succumb to the pressures in a culture, whether by abusing drugs, becoming suicidal, or developing a neurosis are somehow different from the rest of the people in that society. To test this objection, in a study of culture, character, and suicide in Scandinavia I studied "nonpatients," using psychoanalytic techniques in a series of interviews. I found similarities between patients and nonpatients so persuasive that patients seemed to merely reflect, often in an enlarged and dramatic way, the pressures on everyone. When I came back to this country I refined and developed methods for the psychoanalytic study of the nonpatient in *Psychoanalysis and Social Research*. This present study draws most heavily on students who did not seek help, but who did not turn out to be so different from those who do. Students who are serious drug abusers and students in severe emotional crisis illuminate in exaggerated form the conflicts of all the students, although their ways of dealing with their conflicts are causing them far greater pain. Studying both patients and nonpatients can illuminate the ways people deal with pressures with and without help; it can provide a fuller spectrum of the emotional range operative among people today.

I selected fifty male and fifty female undergraduates at random from the entire student body of Columbia College and Barnard College and paid them each fifty dollars for completing five interviews. Only four of the students contacted chose not to participate, explaining that their interest in talking about themselves was outweighed by anxiety over what they might discover about themselves. The students who did participate became as easily involved in the interviews as students who were patients. Virtually all appreciated the chance to discuss themselves and most stayed in contact with me either because they wished help at a subsequent time or because they wanted to read what I had written about them. These attitudes also prevailed among two other nonpatient groups: student revolutionaries and nonpatient homosexuals, although both groups expressed suspicion of psychiatrists. The student revolutionaries who were leaders in the radical movement between 1968 and 1972 and those seen more recently were referred by each other and were seen on the same basis as the other nonpatient subjects. Four of the fifteen nonpatient homosexuals were seen as part of the fifty student male group selected at random and eleven others were referred by the original four.

I studied over one hundred students who were involved in drug abuse, seeing at least twenty students who specifically abused each of the four drugs discussed in detail, as well as another group of twenty students who were involved in a pattern of mixed drug abuse. Students who used drugs occasionally and students who did not use drugs at all were studied in similar detail and used as controls. Most of the drug abusers were men except in the case of amphetamines where seventeen of the twenty students were women.

At least twenty students were seen in each of the crises discussed, although over fifty were seen as part of the study of student suicide. Students in crises and students who abused drugs were seen as often as necessary to form an adequate psychodynamic picture of them; many in these two groups were seen in short-term therapy—several months to a year—when indicated.

All of the interviewing of all the students in the project was done by me. The one exception were the impotent students, of whom I saw only eight. The remaining twelve were seen by St. Luke's psychiatric residents, whose treatment of them was supervised by me as part of a special study. Psychological tests (Wechsler Adult Intelligence Scale, Rorschach, Thematic Apperception Test, Sentence Completion, Figure Drawing, and Word Association) were performed on all groups, including the nonpatients, and used as an independent check on the data derived from the interviews.

The four hundred students seen at Columbia University in the course of this project came from all over the country. They came from every major religious background and every socioeconomic class. In the course of the project I have also seen close to a hundred students from other major universities. From such observations and from discussions with colleagues, I believe that the trends being described are pervasive throughout the country.

Presenting the findings in the clearest possible manner presents special problems in a study in which many thousands of pages of case material must be condensed. The procedure followed has been to write up and analyze the individual cases in detail, establish the predominant trends, select representative cases for each group studied, and to try to condense and disguise those cases without sacrificing their basic content. I hope to have presented enough data to show how I arrived at my conclusions, and even enough for the reader independently to form his own.

As the first such study to be done of this culture using psychoanalytic techniques and relying on psychoanalytic interviewing to study patients and nonpatients, it is bound to have many shortcomings. A focus on an individual's problems often blurs a view of his or her strengths or assets. The situation is further complicated because one of the great strengths of young people today, shared by virtually all the students I saw, is the ability not to whitewash themselves, to be open about their fear of themselves and other people. As a result the conflicts and problems of young people sometimes emerge more vividly than their assets.

There is no better confirmatory evidence of what trends and themes pervade a culture than the national literature. In my past work, novelists and poets provided an invaluable complement to what had been discovered from the inner lives of individuals. For example, Norwegians are less driven than Swedes in their need for performance and achievement. This attitude is reflected in the Norwegian folk tales of Asbjørnsen and Moe, which are an integral part of Norwegian culture. Askeladden, the hero of the tales, is an idle dreamer who sits by the fire while his brothers work hard, but it is he who acquires wealth, power, and a princess as rewards for his goodness of heart. It is no accident that in Swedish folktales it is only the hardworking nose-to-the-grindstone brother who wins success. Similarly, American fiction over the past twenty years provides a fascinating reflection of the themes and preoccupations of people in this culture today.

The portrait of emotional life that took shape as I did this study showed a brokenness and unhappiness that re-

flect intense disengagement between people, the abrasiveness of sexual life, and the endangering of our power to
feel positive emotion or to feel at all. But to simply blame
the younger generation is to misunderstand the ways in
which the generations are linked in their problems, and
the degree to which a willingness to be unsentimentally
clear about one's fears can be a sign of strength. Many
young people do emerge from the conflicts described to
find a satisfying, productive, and loving life. But emotional survival is hard today and even those who deal with
today's turmoil with the least difficulty show scars of
battle.

In his brilliant essay *Civilization and Its Discontents*,
Freud asked, "What would be the use of the most acute
analysis of social neurosis since no one possesses the power
to compel the community to adopt the therapy?" For all
the pessimism implied in that question, Freud had an intense commitment to civilization, to the continuum of
human life on which his own work had an enormous impact. It is true that no one can compel a culture, or for
that matter an individual, to accept treatment. But the
pain, turmoil, and distress both of the individual and society can often drive people toward a willingness to solve
their problems and to seek some positive change. What
is crucial is the awareness of the point and pattern of personal and social distress. Doing this study has convinced
me that profound emotional distress is encouraged and
reflected in the social turmoil everywhere around us. Yet
I believe this turmoil is correctible if we recognize what
it is and where it leads.

Acknowledgments

A GRANT FROM the National Institute of Mental Health (MH 20818-02) made this project possible. A grant from the van Ameringen Foundation made possible the specific study of student drug abuse. Columbia University and St. Luke's Hospital granted me use of their facilities to see students and graciously facilitated my work in every way possible.

Williams and Wilkins Co., publisher of the *Journal of Nervous and Mental Disease*; Marcel Dekker, Inc., publisher of *The American Journal of Drug and Alcohol Abuse*; and the *New York Times Magazine* gave me permission to use material from articles of mine that originally appeared in those publications.

Because discussion of one's own culture is an emotionally charged, controversial process, it is more than routinely necessary to make clear that the constructive help I received from friends who are acknowledged below does not imply their agreement with my conclusions. I am particularly grateful to Ruth Easser, who read the manuscript in various stages of its development. She made valuable suggestions for its improvement which I have utilized to the best of my ability. I would also like to thank for help and advice with the manuscript: Martha Duncan, Aaron Esman, Robert Michels, Paula and Malvin Ruderman. I was fortunate to have the help at W. W. Norton and Company of George Brockway, Lisl Cade, and Sherry Huber.

Joan Schaeffer did most of the psychological testing of the students, often spending evenings and weekends to complete the work. Carole Bundy gave generously of her time to type the preliminary drafts and final version of the manuscript.

No group I have ever worked with moved me more than the students in this present study. I am grateful to them for sharing their experiences with me.

Josephine Hendin, my wife, was my collaborator in this study. She is concluding a comprehensive treatment of the contemporary mind as revealed by modern fiction. The cultural themes that emerge in this study were the product of continual discussion between us. Her inspiration was always in the direction of expanding and deepening the scope of this work.

PART ONE

Beyond Emotion

1 | **Beyond Emotion**

THE LIVES OF college students express with elo-
quence what it means to be alive in America today. For
the past six years I have studied students in acute personal
distress and others who were chosen at random from the
college population. Their lives are moving revelations of
the forces which are operating in this culture in the deepest recesses of personality. The new generation is this
culture's best barometer, registering its social unrest, its
conflicts, and its impact on the individual psyche. The
many lives that follow are a psychoanalyst's look at our
young men and women, at who and what they are, what
they feel, what they strive for, and what pressures move
them and us. The collective thrust of their lives points
toward one overwhelming fact: this culture is at war and
young people are in the front lines.

The war that is going on now is a war of qualities, of
difficulties in which there is no one who is not a casualty.
Some are the obvious victims: the suicide rate among
young men and women has risen more than 250 per cent
over the past twenty years. Drug abuse in the past two
decades has become a significant destructive problem on
college campuses and has now stabilized at an alarmingly

high level. Impotence is among the most frequent symptoms bringing college men to seek psychiatric help. But the casualties of this culture's stress and abrasiveness are not only those who come for help or wind up in hospitals. Young people today who are not patients find themselves increasingly driven toward the defensive maneuvers that can outwit depression, stave off impotence, or check rage.

Since I began this project I have seen students go from a concern with revolutionary politics to taking drugs, to getting into graduate and professional school. While from a distance these shifts seem to many people to point toward three different generations of students, in actuality they do not. I have seen the same student move at different times in each of these directions. The current concern with success has been called by many a sign of a return to fifties materialism, perhaps because we would like to believe that the unrest of the last ten years has ended and we can return to the relative tranquillity of the past. But the young person concerned with security now has more in common with revolutionary and drug-taking students than with young people of twenty years ago. Underlying violent protest, experimentation with drugs, and the pursuit of establishment success are the more profound changes that have occurred in people over the past twenty years and have transformed the young.

What has changed dramatically is the pitch of anger between the sexes. The openness, the casualness with which young men and women regard each other presents a picture of surface camaraderie that leads many people to believe we are ushering in an age of unprecedented sexual harmony. But in actual experience greater openness between the sexes often means greater openness about their fear and anger toward each other, and a general cynicism, disillusionment, and bitterness that one rarely found among the young twenty years ago.

With some frequency young men today speak of their relationships with women in terms of "ripping her apart emotionally" or "fucking up her mind." Some men withdrew from women to avoid having to deal with such feelings. Others were extremely passive with women, abdicating continually to their girlfriend's needs while inwardly seething. The extent of their anger toward women contributed to the impotence of many young men who saw themselves as "firing salvos" at women from a distance. This anger was expressed in its mildest form by the many male students who chronically belittled, put down, and criticized the women who cared for them.

Faced with such hostility from men, women look for means of protecting themselves. Yet the defensiveness of women students transcended the search for protection from male anger and was itself only one aspect of an attempt to live a life in which no man can make much of an impact. For most the fear of involvement was profound, pervasive, less a sexual terror than a fear of being totally wiped out, of losing the fight for self-validation. Many equated relationships with inevitable slaughter. One young woman who was a successful student dreamed of herself as a pregnant woman with a small child who was suddenly attacked and shot in the head by a man. She dramatized the widespread vision of women students that motherhood was the male attack on women, the lethal shot that ends your life. Most young women avoided real intimacy with a man, feeling that caring itself was self-destructive. Their lives were marked by the attempt to barricade themselves behind work, in casual sex, or in withdrawal from men entirely.

Relations between the sexes were often an uneasy truce between enemies. Men and women seemed to come together expecting little support or tenderness, and even when it was offered they were afraid to accept it. Most often both sides got even less than they expected, and the sense of letting each other down continually was pervasive. The determination of many women not to become involved, not to be drawn into feeling compassion, to suppress desires, and to be neither protected nor protective served as a weapon against all men, however they behaved. Similarly, many men were most critical and abusive toward the women who cared for them. Many needed women who could stop or check their anger, and women who could not, those who were most vulnerable, invariably were most hurt. One young man dreamed of continually beating up his girl in a boxing match while feeling amazement that she let him. Men, to put it simply, often felt caught up in a hostility they could not control; women felt overwhelmed by a vulnerability they feared was limitless. The fears of each drove them further and further apart and made their moments of connection explosive.

Work provided men with no surcease from combativeness, but was instead the most blatant statement of life as competitive war. The pitch of anger involved in life in this culture today is evidenced in the degree to which young men, whether or not they claim to value the competitive life, are haunted by feelings of being humiliated losers if they fail, or murderous fighters if they succeed. Fewer and fewer students can compete with any enjoyment. Many withdraw even from the sport that meant most to them because their pleasure was spoiled by conflict over winning or losing.

Many women students considered work the solitary

source of meaning in their lives. They were plagued by a sense of vulnerability that made them feel that only through fulfilling great expectations for academic or professional achievement could they win the right to be noticed or treated as a person. The more such students felt they had no right to feel or to be seen if they were not successful, the more they were enraged, conflicted, and driven about their work. To win the war against themselves some women took amphetamines to detach themselves from their anger and go on competing. Overwhelmingly used by women students, amphetamines were the drug they hoped would make them able to adopt the relentless, efficient, invulnerable style of competition they felt the world required.

Encapsulated in conflict over their individual lives, unable to come to each other for sustenance and support, young men and women are faced with having to deal with spiraling turmoil in every aspect of life. Over the past six years I have done studies of students in crisis over politics or drugs, students who felt chronically depressed or were suicidal, who were flunking out of school or were in conflict over their sexual lives, as well as a large number of students who were not patients. In many different ways and with remarkable adaptive variety they shared a common terror of themselves. The students I saw wanted to escape their own emotions, to blot out, space out, bury, or flee how they felt about their lives. Students in crisis in their more intense distress held an enlarging mirror up to the anger, pain, and turmoil other students experienced. Many on drugs hoped to find in the drug of their choice the means of altering the particular feelings that most terrified them. Nonpatient students joined both these groups in a sense that feeling itself is a danger and that life's best achievement would be the fastest, highest possible flight from emotion.

The students I saw tried many escape routes. The main ones moved in two seemingly different directions: one toward numbness and limited, controlled experience; the other toward impulsive action and fragmented sensory stimulation. At times the same student alternated between one and the other. To perform, but not to feel, to acquire sensory experiences without emotional involvement were hopes which reflect the consuming wish not to know or acknowledge one's feelings. Spaced-out is the contemporary metaphor for the extreme degree of emotional detachment apparent in both the benumbed and those who fled toward sensation. As the lives that follow will show, the flight toward detached sensation or a machinelike emotional numbness was a widespread maneuver designed to achieve imperviousness to the turmoil within.

What distinguishes this generation is its active pursuit of disengagement, detachment, fragmentation, and emotional numbness. For me and my generation, which prized commitment and involvement as the source of pleasure and satisfaction in life, alienation from self was seen as an evil to be fought and the source of endless unhappiness. Yet it does not signify this to young people today whose expectations from life are quite different from their parents', who see emotional involvement as the surest route to disaster, and who see fragmentation or detachment as the best means of survival. The voices, fantasies, and lives of these young people make it impossible to ignore the benefits they hope to derive from their pursuit and not to recognize that the quality of life in this culture has changed and has changed us along with it.

Is our technological society to blame for our condition?

Certainly this mechanized society is everybody's favorite villain, conventionally blamed for our depersonalization, our sense of ourselves as cogs in a wheel or robots. The specialization and increasing social complexity of our lives are also simplistically blamed for imposing the sense of fragmentation that pervades young people's lives. But the essence of fragmentation—the sense of life and relationships as a succession of experiences without meaning or purpose—is embraced by young people as a necessity, the means of concealing their own feelings and avoiding the emotions of others and of eliminating intimacy in friendship or sex. Nor is what troubles young people creeping mechanization. Many I saw wanted to be virtual robots. Feeling unable to cope with their emotions they would like the invulnerability and efficiency of an IBM machine. They wish they could switch themselves on and off. The same students who complain of being programmed by parents and schools are often attracted to the behavioristic utopia Walden Two. It is not the idea of being programmed that bothers them, but of being badly programmed. They *envy* machines.

The social and physical reality of our culture provides raw material for the imagery of our art, our dreams, our intellectual life. It is what people do with this raw material that tells us about both them and the significant forces in the culture. Machines do not make people mechanical any more than reaching outer space has made them space out. If outer space has entered the inner being of our youth as the most powerful symbol of their emotional distance, if a machine has become their ideal, the problem lies with the quality of life that is so full of pain and distress that people become irresistibly drawn to machines and astral distances from each other.

Kurt Vonnegut is a culture hero among the young because his work captures in a wildly imaginative way their daily ironies, problems, and solutions. In *Slaughterhouse-Five* Billy Pilgrim is the innocent who learns the benefits of detachment. People from outer space teach him the astral point of view: Some days we Tralfamadorians "have wars as horrible as any you've ever seen or read about. There isn't anything we can do about them, so we simply don't look at them. We ignore them. We spend eternity looking at pleasant moments—like today at the zoo. Isn't this a nice moment?"

Some of the students I saw dealt with their parents' or their friends' anger by tuning out and listening to imaginary music while they were being berated. One young man indicated his curiosity about his IQ score, which was routinely included in the battery of psychological tests he had taken. At the same time he would satirize IQs, telling me Spiro Agnew had an IQ of 135 and Raquel Welch had an IQ of 150. When the degree to which he used irony to hide what he cared about in his therapy and his life was pointed out, he replied that that was a talent he did not know he had, and now that he learned about it he would use it more. Many students fool themselves as well as others in the belief that not caring about what bothers them is the answer to what bothers them.

Does this technique work when you lose someone you love? It does for some students and it does for Billy Pilgrim: "The most important thing I learned on Tralfamadore was that when a person dies he only appears to die. . . . When a Tralfamadorian sees a corpse, all he thinks is that the dead person is in bad condition in that particular moment, but that the same person is just fine in plenty of other moments. Now when I myself hear that somebody is dead, I simply shrug and say what the Tral-famadorians say about dead people, which is 'So it goes.' "

Vonnegut conveys the protection afforded to people by cool, detached, uncaring resignation. He also captures the widespread sense of entrapment in painful personal situations, in one's own personality, and describes a way out through a fragmentation and distance that do not so much change the jail as alter the prisoner. Winston Niles Rumfoord in *The Sirens of Titan* goes into space to escape his cold-hearted wife. He encounters a phenomenon that fragments him to a stream of molecules waving between the sun and Betelgeuse and permits him to materialize on Earth only once every fifty-nine days, while he is permanently whole only on the remote planetoid Titan. Fragmentation is an ideal escape; distance makes survival (intactness) possible! Vonnegut's novels humorously capture some of the deepest wishes of young people and reflect the impulses behind the new mythology of detached sex.

Opening the body to sensory stimulation without intimacy or emotional involvement seems to many young people both the answer to the pain of close relationships and the most pleasurable possible use of fragmentation. Casual sex did offer some students satisfaction. Yet for most the complexities bound up in detached sexual encounters often served to reduce the pleasure and intensity of the physical experience and to create unrest over the destructive and self-destructive motives converging around casual or indiscriminate sexual involvement.

Drugs that heighten sensory awareness seem to some students the means to experiences larger than life. Many students initially took psychedelics believing they would be made able to make contact with other people in a freer, more open way. Yet those who remain with such drugs find they ultimately help them sever their connections with other people. Certainly psychedelics acquired a cult quality because they offered the promise of physical, sensory experience beyond emotion. As Timothy Leary wrote in *The Politics of Ecstasy:*

> The emotional human being is an evolutionary drug addict continuously and recklessly shoring himself up with adrenalin and other dark ferments. The way to turn off the emotions is to turn on the senses, turn on to your body, turn on to your cellular reincarnation circus, turn on to the electric glow within yourself and engage only in turn-on ego-games.

Leary's mysticism of cells and Ken Kesey's Merry Pranksters were the intellectual and pop underground versions of the will to make emotion irrelevant. If B. F. Skinner described a technology of behavior that could make feeling irrelevant through totally ordering and controlling experience, Leary and Kesey pointed the way to escape beyond emotion through the total abandonment of control and the greatest possible fragmentation.

Norman Brown and Herbert Marcuse provided the intellectual rationale for the fantasy of sensation and fragmentation as liberation. Using Freud's *Civilization and Its Discontents* as a starting point, they arrive at a utopian end to our social problems in the elimination of instinctual repression and the advent of a polymorphous, perverse sexual energy so fulfilling that it will free us of anxiety over death. It is not surprising that a generation that was into the psychedelic fragmentation of Timothy Leary and Ken Kesey, that developed vibrant music to blow the mind and liberate the senses, that made cult heroes of Yippies Abbie Hoffman and Jerry Rubin would make prophets of Brown and Marcuse, who provided a theoretic and intellectual base for the belief that living in the moment could be the greatest possible escape from the deadness in society and in oneself.

No one had difficulty recognizing the significance of the sensory escape, of living in the moment when it applied to blacks in the ghetto. Their refusal to postpone immediate gratification is easily traceable to the hopelessness and despair of their lives. Obviously the loss of hope, the lack of faith in the future experienced by white middle-class college students has not the same economic and social base. But they too increasingly feel a lack of control over life, are bothered by a sense of impotence, see life as a trap, and mostly by default come to feel that satisfaction means taking what pleasure you can while you can. No sensory acquisitiveness can change such basic despair.

To be a precise, flawlessly constructed machine or a mass of waving, sensing cells is a wish which reflects the common rejection of feeling, commitment, involvement. A culture that swings between the robot or the impersonal molecular flow will inevitably settle on death. One sees in many young people a vision of life as a grueling war of attrition with death. This is death as a daily experience; this is the routinization of mortality itself. The other side of their struggle to flee emotion is the daily necessity to bury their pain, their rage, and their deepest feelings. Life dominated by so much buried feeling comes to resemble and feel like death. Blurring the differences between life and death serves as protection and insulation against both.

But the price of such protection is often an unendurable woodenness. Many students who feel benumbed as the living dead attempt to use the flight into fragmented sensation to escape their constriction and to further blur the distinction between being alive or dead. Death, as Leary and others have said, is another arrogant ego trip. What is preferable is fragmenting the ego, becoming one with the molecular flow of the universe, and turning death itself into a sensation. The perpetual sense of death and rebirth through the LSD trip makes death seem less of a loss, makes life and death less real, less threatening. It is the penultimate way of getting beyond both mortality and emotion.

As the lives of students who are severely depressed and who make suicide attempts suggest, the fascination with death is often the climax of having been emotionally dead for a lifetime. How much life equated with death is life devalued is underlined by the risks taken and injuries suffered by many students with cars, motorcycles, or drugs. Such risk-taking invariably occurs in moods of depression, in which it makes little difference to the student whether he lives or dies. For a few students only the excitement of daring death produced a sense of life. Yet this is a sign of a capacity for emotion and pleasure already so damaged that it will only respond to the ultimate stimulus.

The sense of death penetrating life that moves through the dreams and experiences of many students I saw is carried to its most extreme statement in Thomas Pynchon's *Gravity's Rainbow*, where death personified seems to be the main character, and life, love, and civilization are a series of temporary accidents that befall him. Blicero, one of death's representatives, finally wishes to escape the cycle of human relations, the small destructions to be experienced between people, and to ally himself with the larger force of death. He sees in his literal disintegration the transcendence of the merely human power to suffer and to hurt, an escape from the chain in which "fathers are carriers of the infection of death, and sons are the infected." What Pynchon's fiction reflects is the feeling of so many students that their emotional death is so profound, their lives so benumbed, that life's purpose must be exactly the proliferation of destruction in all its many forms. What Pynchon carries to the final extreme of pessimism is the sense that today neither God nor man controls human activity or human feeling. It is now death that is seen as the prime mover, the source of the human relationships that increasingly seem bound on the wheel of destruction and self-destruction.

It is no accident that at the present time the dominant events in psychoanalysis are the rediscovery of narcissism and the new emphasis on the psychological significance of death. This culture is marked by a self-interest and egocentrism that increasingly reduce all relations to the question: What am I getting out of it? Nothing blocks involvement more effectively than a sense that anything felt or done for another person is a wearisome burden or that nothing is worthwhile that does not immediately result in some gain. Society's fascination with self-aggrandizement makes many young people judge all relationships in terms of winning and losing points.

For both sexes in this society, caring deeply for anyone is becoming synonymous with losing. Men seem to want to give women less and less, while women increasingly see demands men make as inherently demeaning and regard raising a child as only an unrelieved chore with no objective rewards. The scale of value against which both sexes now tend to measure everything is solitary gratification. The current concern with narcissism is clearly the outgrowth of the new types of problems we are witnessing.

It is also no accident that death as a motivating force

in human behavior is a major preoccupation. From a nation that has been described as death denying, we have become one that is death obsessed. For Freud there was a fairly even balance between the forces of death and life. But for contemporary writers as brilliant as Ernest Becker the struggle with death is seen as the ultimate mover of all human behavior. The concern with death and narcissism are two aspects of the flight from emotion, they are alternations between the flight toward numbness or sensation. Preoccupation with death comes from the burial of feeling; sensation can be used to overcome subjective death feelings. But death is also the ultimate blow to everyone's narcissism, and a culture that is into life as pure gratification is bound to find death an enormous stumbling block.

As deadness has always contained the rage of poor blacks, so deadness and numbness serve to contain the buried rage of the students I saw. As numbness has been broken by eruptions into overt violence in the ghetto, so is the constriction of students broken by eruptions of cruelty, violence, and death. But middle-class rage erupts more often into fantasy and fascination with violence than into literal riots.

Students seek out reruns of films like *El Topo* or *Night of the Living Dead* and often get stoned to watch them to be able to enjoy with the protection of detachment, the spectacles they offer of blood, dismemberment, and zombies. Films like *A Clockwork Orange* appeal to many because they are sophisticated about automatic, heartless violence done smoothly to the tune of "Singing in the Rain." The audience identifies with both the experience of being brutalized and the recognition of being able to brutalize without emotion. Yet such films imply that as victim or perpetrator it is better not to have an emotional center, but preferably a heart as halfway between the organic and inorganic as a mechanical orange. *The Exorcist,* with its voice of hate from beyond the grave, its image of an innocent but murderous child held helpless in the grip of a fury she cannot control, reflects the sense many people share of being trapped in anger.

Engulfing emotion, the free and uninhibited hate of the demon within is the unfaceable demon for many people today. In reflecting the nexus of anger, pain, and destructiveness films and fiction serve to turn what infects our lives into an entertainment, a removed spectacle that can be watched with the recognition and detachment of moviegoers. What they offer is the oblique experience of ourselves.

Emotion—direct, personal, raw—has become the new taboo. Social criticism, which should help us gain perspective on what is happening, seems itself to be in flight from the emotions of our time and the lives people are living. How else to explain the degree to which writers as distinguished as Talcott Parsons and Erik Erikson see nothing particularly disturbing in the quality of life in America today.

Erikson and Parsons assure us that our youth is in no more distress than in past generations and base their conclusion on the feeling that the same percentage now as in the past accepts the values and challenges of society. Parsons sees most of our youth as accepting the dominant value of our culture, that is, the individual actively pursues achievement while feeling himself the instrument of the general social welfare ("instrumental activism"). Clinical observations of the egocentrism rampant in youth today, the urge to get what one can with minimal effort and little regard for others would seem to contradict this thesis. Even if it were true, it ignores the inner feelings of youth about their lives, what Kenneth Keniston has called "the double consciousness" that enables them to go through the motions of adult life without commitment to it.

Erikson sees the turmoil of college students as but a phase in a search for identity in which many roles are played. Certainly there is a provisional and experimental quality to much that young people do. But the underlying detachment and fragmentation that unites politically or vocationally committed youth to dropouts or drug abusers is not proving transitory. If anything, the values and attitudes of youth are having increasing influence on their parents. Nor do increasing numbers of young people want the sameness, the continuity, the unity of personality that Erikson sees as the cornerstone of identity. It is probably more accurate to say that young people are in flight from identity, from what they see as the trap of involvement and commitment. "Confusion about identity" is an abstract way of saying that people are out of touch with their feelings. Confusion about who you are is always at root a confusion about what you feel about people, life and work. Far from being an adolescent quest for self, disorder is as much the mark of young adults. Whether or not they accept social goals in their twenties and thirties, their adult lives are marked by a detachment and fragmentation that tells us their unrest is far from transitory.

The romantic idealization of youth that characterized so much of what has been written about them in the past decade in such books as Charles Reich's *The Greening of America*—the vision of young people as having a unique freedom and joy in living that simply is not borne out by knowing them—says more about the dissatisfaction with life of the older generation than it does of the joy of the younger. James Kunen, writing *The Strawberry Statement* as a Columbia student, put the situation in better perspective: "My friends and I became preoccupied with the common nostalgic assertion that 'these are the best years of your lives.' We could accept the fact that the college years are exhausting, confusing, boring, troubled, frustrated and meaningless—that we could take in stride; we'd seen hard times before. But that everything subsequent would be worse was a concept difficult to grasp and, once grasped, impossible to accept."

An unromanticized vision of youth is not a pessimistic one, but rather one that acknowledges their relation to us, their literal and psychological kinship with the past and larger social present. Failure to recognize this kinship can lead to the misguided idealization of one generation at the expense of the other. Keniston's romantic idealization of *Young Radicals* was possible because he believed "many young Americans feel toward their parents a sympathy, a compassion, and a pity that most of us can feel only toward that from which we feel ultimately detached; and with this sympathy goes a strong sense—an implicit realization on the part of *both* parents *and* children that the way parents conducted their lives may be neither good nor bad for their children, but simply irrelevant." Study of the lives of young people reveals that behind such feelings lie pain and rage, the sense of having been treated by their parents as irrelevant themselves.

As Bruno Bettelheim put it in a sensitive paper on the problem of the generations, "whenever the older generation has lost its bearings, the younger generation is lost with it." If youth were as free of their parents as Reich or Keniston would have us believe, we would be absolved of having passed on to them what we may dislike most about ourselves and our lives. Moreover, we might even look to youth, as Reich did, for the way to save ourselves. This is a kind of false use of the young, an optimism based on such thorough denial of the ways in which the present and past are inevitably connected that it is doomed to fail. Now that it has, it is not we who are to blame, but again youth for giving up the revolution and moving into a "new materialism." Recognizing the ways in which our young are bound to us is the necessary first step toward freedom from our demons and theirs.

The most remarkable of Freud's many astonishing contributions was the tool of psychoanalysis itself, the means of penetrating what was actually occurring in an individual mind and of establishing the impact of one generation on the next. Analytic study of the lives of students today reflects how much they feel trapped by society, by their own past, and perhaps most by their own personalities. All had extraordinary difficulty in dealing with their own feelings and the facts of emotional life in this culture. How to face the many competitive situations in college when competition is intolerable? Why is it intolerable? How to live with a man or woman when closeness is terrifying? Why should intimacy terrify?

Students resort to a variety of ways in dealing with or in fleeing from the emotions that torment them: Some students flunked out of college, others drove themselves to achieve better and better grades; some collapsed into an extreme dependency, others pushed themselves into independence and denied they needed anyone at all. Some avoided what they saw as threatening involvements with

men and women, others engaged in a series of pleasure-
less relationships that were equally designed to protect
them from involvement. But all these students faced with
dread the emotional facts of their own lives.

Virtually no one grows up in this culture today without deep and painful conflicts over involvement and commitment. Even those who are dealing best with life show
the numbness and pleasurelessness of the general flight
from emotion. Men and women are equally affected in a
culture that makes it hard to be either. The next three
chapters explore the lives of men and women who were
chosen at random from the college population. They are
young people struggling in a sexuality that was never under greater stress; they are young people from all over the
country who are the individual faces of social distress.

PART TWO

Chosen at Random

2

Don't Get
Slaughtered

VULNERABILITY IN EVERY corner of life is the
fury most young women I saw are trying to escape. Drawn
at random from the college population, bright, lively young
people, these women saw life as a series of dangers they
wanted to avoid. They had grown up after the sexual revolution; independence in work was a common goal. They
did not politicize their situation as women nor define male
oppression as the social factor they must overcome. Nor did
they focus on the damage done to them in girlhood, though
many had gone through painful childhoods. What they
pursued with all their available energy was an emotion-
free oasis where neither love, nor anger, nor depression
could touch them.

Many women who were profoundly troubled began our
initial interview by telling me that they were thoroughly
pleased with their lives. "I'm happy at college; I'm the
oldest child, which is the best position in the family, and
I have a wonderful family," said one student. "I'm abnormally normal, thanks to an incredible family life," began another. Yet these declarations reflected less their

actual feelings than their determination not to be or even seem conflicted, confused, or depressed about anything. "If you act happy, you'll be happy!" insisted one student. "I painted my room a bright yellow so as not to seem depressed," said another. These women take great pains to appear confident and totally in charge of their lives in the hope that they can become the roles they play. What they often achieve is a distance from the sources of their own unhappiness so great that some would begin to cry without knowing why while they told me about the lives they said were perfect.

Young women often buried their unhappiness behind a show of self-confidence, certainty, and invulnerability. Although their judgments of what was possible for them in life were far from optimistic, at twenty they were sure there were no other alternatives for them. "This is the way I am, this is the way life has been; this is the way it will be," they insisted. Set in their expectations, they had little willingness to live with uncertainty. They were determined to be sure chance would play no part in their future.

These young women had little actual confidence in their ability to deal with the unguarded, unchecked flow of experience. Their sense of being unable to shape their own lives in the rough and tumble of an intense affair or a risky career forced them to walk a narrow path that allowed no deviation. They were determined not to get hurt, not to fall into what many saw as the deception of marriage and the snare of motherhood they regarded as the final seal on the marital trap. They saw any deep involvement with men as inevitably destructive. They admired women who seemed in control of their men or women who took their involvements casually. Some avoided anything but casual dating, insisting that any sexual or romantic attachment means inevitable pain. Most preferred friendships with occasional sex to the intense intimacy of love. Yet the attempt to remain emotionally detached in or out of sex was the other side of the fear that being deeply involved meant being "slaughtered." Men were not political enemies for these young women. Nor were they sexual tools. They were not exactly people either. Relations with men were the battleground on which these young women fought against their own vulnerability.

Work as the barrier against need, as the testing ground of individual worth, as the best defensive weapon was very much in the minds of these young women. Those who were unable to form strong interest in a career were tormented, believing that they would be doomed to wretched and unhappy lives. Given an assignment in a French class to describe how she saw her life in ten years, one such sophomore wrote two versions: in one she was single, happy, and pursuing a career she liked. In the other she was trapped by yowling children and miserably married. She was typical in her feeling that life divided between unencumbered happiness at work and total self-destruction in motherhood and marriage. She quietly predicted that she would have the worse fate because she had no strong work interest to shield her.

The self-protective significance of work was dramatized by the many women I saw who used it to forge an emotional armor. Even success in demanding majors did not give them the confidence to feel they could enter into any intimate relationship with a man, set limits, and happily survive. As a result their vigilance was relentless; they remained on perpetual alert against anything that might interfere with the work to which they tied their entire emotional lives.

Ellen, a college senior committed to law, began her story by saying that she might have a prejudiced view of herself, that others might see her differently, but that she had a certain position and that was the way she was. This instant defensiveness, this warning not to challenge her life reflected the degree to which she had barricaded herself and the vulnerability she had tried to bury. She said she had been unhappy and insecure in high school, but had since learned how to seem self-assured and was now determined to be happy. By way of example, she told me that when lost on the subway she held her head high, acted like she knew where she was going, and could look as confident as anyone else.

On another occasion she spoke of helping a crippled man in a wheelchair through the underground passages at school, how anguished the man had been, how unable to ask for help, and how miserable he was at needing it. She was terribly pained by the incident and it was clear that she identified with the man and saw herself as crippled and unwilling to admit her need for help.

Ellen put her hopes for the future entirely in her success at college and her aspirations for law school. While her achievements might have been a genuine source of confidence for her, she had so little belief that emotional ties could be anything but disastrous that she was not encouraged by her achievements to enlarge her life. Instead she used her success to justify not getting involved with any man, insisting that any romantic or sexual involvement would stop her career. She said her younger sister would go over to her boyfriend's apartment at midnight if he called and Ellen felt her time was as important as any man's and "why should he assume I will come over!" Her sense that being involved herself would mean running over on command regardless of her feelings dominated her perception not merely of love, but of all human relations. How to explain such pessimism?

Ellen had been a virtual Cinderella in a family where there was perpetual war between her parents, broken only when her father retreated into his den to work or read. She was the oldest and brightest of four children. Her father, who was otherwise aloof, responded to her academic achievements and preferred her to the others, even if at a distance. His preference infuriated her mother, who made Ellen's life at home miserable. She had to do all the chores in the house while her sisters did nothing. Her mother bought them new clothes and her none. She had recently bought new luggage for her two sisters, but none for Ellen. Ellen did not want to acknowledge her mother's feeling and said her mother probably forgot the luggage.

Ellen handled her anger and pain by magically severing herself from her emotions. Her refusal to become involved with a man was bound up with the general withdrawal from emotional closeness that marked her life. Her dreams suggested the magical quality of her burial of feeling. This past summer while working in a bank, she had been falsely accused by an older woman of lying in connection with a telephone message. Ellen walked away from the situation without answering—something she usually did when she was angry. When back at school, she had a dream in which she told her roommate she could not stand the way the woman was behaving to her, but then said that she had to purge herself of her sins. She and her roommate took a pot and went walking in the woods until they found a brook called Ribbl-Bibbl. She threw the pot in a big sweeping motion into the brook and then she felt much better.

Ellen said she has learned to walk away from any angry situation and to feel that "you can never change people, so what's the use," from her relationship with her mother, "who just ignores anything you say and talks right on past you." Her father also handled her mother by not answering back. The profoundness of Ellen's vulnerability was expressed in this and other dreams in which she rid herself of anger through magic words, gestures, or incantations which did not express her rage but somehow washed it away. Ellen's dreams also suggested that her mother's anger, however unjustified, caused her to feel sinful and guilty. Her magical words were ways of purging herself of both her guilt and her rage.

Ellen was grimly determined to please her parents. She unconsciously appeased her mother, who was puritanical in her sexual attitudes, by avoiding sexual involvement. Her sisters, who got along better with her mother, were not so bound by her restrictions. She succeeded in pleasing her father by her achievements at school, but was frustrated that her relationship with him was at a distance. She dreamed that her father was supposed to be watching her five-year-old brother. Instead he was reading the paper and her brother fell off the cliffs at the back of their house. At first they thought he broke his neck or was paralyzed, but he turned out to be just numb.

Although Ellen was critical of her father's lack of interest in her brother, she also identified with her brother and had felt comparably hurt. She too had managed to survive, although at the price of emotional numbness. She mentioned again the incident in which she helped the crippled man and how much she felt for him. Numbed and paralyzed by a lifetime of rejection and aloofness, Ellen was now routinely following the rules set by each parent and working hard to get the little she could from them.

Ellen was quite alarmed at the prospect of any change in her life. She was determined to hold her ground, feeling she could only do so and get through law school by avoiding any romantic involvement. Actually the one young man she had liked at college and who was fond of her was very encouraging about her legal career, but Ellen could not trust her own assessment of him or any man.

Ellen's involvement in our sessions caused her some apprehension that was reflected in a dream. She and her family were all upstairs, while downstairs the house was dark and some man was knocking at the door. He looked evil and they looked out the window at first and did not answer. Finally they decided to let him in, and he came in and a number of other evil-looking people came in and these people wanted to change things in the house. Ellen became alarmed and decided to call the police. The phone that she used downstairs only rang in her room upstairs and was not reaching outside. Ellen started blaming the house, saying she always knew they should have sold it and that she had never wanted to live in it. Then the man ripped the phone out of the wall.

Ellen saw me as the man she had let into her house and into her life. She spoke of the apprehension she had about changing any of her defenses. While critical of her house in the dream, in fact she and her father liked the house and it was her mother who always criticized her father for liking it and not selling it. Ellen was afraid that becoming involved with anyone would unleash her anger and discontent. She has kept her feelings to herself—in her dream her phone rings only in her own room and has no outside connection. While the image of my ripping the phone out of the wall reflected her anxiety about our sessions coming to an end, she was also quite relieved since she feared that if she let one man be close to her, it would open her up to others.

Self-protection was the driving force in Ellen's life, manifesting itself in her attempts to close off her feelings and in her use of work as a shield. Many students have experienced the early rejection Ellen had and have been left with a feeling of their unlovability and a dread of any closeness. While most do not avoid attachments as completely as Ellen, they tend to pull back from them when they threaten to become intense. Their conflict is even more sharply focused when they have no strong work interest to protect them.

Unlike Ellen, Diana is unable to involve herself with work or to use it as a protective barricade. Her parents had never taken her education seriously and sent her to "a good college to meet a more suitable husband." Diana reflected their attitude toward her work. While she had now in her junior year developed some interest in history she said it was too late, that her grades during her first two years were so bad she could never get into graduate school. This attitude reflected her general sense that events in the past have permanently damaged her.

Attractive and vivacious, Diana had an active social life which excluded the possibility of a close attachment. When I met her she was in the process of ending a relationship because she had begun to care more for the man than she felt was safe. She was sure that any man who got to know her well would find her unlovable. A sense of basic unlovability had been with her since childhood and sprung from her feeling that had she been desirable her parents would not have treated her as they did. She had been alternately given out to board with another family or had been watched by housekeepers. She told herself that economic necessity—her mother and father worked together—had dictated her abandonment and was solely responsible for her unhappiness as a child. She nevertheless began to cry when she said that her younger brother was never sent away. To this day she was concerned that her mother should not know how unhappy she had been because it would make her mother miserable. Her anger and her fear of losing her parents, however, were reflected in frequent dreams in which her parents died.

While Diana had fantasies of being an actress and wished to be able to command attention merely by having a temper tantrum, in actuality, like Ellen, she was determined to remain aloof from her turmoil and was committed to a show of coolness. In fact her cool, controlled outer manner was admired by some of the other young women who saw her as in control of her relations with men and satisfied with her life. Diana herself, however, was fully aware of how unhappy she was behind her outer façade.

How profoundly Diana had been damaged by her life, how much her surface calm concealed turmoil was reflected in a dream in which she was drinking a glass of water and discovered a bloody rat whose tail was bleeding in the bottom of the glass. The sense of surface coolness covering a submerged rattiness, concealing a bleeding, rapacious animal pervaded Diana's life. The crippling female self-hatred of the "bleeding tail" image of her dream was reflected in her feeling of the inequitable treatment her parents meted out to her and her brother. She saw herself as a vessel of the anger, pain, and frustration of a wounded, despised predator, the rat she feared would emerge through emotional involvement with a man.

Diana expected to marry, although she anticipated an unhappy future. She was typical of the women I saw in her determination never to have children, and commented that she could never give them away as her mother did to her, but felt she could not stand their demands either. It was clear that having children would revive her own frustrations, that her own angry neediness made her feel unable to tolerate a child's appetites. Like so many of the students I saw, she lived in private fear that if anyone knew how rapacious and angry she was, they would immediately abandon her.

Ellen and Diana were typical of the many students I saw who tried to control their emotions through denying that they had been hurt and through burying their outrage. To be able to see their past damage as an accident or an unavoidable necessity for which no one is to blame made it possible for many women not to acknowledge the pain of having felt unloved and unwanted. By avoiding reproach, they hope to avoid the hurt and anger they fear might one day engulf them. They can describe even nightmarish childhoods blandly. Yet nothing more totally cements these young women into unhappiness than their inability to deal with rage.

The great vulnerability of these young women was magnified by a lifelong repression of anger reinforced by cultural sanctions against any female expression of rage. Self-containment had rendered these students unable to deal with their own anger or with anyone else's toward them in any situation. The slightest expression of criticism of their mothers tended to arouse inordinate guilt. One student, after describing her relation with her mother in what seemed the mildest of ways, dreamed that night that she was John Mitchell, after she had watched him testify at the Watergate hearings. She said she had felt sorry for him since he was obviously guilty, but had to lie to protect the president. She was torn by guilt over not having similarly protected her mother. The dream image of being an accomplice in crime with an authority one must protect reflected a widespread sense among these young women of being bound to their mothers in some damaging, illicit act. That the crime is a crime against themselves is something they hesitated to acknowledge or face. Yet most of these young women had figuratively jailed their feelings to permit others to go free of blame.

Women like Ellen tried to avoid bitterness and pain in riveting their lives to productive work. The alternative to Ellen's isolation or to the surface gaiety of women like Diana was seen as collapse into total dependency, vulnerability, and helplessness. Nor was this vision of what was possible for them unrealistic. Its horror was that it was often exactly what happened.

Many women I saw lived out the nightmare women like Ellen and Diana feared. Such women had been habituated to obedience and self-abnegation by mothers whose interest and affection were synonymous with a need to control, direct, and dominate their daughters' lives and by fathers who had let them down by permitting or encouraging this to happen. Just as these students felt that to preserve the security and affection they got from their mothers they had to be submissive and could set almost no limits on their mothers' control over their lives, so they were unable to set limits with their boyfriends, friends, or husbands. They were often irresistibly drawn to men who needed to control them without any regard for them as people.

Often their compliance was so complete that they were unable even to form strong independent interests, or to pursue them if they had. They frequently had the illusion that through relationships with men unacceptable to their mothers they could rebel against their mothers' domination. Yet in such relationships they invariably seemed only to exchange one master for another.

Rachel was one of the young women who began by saying that she was "abnormally normal" and felt she handled things better than her friends because of her wonderful life with her family. She admitted her family's harmony was shaken when her sister became heavily involved with drugs a year ago. She spoke of her sister as unable to sleep when she was upset and of herself as sleeping better than ever when she was disturbed about something, explaining that she could push her problems out of her mind. But she took pains to convince me she had no problems and later said she was unsure how I would feel about her once I knew that she did. Most of her praise of her family focused on her mother, whom she idealized as perfect. Yet her mother had no such feelings about Rachel.

A tall, attractive girl, Rachel might be five or ten pounds overweight, something which one would not notice were it not that weight was a central issue in Rachel's relations with her mother. Her mother insisted that "no one can like herself who is not confident about her body." She also demanded that Rachel weigh herself daily at home and inform her mother of her weight. She criticized Rachel's lack of confidence at the same time she undermined it. She objected to Rachel's taking a study program in Europe for several months on the grounds that if she went she could not watch her weight. That summer Rachel wanted to join her boyfriend in Israel. Her mother argued that she should not go because she would look ridiculous in a bathing suit, since she was so heavy. They made a deal that she could go if she lost a certain amount of weight. Rachel was unable to lose the weight and did not go. This sense of Rachel's basic unacceptability and the refusal to acknowledge anything about her but her body effectively served to undermine Rachel's feeling about herself and to keep her tied to her mother as the only arbiter of her worth.

How long a history of insecurity Rachel had is suggested by a dream she had when she was eight. She dreamed that their dog Princess was somehow walking across the swimming pool. Their other dog, Molly, tried to follow her but Molly sank to the bottom and was all smashed up and water-logged. Rachel remembers looking at her forlornly.

Princess was now nineteen and Molly was her one puppy that they kept. Molly was Rachel's dog—the one she was attached to, identified with, and had cared for. After telling me the dream she went on to talk about her mother as somebody who was thin, elegant, and perfect— almost able to walk on water. She could see that Princess represented her mother and that Molly was herself. The exaggerated image of her mother, the conception of the misfortune that befell her from trying to follow in her mother's footsteps, and even her heavy, water-logged self-image suggested the battering that she took by virtue of their relationship.

Rachel now took a similar battering in her relationship with Daniel, a young man who demanded that she be as involved with orthodox Judaism as he was. He insisted that if she ate nonkosher food she would be contaminated and he then would not have sexual relations with her for fear she would contaminate him. She handled this by lying to him as she did to her mother about what she ate. Although she was far from enthusiastic about Daniel, he was able to persuade her to give up her studies for a year and join him in Israel while he pursued his Hebrew studies. Rachel's mother objected to Daniel and said Rachel clung to him out of insecurity. She had, however, cultivated Rachel's insecurity as a way of making Rachel cling to her.

Some students see marriage as a way of escaping their mothers' domination. Linda was a twenty-one-year-old senior whose parents separated when she was a child, and who, along with her older sister, was raised by her mother. She saw her mother as having sacrificed herself for her family, but as also having used these sacrifices as a way of controlling her daughters. She felt that her sister, although in her mid-twenties, had never escaped a paralyzing dependence on their mother and was very afraid of her own tendencies in that direction. During her freshman year, she married Jack, whom her mother opposed because he came from a different social and religious background, had no ambition, and participated in radical political activities. Her mother's opposition gave Linda the sense of rebelling through her marriage, yet in marrying Jack she had virtually married her mother.

Like her mother, Jack insisted she share his interests and showed no enthusiasm for hers. While Linda was not a political radical, Jack demanded she become involved as fully as he in the violent political activity that consumed virtually all his time and often caused him to come home beaten and bloody from encounters with the police or with other revolutionary groups that opposed his.

Linda lived in perpetual fear for his safety. Jack blamed all the difficulties between them as well as his own insecurity in the movement on the fact that she was not more involved. Linda eventually accepted this and threw herself into the movement with no improvement in their relationship.

Linda wanted to get a graduate degree in biology, but gave up her plans because of Jack's opposition. He insisted that she would be working on projects in which the government had an interest and that getting a scholarship to graduate school meant being the puppet of the government. It was clear, however, that he did not object to her being a puppet as long as he was pulling the strings.

How much Linda perceived that she had replaced her mother with Jack was reflected in her dreams, which frequently called attention to the relationship between them. In one, Linda was wheeling a crippled woman who said that she was afraid to lose Linda. Linda was also limping in the dream. Then this woman became ill and Linda had to call the police. The policeman who came was the woman's son. Linda went to bed with him. He wanted to marry her, and a friend told her that he was no good for her.

Linda's associations related the woman to her mother, who has been afraid of losing her, and the man to both Jack and her father. Linda has handled her Oedipal situation by seeing to it that she found a man who gave her no more than her father did her mother. Instead he becomes a replacement for her mother who tells her what to do and polices her behavior. Striking was her image of herself as being crippled by her relation to her crippled mother and her sense that she had escaped one damaging situation by jumping into another that was equally bad for her. Linda repressed most of her anger toward Jack but expressed it in frequent dreams of leaving him for another man, and it was clear that she could not conceive of herself as not in relation to somebody who was playing the sort of role with regard to her that her mother and Jack have played. She shook off the fact that Jack never said he loved her by insisting that he did love her but did not know it. She became panicky about the possibility of his leaving her or her ending the marriage. When this panic was explored she said that a separation or divorce would prove her mother was right and, more crucially, would lead to her going back home and becoming like her sister, who was totally under her mother's thumb. Despite her fantasy that perhaps she could find some other man who would be kinder to her than Jack, she saw the actual alternatives in her life as being dependent on Jack or being dependent on her mother.

Women like Rachel and Linda grow up feeling crowded by their mothers. Linda had a recurrent dream in childhood of a large whale that filled up her room so that there was no room for her. She saw her mother as someone who directed everything she should do or feel as a child, so she felt there was no room for her to move in. Such women are easily crowded out of their interests, are virtually habituated to put themselves second to someone who is in charge of their lives. While marriage or a relationship with a man their mothers disapprove of often gives such women the illusion they are breaking away from their mothers, they eventually discover they are merely perpetuating the style of submissiveness and self-denial they have always known.

Is it possible to change the nature of relations to men, to escape the seesaw between withdrawal through fear of intimacy and immersion in an intimacy that consumes and annihilates? A few young women had developed a relation to men that permitted them to enjoy a sexual relationship while continuing to function effectively in school. They had made female vulnerability an object of study or scorn and had great contempt for women who were unable to achieve the peculiar compromise with life they had worked out. Such women expected and wanted no real intimacy. They had affairs that were cool and casual, even with men they planned to marry.

Marion, a tall, attractive college senior, said that some of her friends felt you have to be slaughtered in a relationship with a man for anything to develop. She did not agree and saw no reason to get hurt. Marion had lived for the past year with a man who had just gone off to graduate school in a nearby city. She expected that she would eventually marry him, yet she was rather casual and unromantic in her attitude toward him. She made the point that she has always been close to or come to care for the people she was near and felt that people were replaceable. If the fact that she and Earl were in different cities meant that they would drift apart, that would be no problem, she said, there would be somebody else. While she has been involved sexually with Earl and she said she enjoyed their sexual relationship, her story was filled with images of relationships that were destroyed by too much closeness. She saw being dependent as a weakness for which she had some contempt.

Marion considered her relationship with her mother to have been the closest relationship she has ever had. She could not conceive of a relationship with a man that would have a comparable intimacy. While Marion had been her mother's confidante from the time that she was seven or eight, the other siblings in the family hated the mother and never developed this relationship with her. In addition, in Marion's case her closeness to her mother was engrafted on an earlier experience of rejection which all the children shared. She said her mother hated having children—she had four—and was hardly ever around them. Marion had no memory of her mother in the first six or seven years of her life, only some vague ones of a servant who took care of her. She related without any apparent bitterness that her mother had told her that none of the children learned to talk till after they were three because the mother and father never spent any time talking to them. They learned to walk early because they were just put in the center of the room and had to manage for themselves.

When Marion was eleven her mother started working and Marion took care of the house. She did the cooking and cared for the younger children. When her mother came home from work, they would talk together, go out for long rides in the car together, and occasionally read poetry to each other. When Marion was sixteen her mother told her she was considering leaving her father for another man. She discussed her divorce and remarriage with Marion, who told her to go ahead. Yet the degree of pain and fear of abandonment that was hidden behind Marion's rapport with her mother was reflected in an incident which occurred at this time. Marion had been at a party, where for the first time she had had a number of drinks. She came home, had another beer with her mother in the kitchen, and then proceeded to become hysterical about the idea that she and her mother might be separated by the death of one of them. At one point during the evening, she wrote out a will leaving all the things she valued to her mother. At another, she proposed a suicide pact with her mother in which they would lock themselves in the refrigerator and die together. Her panic indicated fear that if her mother left her father for someone she really loved, it would mean the death of their relationship, since she would no longer come first in her mother's affections and would be replaced in importance by a man.

Let no man come between us is the message Marion both gave and received from her mother. A coercive use of the threat to break family ties recurs in her story. When Marion's younger sister fell in love, her mother, who feared her daughter would run away with the man, attempted to destroy the relationship by telling her, "I did not run off, I chose for the family. You must too." The sister bitterly resented this pressure and has been estranged from their mother ever since. Marion hoped going away to college would help her become less dependent on her mother. Yet last year while drinking with Earl, she became intoxicated for the second time in her life and began crying bitterly about the unhappiness in her mother's life.

After her first year in college Marion had a dream that she described as the most memorable of her life. A woman who was pregnant and had a little child with her was entering a store when she was shot in the head from behind. Then Marion became that woman and the same thing happened to her, but somehow she was not killed. She was putting on very nice-looking bed clothes to go to the hospital, but she did not want the ambulance drivers to see how concerned she was at looking nice when she was so seriously wounded. She hastened to avoid embarrassment by finishing her preparations before they arrived and saw her bloody head. In the latter part of the dream a man

who had been her drama teacher was chasing her and trying to shoot her.

In discussing her dream Marion spoke first of people
who deny pain and death: of her younger brother, who
denied he had epilepsy; her father, who was dying of cancer and denied the terminal nature of his illness. Yet it
was clearly Marion who in the dream and in life denied
her pain and anger and tried to ignore her wounds by
concern with how she looked to the world rather than with
how badly she has been hurt.

In her dream Marion literally became her mother and
dramatized the danger of sharing her fate. Marion never
wants to be a mother; never wants to bear the brunt of the
total dependency of a child. Her mother has told her that
she went to pieces when she had little children, hated
them, and really turned them over to a woman she hired
to help raise them. Marion intended to marry but was
quite determined never to have children, and in some
way she seemed to sense that she could maintain a surface, casual, invulnerable position as long as she avoided
the kind of involvement children would bring. She told me
a story she had read of a woman who had no husband,
but wanted a girl child as a companion. She had a boy
instead, tried to be friendly with him, but the story ended
with the boy puking all over her. Marion was determined
not to have her life messed up in this manner.

Marion associated the drama teacher in her dream with
her father. Both he and her father were people who liked
her but were never able to express this and always seemed
uncomfortable with her. She described her father as someone who was outgrown by her mother, who could never
handle emotional situations, who could not be affectionate
with her and was uncomfortable when she tried to kiss

him. While she saw a man's interest in her as potentially fatal—a man could destroy her as she felt her mother was destroyed by marriage to her father—she seemed to feel that by avoiding children she can avoid her vulnerability to such danger.

Marion had a strong sense of the necessity for living within an emotional framework she could manage. Work was an integral part of that framework. She had known for some time that she wanted to be a gynecologist, stressing her interest in working with and helping women. In effect, her interest in pregnancy as a phenomenon to treat medically served to express both her fascination for women in a vulnerable state and her determination to be vulnerability's objective observer—the doctor in charge and not the patient in need. Since Marion was confident that she would not permit the man she married to disturb her emotional equilibrium, she did not share the fears of some of the young women that a man would interfere with her ambitions.

Not letting a man become too important, treating men as replaceable or interchangeable were Marion's solutions to the intimacy other women feared. Her attitude seemed to reflect her denial that she had lost the irreplaceable person in her life, the mother who had never been available when she was a child and whose absence then she sensed could not be corrected. She was aware of the continuing primacy of her present relationship with her mother. She said she could never tell her mother that she was in love with a man. She felt that she would be saying the man was more important than her mother, something neither of them could accept.

Marion's cool external façade was only partly successful in warding off the impact of her father's terminal illness, although she discussed his death matter-of-factly. She was deeply hurt that her fiancé would not come home with her during this period, for going home had become a strain. But the tension was largely due to the fact that her father's illness had caused her mother to become increasingly dependent on her in a way that Marion had found intolerable. For the first time she envied her sister, whose long-standing anger toward her mother freed her from this pressure.

Marion dreamed she was a slave in a plantation in the south and was about to be sold. Her sister, who was there, was not a slave and helped her to escape. Marion related the dream to the sense of bondage she felt in going home. Yet it also seemed to reflect an increasing awareness of how much her mother has "sold her down the river" in depending so absolutely on her. While she seemed to be hoping that following her sister could make her free, her sense of bondage was deeply rooted in the devouring intensity of a relationship that had begun when she was old enough to respond to her mother's complaints and share her unhappiness, and that over the years had evolved into an unspoken pact that no man would ever break their bond to each other.

Young women who had been rejected, who had been dominated, or whose initial rejection had ended in their becoming their mothers' confidantes dramatized the major injuries done to young women since their earliest lives. The perpetually rejected had been sacrificed to the fact that their mothers did not want them, the controlled were subordinated to whatever their mothers wanted, the confidantes had been used, after an initial rejection, to allay their mothers' guilt over that rejection. The price of the mother's friendship was that the daughter bury her anger and resentment and become the mother's accomplice in hatred of motherhood and not her accuser. For most young women life had involved subordinating their feelings and interests to mothers who had no regard for them as individuals and whose interests and needs did not coincide with their own.

Having been denied the right to independent feelings and interests from their earliest life, young women had enormous conflict about any independent feelings or interests they developed. As no one had really felt for them, so they too have an impaired capacity to feel for other people. When cultural pressures against women expressing anger or self-assertiveness are applied over the emotional burial that has already taken place, they seal off the power of many young women to use their feelings constructively to shape their lives.

The cynicism of so many women students has its source in the experience of mothers who had been embittered by their own disappointment and had by pronouncement or martyred, silent example instilled in their daughters a hatred of motherhood and the wish that they be invulnerable to men, in fact to everyone but them. In channeling their daughters toward careers of their choice, toward men of their choice, toward looks of their choice, toward muted emotional lives, these mothers were bent upon solving their own vulnerability through barricading their daughters.

The widespread dread of marriage among young women stems largely from their own painful lives with their families. Many have watched unfold before them since childhood the spectacle of their parents' disillusionment with each other and their mothers' entrapment and discontent. Some students described their parents' marriages as going well at the children's expense. What had preserved the marriage was the sacrifice of children, who were either sent away or raised by housekeepers. In other marriages, the professed happiness of the mothers was belied by their need to so devour, dominate, and control their daughters. The daughters who become confidantes are virtually educated in the dangers of involvement and in the methods of avoiding it.

Most of the young women I saw felt resentment over their fathers' unavailability. In several families fathers were cut off from the family through their wives' condemnation of them as unable to meet their economic, social, intellectual, or emotional needs. Isolated by this dislike, often unable to deal with the demands of children himself, the father retreated further into work. What resulted was an end to any real family life and a polarization between the father, whose own needs for affection and approval had been dismissed, and the mother, who felt trapped by her children and unable to have the freedom her husband enjoyed.

How violently disruptive of the tension between fathers and daughters a marital war could be was dramatized by one student who had become her mother's confidante and began to see her father through her mother's disillusioned eyes when she was eight or nine. She told of an argument she had had with her father when she was ten which ended in their not speaking to each other for three years and communicating only through her mother. The student had never questioned her mother's role in permitting the situation to last that long and in making no demand that her husband and daughter speak directly. This is only the most literal example of the degree to which communication between father and daughter was controlled by the mother, while the father's feelings toward his daughter are spoiled by his anger with his wife.

Some young women remembered having had warm feelings toward their fathers as very little children, but this affectionate relationship was spoiled as they grew up and started to be a bit more independent. One student who had been particularly close to her father recalled how hurt she was by her father's refusal to stop calling her Chicken Little, which she hated and which reflected his need to continue to see her as a very little girl. Relationships that survived through this period often foundered in the girl's adolescence with her emerging social and sexual life. Obviously unable to deal with their daughters as women, many fathers became critical or simply withdrew. What these young women felt most bitterly was that their fathers were unreachable in emotional terms. Ellen knew her father preferred her to the other children because of her scholastic success and her musical accomplishments, but she resented that she had to impress him through her success and was bitter over his withdrawal from her and the family.

Withdrawal was precisely the message these women had gotten from their fathers. If their relationships with their mothers were at times suffocating, their contacts with their fathers were usually sterile. The sense that life for them alternated between the consuming, controlling love of their mothers or the detached approval they sometimes got from their fathers ran through the lives of these young women. To be a child in such a family meant being caught between two styles of unhappiness, to be a casualty in their parents' discontent with each other. To be a woman meant facing the possibility of a similar entrapment between the child you did not want and the husband you no longer loved. Virtually all these women feared that they would be like their mothers. Diana was typical of many who said that they would not want to send away or emotionally abandon their children as their mothers had done to them, but did not feel they could live with them either. Many young women sensed that too many of their own needs had gone unsatisfied for them to ever be able to handle those of a child. This vision of children as purely needing and giving nothing—certainly not pleasure—reflected their own recognition that they had, as children, given no pleasure to their mothers and even now were valued for the extent to which they fulfilled fantasies their mothers had for themselves and which they insisted their daughters fulfill whether they wanted to or not.

Coolness and casualness with men, even, or perhaps especially, with those they plan to marry assures these students of protection against the disillusionment their mothers have suffered. One student compared her feeling for her fiancé to her attachment to her Irish setter and said, in response to my surprise, that she was very fond of her setter. This coolness was the mark of women who wanted a no-risk life, who tried for a relation to the world that had as its goal the maximum possible gain with the least possible investment of self.

Women students often avoided empathy for or understanding of their boyfriends' concerns or anxieties as a way of keeping their distance. Typical was one young woman who complained of her boyfriend's sudden drinking and missing class, but did not connect it with the fact that he had just learned his father was dying. The women were not available to the men or to each other in emotional need (nor were the men to them). Physical care or financial help were easy to give, but not empathy or concern. These young people constantly let each other down in the same ways they felt their parents had let them down. Many feel their parents never wanted to know if they were in trouble. "They like to see me as having no problems" was a familiar remark. Or "they were more concerned with my cutting school than with my being miserable." As one student put it with devastating simplicity, "My mother was overprotective without any real warmth."

Most young women I saw have no romantic expectations from men. Many were able to enjoy sex only in situations when they could define and limit the intensity of the relationship. Women whose tensions and anxiety made sexual pleasure impossible with men they cared for deeply, enjoyed sex with men they liked without admiring or needing. Sometimes these women planned to marry, feeling they could enjoy marriage if they felt their husband were disposable and if they did not have children.

The extent to which young women want to bury their feelings, their vulnerability, their need is reflected in both their actual and their professed sexual mores. The flight from intimacy and love has been virtually institutionalized in the changes begun by the sexual revolution. Young women are now under pressure from each other to become sexually involved with men. Sexual experience confers status; living with a man even more so. Being casual, experimental, and detached about it most of all. The young women who wish to remain virgins, who wear dresses or make-up to class are often attacked by other women for both making themselves into sex objects and for trying to feel "superior" because of their virginity. Many young women deal with this pressure by doing what many young men have done for a much longer time, that is, lying about the sexual experience they have had.

That this is a generation of swingers is an illusion. About half of the young women had active sexual lives, but only a few tried to take sex in a totally casual way. They were not only a minority but a troubled one whose sexual behavior did not reflect the new permissiveness in society so much as their own confusion about themselves. Gail liked to think of herself as Mae West, sexy, hard-boiled, and funny about her sexual contacts. She would pick up a man who attracted her at school, in a shop, on the subway and spend the night with him. While she sometimes succeeded in conveying the Mae West image to friends, casual sex never enhanced her mood, but always left her feeling down, degraded, and depressed. But becoming involved with men in a careless, almost random way had a purpose for her that was not uncommon.

When she met a man who really interested her, Gail experienced enormous anxiety that she would be rendered vulnerable and would be hurt by him. She dealt with her fear or any actual hurt by immediately going to bed with someone else. In the process of running from one such relationship she went to bed with two different men in the same weekend. Nightmares following these sexual contacts and her failure to use any contraceptive device was also a sign of how profoundly and effectively she used sex to end or diminish something that really excited her and to hold on to a depression that was long-standing in her life. She alternated between feeling invulnerable on the one hand and so depressed on the other that it did not matter what happened to her. About to rent an apartment in a dangerous neighborhood, she told a friend who was trying to dissuade her that "the worst that could happen is that I would be robbed, raped, or murdered and so what."

Her depressed vulnerability tied her to a mother who always did put down her enthusiasms, who could only become involved with her when she was depressed and needy, suffering and in pain. Putting herself in the path of disaster was Gail's means of remaining in the vulnerable, needy position her mother had placed her in. While her sexual behavior outwardly seemed a rebellion against cautiousness, against vulnerability, it involved for her an intensification of the suffering that left her more bound to her mother than ever.

Casual sexual involvements were used by some young women to hurt or degrade themselves after they felt they had been hurt by a young man they cared for. Told by her boyfriend, who had been hospitalized, that he could not have sex with her for a month and she should find someone else while he was sick, Marlene was not aware of being either hurt or angry by his assessment of her concern for him and the lack of feeling for her implied in what he said. She proceeded to go to bed with his best friend, who was married. She was unaware until afterward that she felt disgusted with herself for doing so. Many of the women I saw were as unable as Gail or Marlene to be aware of their anger and to express it directly. When treated badly they use impulsive sex in a revengeful, self-punitive way while often believing they are simply responding to a sudden sexual impulse. Yet the despair that preceded these contacts and was intensified by them was a more reliable indicator of their mood.

Out of a sense of futility and depression Elizabeth played Russian roulette with sex. She spent a summer hitchhiking across the country and becoming involved with several of the men who gave her rides. She knew she was taking a chance, but felt playing roulette with her life was a true expression of how she felt—whatever happened meant little to her. She had had a sexual involvement at sixteen when still in high school with a married man of thirty-one, hoping this would involve her parents in her problems. She was disappointed that her parents did nothing to stop the relationship. Nor did they react to a suicide attempt she made at this time. In college she still felt that nothing she did involved them. Yet she preferred not to blame them for her own sense of not counting for much and for her inability to feel worth protecting. Sexual roulette was another expression of her childhood feeling of having been accidentally damaged by her parents' treatment of her. Her most vivid childhood memory is of being burned when her mother accidentally spilled boiling water on her. Now the "accidents" that hurt her originated in the bad chance encounter with a man, the unfortunate night in bed. A sexual life that was a series of unpredictable events permits her to see her unhappiness not as of her own making nor as the product of a catastrophic and lonely childhood, but as the gift of chance, anonymous and uncontrollable.

What the sexual revolution produced were changes in behavior and attitudes; it legitimized an active sexual life for the young and unmarried. Yet what happens between men and women in bed is influenced less by sanction than by personality, by conflicts over involvement, intimacy, dependency, and assertiveness, and by fears of vulnerability that shape the subjective experience of sex and affect its enjoyment. Society's increased tolerance of the sexually free woman has not yet been marked by any simultaneous increase in the young woman's confidence in her ability to handle relationships.

Just as sexual freedom resulted in a tremendous pressure on young women to have sexual experience, so liberation to work has turned the development of a career into a necessity. Work is now for young women a primary test of their worth as people. Women who find strong career interests often use them effectively to protect themselves against dependency and vulnerability, to support their withdrawal from men, or to justify limiting their involvements to casual sex or muted affection. Women who have no strong interests saw themselves as deprived of every emotional refuge and felt a merciless fear and humiliation that they would be doomed back into the married, mothering masses of women who had failed. Both women who had a career interest and those who did not were pessimistic about their ability to happily include another person in their lives. Few seemed to believe that it would be possible to find both work they love and a man they love, to be independent in a career and acknowledge their need for another person. At this point in their lives they are either following a path of isolating work or hoping they can find that straight and narrow road. But the road to satisfying work is as tortuous as the way to conflict-free sex for these young women. Convinced that pleasure lies in a career that will make them whole, independent, and invulnerable, these young women often find themselves caught in an impotent agony over their inability to develop any strong interest in any field. What inhibits them?

Some young women are still brought up to see their education and work as a kind of diversion, as play-acting at a career before they marry. Diana was typical of the many girls who were sent to college to find the right husband. Although she dreaded marriage, she was so habituated to regarding her work as only a pastime that she gave very little of herself to it. Women who never develop any strong interest clearly get the worst of both worlds, since many feel as keenly as their friends the imperative to independence, dread the idea of marriage and motherhood, and yet find themselves deprived of any way of withstanding it.

Other students whose parents have educated them to the primacy of marriage and motherhood find that college opens up their vision of what life can hold for them. One young woman worked hard in school, loved it, and wanted to study law, but she was under continual pressure by her parents to return home and study art, which had always been a hobby of hers. Her parents evidently recognized that college has challenged their ability to shape her possibilities. They wanted her back within their sphere and advocated art because painting was, they felt, an ideal pursuit for a woman: it could be done at home, in spare time, by a wife and mother. They knew she had no real aspirations as an artist.

Some young women are pushed toward particular fields without regard for their interests and needs by mothers who would have liked to study such things themselves. Such students have been raised not to follow their own enthusiasms or impulses. Their mothers have often been among the most controlling, choosing everything for their daughters from their ideal weight to their ideal future. Such mothers accustom their daughters to giving up their own interests for theirs. This pattern of abdication prevails in the work lives of these students, who can be easily made to act against themselves. Linda permitted her husband to talk her out of graduate school in biology and into political violence she does not support. Several students whose boyfriends had done poorly and dropped out of college let themselves be talked into dropping out, although their grades were excellent and they enjoyed school. Men were able to persuade them to adopt a way of life they did not respect because they had gone through a lifetime indoctrination at the hands of their mothers and fathers in putting themselves second. Such women are perennial second fiddlers who invariably put themselves and their lives aside to play the tune their mothers, or boyfriends, or husbands choose.

What work signifies to other young women is merely "mad money." Work has no primacy for such women but is "something to fall back on" if a marriage fails. It is protection against the economic dependency their mothers have often pointed out is the glue of marriage. Out of a passion for security such students often give up their real interests in risky careers for secure ones that do not interest them, but have been chosen purely for their "market value." This concern for economic security often defeats its own purpose since it is hard for the student to succeed at something she does not really care about.

The types of work which arouse the most consuming commitment arc often those which permit a woman to play in her professional life the role she would like to occupy in her emotional life. Law had a particular significance for women like Ellen in providing a sense of being at home in the world, of being able to define, set, and defend limits according to an external standard. Medicine offered many young women the opportunity to deal with the pain in other people's lives as they never had their own.

To be unique, powerful, commanding, different from the "masses" of ordinary women was the wish of most of the young women I saw. Diana's fantasy was of being an actress in control of the center of the stage, where she could invite such attention that she would feel free to throw a temper tantrum and be admired for it. Many of the young women began their sessions by telling me that they were unlike all the other women at college. Some said they kept different hours, others that they had a different life-style, Marion that she did not get "slaughtered," Ellen stressed her legal ambition and different sexual and moral life-style—all clearly felt they could only be admired for their accomplishments, for being unique at something. They hoped they could coerce or command from the world the attention and affection they wanted.

The pressure to have a career and an active sexual life —whether ready, willing, or not—the conflicts generated by new directives replacing the old are so great that it is not surprising that many young women try to hold on to their mothers as the arbiters of value. One student worried, "Who will replace my mother in knowing what is right?" The idea that she herself might develop sufficient judgment to make decisions did not seem possible to her. Many lamented that "no one tells you the right thing to do or the right way to live." They go to lectures, take notes, study, always wondering if they are doing it all "correctly" with the vague, nonspecific feeling that they are not doing what others expect of them.

The sense of being "wrong," of doing an inadequate job, or making the wrong decision dogged many of the young women I saw and pushed them into extraordinary compliance and concern for fulfilling other people's expectations. They continually expressed worry over whether I was "getting enough" out of my sessions with them, presumably believing that my interest in them depended on whether or not their lives coincided with my expectations. Through their worry ran their sense of being basically unlovable, of being angry and demanding and full of the "wrong" emotions beneath a compliant, controlled exterior. They do not believe that if they are themselves, make demands, or assert their feelings that anyone could possibly be interested in them. Clearly what they fear in giving the "wrong" answer is revealing themselves. What they do not want to show is how damaged they feel they have been by their early lives. Images of having been crippled, scarred, injured, and burnt pervade their childhood memories.

Willful detachment and coolness were for many young women the corollaries of both the inability to deal with strong feelings and a means of solving that inability through pretending not to care. Marion seemed unshaken by her recent discovery of her father's terminal cancer. She was openly contemptuous of her uncle, who, coming to see his brother, wept for him. Marion felt such displays are excessive. She permitted no one to mean enough to her to excite tears for any misfortune. She said she had cried only twice in her life, in pity for her mother and in fear of losing her. This is not only the sign of the solitary focus of her feelings, but an indication of how profoundly insecure she feels about the consequences of caring for anyone else. Dreaming of herself as her mother's slave, does she see any other close relationship as involving only a second bondage?

But bondage is not only a fear that haunts modern women like Marion. Even students from the most traditional backgrounds, whose families were classical examples of those in which mothers had continued to love and admire their husbands while subordinating their lives and interests to them, now regard their mothers' lives as models of what to avoid, not pictures of an acceptable life. Bonnie, a midwestern young woman with the pertness and prettiness of an All-American cheerleader, said she was brought up to "wear make-up, do what you can to be as pretty as possible, and to bat your eyes at boys and hope that some of them respond." In a light, cheery, witty way, she said she had worked hard in high school to be "Miss Popularity" and that "while it was not really [her], it was not entirely phony either."

Bonnie had been brought up to marry and make her husband her life as had her mother, who, though an educated woman, limited her life to helping her successful husband with the lesser details of his work. Although Bonnie loved her mother and admired her father, she had great conflict over her future. She had developed a strong interest in medicine and was being pressured by both her parents to give it up as incompatible with a woman's life. She had derived from her family the ability to love and be loved and to want an involvement with a man she really cared for and admired. But she feared being engulfed and submerged like her mother. She dealt with her vulnerability by ending a relationship with a man she loved and admired to avoid that fate. But it was an open question whether she could withstand her parents' pressure to give up her interest in medicine.

The freedom to be involved with men has not been accompanied by women gaining the confidence or ability to protect themselves when they do. Virtually no young woman today can escape great conflict over her own vulnerability if she does become deeply involved with a man.

Her situation, as we shall see in the next chapter, is made still more difficult by the escalating aggression of young men against women. Nor is it eased by success at school or work. Ingrained in the cultural life of women, and now more painfully exposed than ever, is the inability to set limits, to shape life in the context of an intimate and deep connection to a man. More and more young women today see life as fatal to the woman who is not impenetrably cool. Increasingly, they arm themselves with a vision of reality as threatening. Game, plucky, the women students I saw are determined not to be overwhelmed by experience. But in the search for an antidote to emotion they often find that they have killed their power to care deeply for anyone.

3 | Control! Control!

"To JUDGE FROM my father, men between the ages of six and sixty did nothing but meet new challenges, take on heavier responsibilities, and lose all freedom to explode," wrote Robert Lowell in a memoir that conveyed the fears of any boy who saw manhood looming like oppression, but who was determined to be different from the men around him and remain in touch with his feelings. Like Lowell, college men today speak as though emotions were explosions, outpourings of rage. But the young men I saw did not want to be in touch with the volcanic center of themselves.

Unleashed feeling, the explosion of the heart is so feared by most young men today that what they desire is not freedom but controls, checks to block any opening up of their passion. The students I saw were chosen at random from the college population and represented a great variety of interests and backgrounds. Yet they all saw feeling as destructive, saw passion as harmful to them and those involved with them. Their fear was so pervasive that despite their differences, virtually all of them dreamed of emotion as a fire to be extinguished, as a stampede of cattle that should be corralled, as a disease that would destroy, as a weapon that would kill. If young women saw themselves as potential victims, young men knew and feared their potential for becoming victimizers.

Dealing with the aggressive urge in the charged competitive life at college was extraordinarily difficult for the young men I saw. All hated the "rat race" at school; virtually each claimed he was less caught up in it than his friends. These students were competitive about their noncompetitiveness. What all these students hated in the rat race was precisely the combativeness it aroused in themselves. Some of the young men were able to use their work to contain and channel their anger. One student dealt with his angry tension over grades by deciding to become a professional tennis player. He experienced a violent anger toward anyone he played, but was not disturbed by this because the need to "crush" was sanctioned by the nature of the sport and structured by the rules of the game. Another student, who was a writer, saw his life as a cerebral combat in which he had to withstand the demands other people made on him. He succeeded in treating both his life and his fiction as a chess game in which he controlled everybody's moves. Yet most young men found in the everyday competition at school insoluble situations of war that called for the best possible defenses and the most pointed offensive weapons. They found themselves forced to enter the combat or withdraw, to make a choice which meant coming to terms with what they felt and what they were.

"Some students work hard for grades, others work hard at being dissolute, and I work hard at neither," one student put it, defining the position of many young men who adopted an aloof superiority they did not possess. Like the women who feigned cheeriness and self-confidence, these young men found consolation in an illusion. As another student said, "It made me feel even more superior to be aloof from such a bright group where everyone was something of a cynic."

Putting themselves on the line, getting into life, exposing their emotions aroused enormous conflicts in virtually all the young men I saw. Even acknowledging their feelings to themselves was for them the assertive act that would inevitably lead them into conflict. Many withdrew into an estrangement from feeling that not only blocked out their anger, but their capacity for pleasure. Few young men seemed to be having a good time at life. Their humor was invariably ironic, the words they used to describe their friends and themselves—"grub," "grind"—indicated how dreary they felt their lives to be. What they tended toward in speech was what they tended toward in life: a low-level, mild depression in which nothing was too intensely felt.

The need to contain emotion was particularly marked in the attitude of these young men toward women. Limiting relationships to purely sexual contacts was one way of killing intimacy. Some men destroyed it by criticizing and abusing their girlfriends until they drove them away, and then proceeded to romanticize the same girls from a distance. Some men felt comfortable with women who dominated them, and whose control served to create a necessary barrier by keeping the men's impulses and needs in check. The need to keep intimacy away, to remain aloof from emotion reflected a sense that a close relationship with a woman would end in destruction and self-destruction. These young men feared connecting with their own impulses, with the conflict and anger any strong attachment would arouse.

The relentless, cutthroat competition bound up with American middle-class life has always hit young men in college with dramatic force. Yet students today seem to find such competitiveness less tolerable and do all they can to avoid it, to persist in thinking it is someone else's problem, to deny it in themselves, or to minimize their involvement in competitive situations. As men, they are faced with the traditional demand to excel in some particular work. How to win the prize without entering the race?

The junkie mentality, the belief in ripping off a person or establishment while giving nothing in return, offered some students a way of dismissing or circumventing the traditional ground rules of competition. Such students are not that involved in proving themselves in any particular field, but they want the rewards that should come to the student whose talent and commitment have made him excel. For such students the urge to succeed at any price except work was often coupled with the desire to take as much as they could from life while giving as little as possible of themselves.

Bob was a tall, powerfully built junior who was typical of the students who approached life as takers. He had used his football ability to help him get into college, but refused to play after a season because he did not feel the coaches had done enough to help him find a well-paying job. He would have liked to teach English in college, but felt the oversupply of English teachers would make that a struggle and he did not want to have to struggle to make a living. While the income of a lawyer appealed to him, the aggressive competitiveness of law turned him off. He insisted he did not want to be competitive, that he would not put another student down to get a better mark, that he did not want to use people to get ahead. He avoided being sexually involved with women, because he "did not want to use anyone." He could not conceive of a sexual relation that would not involve his using a woman.

Bob tried to suppress his combativeness and exploitativeness toward women, but was not able to withdraw from it in the rest of his life. He dreamed before our first session that he was pedaling a strange bicycle and another fellow was on the side seat. Some kind of war—a guerrilla war—was going on. He thought he would have to do all the pedaling in our sessions, since he had heard from another student that he would do most of the talking. He foresaw that our relationship would be a war—as were most of his relationships. He had recently been injured while riding on the side seat of a motorcycle while the driver had emerged from the accident unscathed. In his dream Bob made sure he was in the driver's seat. His prediction of a guerrilla war proved correct since he quickly made a combat of our relationship, doing his best to dodge or defeat my questions while never becoming openly angry. He was determined, as he eventually admitted, to reveal as little as possible of himself while receiving the money paid to nonpatient subjects.

The need to rip off the establishment, to beat the system, not by joining it but by exploiting it, was for Bob accompanied by a perpetual guardedness about being ripped off himself. He saw all relationships as intolerably tense combats in which the alternative to taking was being taken. He spoke of himself as being more cautious than many other students—he did not get too involved with women and did not use drugs until his second year in college. Yet his caution sprang largely from his fear of being engulfed in the anxiety other people aroused. Only with marijuana is he able to unwind from being perpetually on guard. He took it regularly as the only available relief from the tension of his combativeness.

Other students are more aware than Bob of the destructiveness in themselves and the difficulty it causes them in entering into involvements in work or with other people. For such students the primary question is how to handle their aggression in competitive situations. Fred began by telling me that he was not caught up in the rat race for grades and spends most of his time playing tennis or taking it easy. He told me it used to be different when he majored in government and felt great scholastic pressure. Since then he had decided that he wanted to make a career of tennis and that had eased the tension over grades.

On the tennis court Fred is "totally murderous." He said that "even if I'm playing my best friend, I feel real hate toward him and want to beat him as badly as possible. If I'm three games ahead, I want to be five." The heat of Fred's rage on the court had its origins in his relation with his father, a tennis pro who had an explosive temper and literally beat his sons with tennis rackets in "teaching" them how to play. Fred described his father as a nonstop talker who tyrannized the family, and whose sense of importance seemed to derive from telling his customers to go to hell and from battering his family, verbally and physically. Fred told me he saw welts from a tennis racket on his brother's back after his father had beaten him for no reason. When soon after in a similar situation Fred was about to be beaten by his father, he screamed, "Don't touch me!" and told him he would never play tennis again if he hit him. He told me he has had a nervous stomach since childhood and has had to take medication for it at times. He was sure he had become ill over nightly scenes at the dinner table, where his father let forth a stream of abuse.

Fred now beat his father regularly in tennis. He said that on occasion he let his father win because his father was so pathetic about losing. Fred's father now dealt with Fred's success in tennis by belittling it. Fred said his father never told him he did well no matter what he had done. When he was fifteen he won his first junior tournament. His father's only reaction was to berate him for losing a set in the final. He recalled vividly how hurt he had felt by his father's reaction. He had recently won his first important tournament victory over a nationally ranked tennis player. He told his friends that his father would say his opponent had not taken him seriously and was not really trying. When his father responded exactly as Fred predicted, everybody laughed. While Fred seemed to have learned how to protect himself against his father's putting him down, his father's cutting, combative belittlement has had a devastating effect on him.

Fred was tense and jittery and complained of never being able to sit still. During the hour he sat with his legs crossed and was always shaking whichever foot was off the ground. He saw his tension as related to his explosive temper, which his mother has said was just like his father's. He hated to hear this, yet sensed it was true. Before he left for college he would become angry with someone and just grab him and start a fight. He was also very irritable around the house if he was frustrated by anything. If he could not solve a problem he would berate anyone who was there, particularly his sister or his mother.

Fred, while friendlier with his mother than with his

father, felt that she too minimized his accomplishments, if only by her lack of praise for anything he did. He spoke of her as calm and self-sufficient and able to put up with pain or illness without complaining. He admired her ability to ignore his father's temper and for being "unsentimental" but this seemed to be his euphemism for coldness and general lack of responsiveness. He stated that he never saw any physical affection between his parents, and that for the last five years they have had separate bedrooms. He seemed to attribute this more to his mother than his father. That he himself had felt early frustration and disappointment in her was evident in his extreme explosiveness toward her and his sister under any stress. He also seemed to both anticipate and react violently to any rejection by women.

Fear of abusing women as his father did his mother kept Fred wary of involvement. He felt total contempt for the one woman with whom he had sexual relations. He once slapped a girl in high school who was "bitchy" toward him and has had similar impulses toward Grace, the young woman he had most romanticized. He was most enraged when he felt a woman was insensitive to his feelings or showed total disregard for them. Yet he was attracted most to women who belittled him, put him down, and criticized him. Grace and other women who attracted him were also invariably interested in other men and unwilling to become sexually involved with him. He clearly felt that by becoming the "victim" in such relationships he could avoid being the oppressor.

Fred found in tennis the vehicle for expressing his murderous anger and for his sense of life as a cutthroat competition. His tension over combat in the classroom declined as he focused his life on the sport that would permit him to express his rage in the context of a competition controlled by the rules of the game. Fred found in entering into his aggression a kind of momentary peace from the anxiety that plagues him in his relations with women and his family.

Tom was typical of students who had a sense of life as a series of competitions or deals in which everyone was out for himself, but who was able to make a satisfying life despite the conflicts he shared with students like Bob and Fred. A tall, nice-looking freshman who dressed well and had an easy manner, Tom talked slowly with an engaging humor about himself. He told me that the night before he came to see me for the first time he had not been able to sleep, thinking of the various schemes he had for selling things as part of the successful music business he had established at college. That his anxiety over his forthcoming talks with me took the form of concern over his sales ability was characteristic of Tom, who had difficulty in seeing people except as customers. He looked upon me as a prospect to whom he was selling his life.

Tom's father sold component parts for music systems and Tom had supported himself at college by opening his own branch of the business. He bought records and tapes and sold them to students as a "come-on" so that they could see the equipment he could build for them at a reasonable price. Tom spoke of his father as the best salesman he had ever met and stressed his respect for him. Yet in all his conversation about him, he spoke of his father behaving in an unreasonable way or making financial blunders, each time prefacing the anecdote with "I haven't lost any respect for my father even though . . ." Tom seemed to be trying to hold on to a picture of his father that was quite at variance with his own observations of him.

Tom's father had educated him to present a charming, anger-free surface and to look down on the customers they both regarded as virtual know-nothings who thought they knew more than they actually did and who had to be led toward the "right" choice. The covert, hidden-even-from-himself quality of Tom's disillusionment with his father's abilities was partly the outgrowth of his habit of concealing his feelings from people out of fear of losing a deal. It was his father who had perpetually stressed how important it was never to get angry at a customer.

A dream Tom had after our first session reflected his feelings about me, the customer to whom he was selling his story. He dreamed he was being chased out of the room he lived in by Ben, a big heavy fellow who was his friend. He ran out into the hall and hid behind something. Ben had a machine gun and Tom had just a hand gun. Tom did not want to shoot him so he threw his gun and hit Ben in the head. Ben turned around and proceeded to shoot Tom with the machine gun. Tom started to go to St. Luke's Hospital. Then he got off the subway and played football, but his stomach started hurting and he did go to the hospital.

Tom said he thought the dream must relate to me since he saw me at St. Luke's Hospital. His friend Ben had been instrumental in his accepting the offer to participate in the interviews and had told him that he had once made money that way. Tom also felt that ten dollars an hour was about what he could earn working for his father and he had considered his coming a good deal for him. He said he had been somewhat dismayed by my silence in the first hour. He made a point in relating the dream that when Ben turned around to shoot him he never said a word, which had been his impression of me during that hour. He quoted a favorite remark of his father's: "If you have nothing to say it's better to be silent than to open your mouth and show how stupid you are." When he realized how hostile this remark was, Tom became embarrassed and tried to reverse himself by also quoting his father to the effect that silence can be a form of wisdom and that it was smart to keep quiet. He went into some detail about the resentment he often felt with customers and how essential his father said it was not to show his irritation. He carried both a basic anger and a need to hide it into all his relationships.

Sports were the arena for Tom's freest expression of anger. In his dream he threw away his gun and then went to play football, where he presumably discharged his anger with me. He clearly felt unable to express his rage toward his father, believing that his father had all the weapons. Yet he had developed many ways of dealing with him short of direct confrontation. He said he sometimes did what he wanted and let his father find out afterward. Occasionally he had persuaded his father, but most often he made a deal with him. Tom said his father handled everything through making a deal.

The contractual nature of relationships has been imprinted on Tom's consciousness. He spoke of one close friend he made at college as someone whom he became friends with since this fellow was a mechanic and he needed a mechanic in his work. Their friendship flowed, in his eyes, from their usefulness to each other. During the time I was seeing Tom, he went home for a few days because he was able to persuade his father to pay for the plane fare if he worked every day that he was home. At one point his father regretted the deal—something Tom learned from his mother—but then decided to honor it. His mother had been hurt that the father weighed the value of Tom's homecoming in dollars and cents. Tom, by way of comforting her, said it did not bother him and that his father had ended up by giving him an extra forty dollars to take back to college. Clearly both father and son subscribed to the same dollars gained or services rendered system of measuring their affection.

Tom claimed not to be bothered by his father's emotional unresponsiveness. Yet he seemed almost tearful as he said his parents did not have too much direct communication because his father could not tolerate any disagreement, and that his mother was constantly frustrated by her inability to talk to him, and by the fact that his father was always working until late in the evening.

Tom was not aware of the degree to which he too warded off emotional involvements with women. He sensed, however, that his relationship with his father might be blocking him in his relationships with them. He told me that while his father was friendly to the women he dated, he knew his father was afraid of losing him to one of them. Tom became involved in ways that seemed to ensure that no conflict with his father would arise. His first girlfriend was a cousin whom he romanticized, while she refused to see him because they were first cousins. When he became involved sexually with a girl for the first time, he used his relationship with his cousin to check the affair, limiting their relationship to weekends and becoming really excited about the girl only after he discovered she and her family were moving to another state. He now romanticized her from a distance.

When I met Tom he was in the process of overcoming the loneliness of being away from home. He spoke of coming from a place where he had a nice home, a car, and a girl he loved to a place where nobody knew who he was and nobody cared. He described the experience as being reborn. He used sports and his enterprising endeavors in the music business in his effort to make a life for himself. Unlike Bob, who was willing to give nothing in return for what he got, Tom was eager to do his share and live up to his part of the bargain. He had all the charm of a young American businessman, wheeling and dealing in an amiable way, keeping his discontent to himself.

The explosiveness that marked competition between men often paled beside the complex rage aroused in relationships between the sexes. Sexual need and desire were for these young men invariably intertwined with intense anger toward women. Many young men felt enormous anger toward mothers who had either been unavailable or who had attempted to control every aspect of their lives. While they were often unaware of the extent of their rage toward their mothers in particular and women in general, most were faced with the problem of dealing with a free-floating fury toward women.

Peter was typical of the students I saw whose hatred and need for women originated in his sense of having been devoured by his mother. When I met him, he was concerned about admission to medical school and even more with not having a girlfriend. He spent a great deal of time having romantic fantasies about the sexual relationship he had had with Mona, a girl he knew through the last year of high school and the first year of college. He said that when he had been with her, however, he was always critical, belittled her, and paid no attention to her needs.

He also felt she could not understand his need to "grub for exams" and the fact that work "did not come easy" for him. He said she was angry at how much he was in contact with his mother—they called each other two or three times a day—and with his reporting to his mother what he did or how much he ate. It was clear to Peter that his mother had kept even closer watch than usual on him during this period.

What was not clear to Peter was the degree to which his own hypercritical attitude toward Mona when she was there and his romanticization of her when the relationship had ended reflected his own unwillingness to break free from his mother. The pattern of abusiveness, nastiness, or extreme criticism toward a girl during an involvement and of affection for her when she was beyond reach was typical of the young men whose problems with separation were greatest. Peter's sense that Mona did not understand how necessary it was for him to study and did not appreciate how hard work was for him reflected the extent to which he had absorbed his mother's unspoken message: You can trust me to look out for you, but no one else!

Peter had taken over his mother's suspicion of all outsiders. When he told his mother about our sessions, her immediate reaction was to be suspicious of me and look me up. When she discovered I was on the faculty of the medical school at the university, she was convinced that my sessions with Peter were a way of evaluating him for medical school, which was her main ambition for him. Peter was embarrassed by his mother's reaction and even more so by the degree to which it had influenced him.

Peter's attitude toward work had a particular significance in the context of his relations with women. He saw work as the only way to both please his mother and be free of her. He saw women as interfering with the work that both held him to his mother and which he hoped would permit him to escape her. His interest in medicine was stimulated by his father, who never pressured him but whose example convinced him he should study medicine: "My father," he said, "has it made. He is a successful physician and spends all his free time playing golf." Pleasure for Peter seemed to be, as it was for his father, being away from the house and his mother's dour presence.

Sexual frustration now pushed Peter toward great tension and great unease over his difficulty in maintaining relationships with women. At one point in telling me how sexually hungry he was he said that he would just like to get involved with anyone and everyone for a couple of months. He remarked, "It isn't that I just want to get sex out of my blood," but he did seem to see his sexual feelings as a disease of the blood it would be good to be free of. When questioned about this, he told me his mother has always told him about her father, who died at eighty-seven of syphilitic heart disease. She said that his mother had died when he was a young man and he had been involved with many women. She indicated that had his mother been around he would not have gotten syphilis. The fact that his disease did not prevent him from marrying or living to eighty-seven was presumably irrelevant. Peter added that she changed the channel on television whenever a program with a sexual theme came on. She always disapproved of any girl he brought home, always said the girl was just interested in getting married or tried to tear her down by saying she was not pretty. She attributed the fact that Peter did not do well during his first year in college to his involvement with Mona, and Peter seemed to agree.

Peter had so internalized his mother's wishes that he mistrusted his own need for pleasure and was made anxious even by male friends he enjoyed but considered able to divert him from his work. He spoke of a friend, Lyle, whom he described as a free spirit who always did "wild things." Peter stressed that "Lyle was OK, but only in small doses" since he had to get back to work. One night because they were going to a massage parlor, Peter took quaaludes to make him feel "looser and freer." He said they relaxed him too much since he could not "even get an erection." His inability to rely on himself and his own impulses—especially his sexual ones—in less concrete ways than this, served to prevent him from achieving both the excitement and the release he craved. He smoked a great deal of marijuana to unwind and go to sleep after studying, and apparently saw an isolated nonsexual relaxation as the only available release for him, while at the same time he craved an involvement with a woman and had fantasies about Mona.

Peter had grown up with the sense that his mother devoted her entire life to his needs and his welfare and that he needed her constant surveillance to survive. The sense of his own inadequacy—his sense that his work came hard for him, that he was too tense with women, that he was too wound up to sleep—originated in the experience of having been so totally controlled he came to believe himself unable to survive without help.

Unaware of his anger toward his mother, or the source of his suspicion of women his own age, Peter lived in a state of anxiety and joylessness. He was convinced that men want sex, but women want status and money, that women could never have anything to offer but their bodies, that this was the nature of life and not his particular vision of experience.

Some students were aware of the extent of their rage at their mothers. Some were not so limited in their hopes from another woman. They consciously seek out a nurturing and warm relationship only to find they are unable to be happily involved because of the burden of anger they carry against their mothers and cannot exorcise from themselves. They are not aware of the extent to which this anger guides them toward women who control them as effectively as their mothers did and take over their mothers' role while appearing to be nothing like the mothers who enrage them.

Jules was typical of the students whose involvement with a woman was determined by guilt over the enormity of his resentment of his mother and by a need to keep his anger in check by being controlled and subordinated to a woman's needs. A well-built college senior with an appealing, sensitive face, Jules spoke of how his first year of college had been ruined by fury at his mother, by his loneliness because he had no girlfriend, and by his poor academic performance. His situation improved when he met Edith, a student who was three years older than he, who was then in law school and with whom he had had a close relationship for the past two years. It was now this relationship that troubled him.

Jules so feared he would hurt Edith if he told her his doubts about their relationship that he only told her about loving her and acted as though he was more sure of what he felt for her than he was. He said she was twenty-five and ready to get married. He was twenty-two and wanted other experiences. He thought he might be able to marry her and be happy, but the thought made him feel middle-aged. She wanted to go on a cruise with him this summer and he saw that as dull and boring. He felt that excitement was missing in their relationship, that much of it involved his continual reassurance of her. He would like to date other women, but felt constricted because of Edith and did not want to do it without telling her. Each time he had tried to suggest they have a less binding relationship, she became quite upset. He felt so unable to deal with her or assert his needs that he had left the question of their marriage "in the hands of fate." He told her that if he went to law school in New York they would probably marry. He desperately hoped she would say that if he were accepted at an out-of-town school he should go. He was sure if the situation were reversed she would feel free to do so. He told me that she had felt free not to see him on his birthday because she had to study, but that he knew he would feel a good deal of guilt about not seeing her on her birthday because he was going to have an exam the next day.

The feeling that life with a woman involved her control over what happened and his total submission ran through Jules's life. His second-class status had been a great source of anger in his relations with his mother, whom he describes as a rigid perfectionist, a psychologist who used her aggressiveness and knowledge to tear him down.

Jules complained his mother did not get along well with anyone but his father, who was "easy-going." He saw her as critical and nosy and needing to humiliate him. She harped on all his mannerisms, asking, for example, why he was picking his face or playing with his hair. If he scratched his head, she would tell him that really indicated he wanted to masturbate, so he should go in and do it. He related an incident when he first came to college and his parents' drove him there. He went downstairs for a minute and told his mother not to unpack. But she did, despite his specific request and even arranged his prophylactics carefully on top of his dresser. He remembered feeling furious about this and clearly felt his mother tried to humiliate him by arranging even the most private aspects of his life.

Jules's anecdotes about his mother indicated how intensely he saw her attempts to control him as inextricable from her need to put him down. He mentioned that he was writing a paper on Dante. She had immediately begun suggesting things he should say. He recalled that in the sixth grade he asked her about a paper and instead of giving him advice about it, she just took it over and wrote it. While he said she was good in school and was just trying to relive her school years through him, Jules felt her way of helping indicated her lack of interest in what he thought and her predominant concern with proving to him how inferior he was.

Jules traced his deepest anger toward his mother to the loneliness he felt as a child. She worked since he was very young and he was cared for at times by his grandmother and at times by a housekeeper. He was not close to either of these women but seemed rather to wait for weekends, when he did have more time with his parents. On Saturdays his mother would always take the children out to do something, and on Sundays the whole family would go to a movie or out to dinner. His only happy childhood memories were of weekends in the city or in the family's house in the country. He seemed to have been unhappy most other times and recalled being very apprehensive as a child going off to nursery school and kindergarten. Once in kindergarten he was threatened by some boys who would not let him out of the bathroom and said they were going to flush him down the toilet. He spoke of how humiliated he felt when, a few weeks later, he wet his pants at school because he was afraid to use the bathroom. The intensity of his fear reflected how profoundly he felt he could be—and had been—figuratively flushed away.

Jules saw his father as the best-loved person in the family, good natured, happy, hard-working, and able to enjoy people. He was, Jules said, less intellectual than his mother, but had a lot of common sense. He felt that he and his father have never been close because his father "blew the relationship by being away so much of the time." His father was only home on Sundays, and one of Jules's most vivid memories was that his father was going to do something with him on a Sunday, and his father said he had to stop off at his office. Jules waited in the car for over an hour. His father came back, but told him that he would have to go up again because he had just been talking with a friend he had met and now he had to attend to the business he came for. Jules felt other people had always been more important to his father than he was. He seemed unhappy that his father did not intercede more with his mother on his behalf, and that he "never bucks my mother directly." Yet he seemed to respect his father's ability to work around her and enjoy her and his life. He spoke of how surprised he always is at how affectionate his parents are, at how much they enjoy each other's company, and how they did things together with enthusiasm and excitement. He believed this happened because his father went along with his mother, even if he resented what he did.

Jules had made a great attempt to develop sources of excitement apart from Edith, who did not seem to appeal to him as much as his mother appealed to his father. He was an officer of his class, had organized a student café, and was active in many phases of life on campus. Yet he said he keeps busy to "keep out of trouble." When asked what he meant by trouble, he said his activities helped him avoid thinking about himself. "When I get introspective," he said, "I tend to be critical of myself and to lose confidence or tear myself down." He felt that he adopted his mother's attitudes toward himself and even toward Edith, whose lack of confidence in herself both drew him to her and made him contemptuous of her at the same time. He had a dream that indicated his tendency toward self-doubt and the role Edith had played in his attempt to deal with it. In his dream he was trying to get into law school. Edith was there and three or four friends, and one person was saying he would not get in and Edith was reassuring him he would.

The person in the dream who kept saying that Jules would not be accepted was male, and that suggested to Jules that the negative male voice might have been his own. This, he said, had been very much the pattern of their relationship. He tended to tear himself down and needed Edith to give him confidence. She on her part was also terribly insecure and constantly needed his reassurance. She had called him at 6:00 A.M. that morning in terror over a final she had that day and spoke of dropping out of law school, committing herself to a hospital, or jumping out of the window. He comforted her as best he could but was bothered by her calling. He thought less of her because she was not "put together better" and thought less of himself for thinking less of her. He saw the limitations on a relationship that kept alive their inadequacies by making them the center of their relationship. Yet he feared that if he left Edith no one else would have him.

Jules saw life as a choice between isolation or involvement with a woman who riveted his life on her needs and his weaknesses. His fear of what would happen if he were able to assert his strengths, unleash his feeling, and get in touch with his own powers was reflected in a dream:

He was at a rock concert. Bob Dylan was going to be the third person on the program. There seemed to be some difficulty in hearing the first performer. Jules considered moving closer since there were a lot of empty seats near the front, which he thought perhaps had to be empty in case of fire. Somebody did move during the number, then everybody started to move forward, including Jules, and pandemonium broke out. He felt some guilt, as though he were responsible for the disorder that erupted.

Jules related some of the literal content of the dream to a beer-drinking contest between his class and another class on campus the night before. Pandemonium had broken out after the contest as students threw papers on fire out of their windows and people ran around dancing in the mud on campus until three in the morning. On one hand Jules had felt guilty for having helped organize the beer-drinking contest. On the other hand he had wanted to get drunk with the others, but Edith disapproved and he did not.

Jules spoke of liking Bob Dylan as someone who, like him, is very conscious of the immorality of the world and suffered because of it. He planned to devote his legal career to help to correct social injustice. He thought it was immoral or wrong for people to throw fiery things out the window and felt he shared with Dylan grief over the breakdown in social morality. He related by way of example how upset he got if his friends stole books from the library or mugs from the cafeteria. When a couple cut ahead of him and Edith on a movie line, he wanted to protest to them that it was wrong. Edith stopped him by saying she would feel very embarrassed and she criticized him for wanting to be everybody's conscience. He saw Edith and his mother as checking his impulses but was unaware of how much they had cut in front of him in every aspect of his life with them. Clearly Edith's coercive fragility had forced him to submit as surely as his mother's aggressiveness. Both his mother and Edith object to his "singing." Both of them were convinced that what he said to me would be reported to the school authorities and in effect told him that if he opened his mouth too much some harm would come of it.

Jules also connected his dream with his literal fear of being on center stage. He arranged all kinds of affairs on campus, but was uncomfortable in the limelight. As he did in the beer-drinking contest, he organized but did not join, he managed to do all the work and not reap the fun. He did not know how to act when his friends arranged a surprise birthday party for him. He said that his mother always took the limelight and annoyed him by coming in when he was with friends and taking over without realizing that he might want them to himself. He cannot get his mother out of the room in such instances nor is he now free to enjoy the limelight even when she is not there.

Discussing his fear of being on center stage and his emotional constriction both excited Jules and frightened him. He had a dream in which there were cattle in a corral and someone was letting them out. He was opposed to their being let out. They were running around and there were soldiers that were going to try to stop them before they reached a town and did damage. Jules intended to join the soldiers. In discussing the dream Jules related the corral and getting out of it to our discussions of his problem in following his own feelings. He told me of an incident where he spoke to a black fellow who cut in front of him on registration line at school and the fellow hit him in the chest. Jules said if he hit him again he would call the guard. The fellow did not nor did he get back in line, but Jules told the story as proof that he could get into trouble if he did not check his impulses.

Emotion as "pandemonium," fun as the "good time that gets out of hand," the beer party that turns into a brawl, the rock concert that goes wild with everyone trying to get to the stage—all reflect Jules's fear that not being contained means unleashing passions that are largely destructive, antisocial, or dangerous acts for the preservation of what is right. His emphasis on the decline in social morality, his inability to simply tell Edith he was not ready to marry were the surface reflections of his fear that were he to join the party, be in the limelight, or get in touch with his passions he would have the force of a wild herd of cattle and start a riot. Jules saw any free assertion of his will as a rebellion against his lifetime of control. He felt our sessions encouraged him to get out of his self-imposed corral. He spoke of traveling and hoped that he could get away from restrictions by being physically away from Edith and his family.

Being protective toward a woman was not easy for Jules. In his reluctance and guilty contempt for Edith's weakness, Jules expressed his anger toward her, his sense that reassuring her was a parental function he did not want to fulfill. This feeling was underlined by his resolution of his problem with Edith. He told me he had decided to ask his father to advise Edith to see a psychiatrist as a way of extricating himself. In going to his father Jules is asking for what he never got from him—protection from the woman who has a destructive force, assistance in dealing with his own fury at her for keeping him leashed and passively angry. What he wanted were directions for dealing with what he saw as the central fact of male life: the anger aroused by a woman.

Is there any alternative to war in work and sex? Some young men had actually found an equilibrium, a level of emotion where it was possible to live relatively anger-free lives with women, and become seriously involved with work in a relatively noncompetitive way. For such students, the goal of life seemed not to be in shaping the world, or defining themselves in everyday life, but carving out an area in which they had total control of their emotions and their experiences.

Hugh was typical of the students I saw who had kept his feelings in check, was fascinated by his work, and was happy with a woman whom he saw as not too important to him. He spoke of his life with an openness, a sensitivity, an uncalculating style that was not an expression of spontaneity, but the result of his control, his perfect pacing of his feelings.

He began by telling me about himself chronologically and factually, giving the dates of his birth, school attendance, and the like. After a while he said he was finished and did not know what else to say. I pointed out the yearbook quality of what he had said. He agreed and then shifted into telling me everything he had done that day in the manner of a diary entry. Only after I pointed this out did he begin to tell me what really mattered to him.

Hugh had written many short stories and has plans for two or three novels. He said that since he was fourteen he spent all his time writing, except when his "social obligations interfered." He was interested in writing that will not just reach all people but will be cosmic in scope. He thought that sooner or later we would have contact with life in other worlds, and he knew that if he met people from a different world the first thing he would want to do is see their library. That would tell him more about them than anything they could say, and he felt he wanted to write a literature that would have interest and meaning not for even the majority of people on earth but somehow for everybody that was touched by the life force. He told me early in his story that if I really wanted to know him, I would have to read some of his stories, which I indicated an interest in doing and eventually did. It was characteristic of him that he seemed to see the written word as a better way of communicating than any other. One also wondered if he did not see all human encounters as being between strangers from outer space, and his fiction as a way of communicating from the remote recesses of his feeling to people he found otherwise unreachable.

I asked Hugh about his use of the phrase "social obligations." He told me first about his relationship with Dick, a friend who had graduated from college and married and whom he felt was intellectually very stimulating. He told me how the phone kept ringing yesterday afternoon. He was busy making some cookies and he knew it must be Dick because his girlfriend, Holly, only called at night. He knew that Dick had been having difficulties with his marriage and wanted to talk to him, but he did not want to interrupt making the cookies so he did not answer. Finally at six he did answer, met Dick for dinner, watched the World Series with him, and "did not get any work done." He said, "Dick was upset over his unhappy marriage and the Mets' loss." Hugh made the point that he liked the Mets but that he was not bothered by their losing. He implied that he did not let himself get bothered by victory or defeat in a larger sense than baseball.

Withdrawal from winning or losing loomed large in Hugh's description of Dick's wedding, where he stood apart, watching his friend dance with an incredible intensity to Russian music. Hugh felt Dick was dancing his life away and would die when all the people left. He said in a sense this turned out to be the case. He also told me that Dick was Jewish and very involved in the Arab-Israeli war. When Hugh had gotten up that morning and heard the news he was annoyed at the Israelis for going so far into Syria and was annoyed at the Arabs for starting the war. Dick had impulses to join the war and fight for the Israelis and while Hugh was Lutheran, he had similar thoughts. He saw the war, he said, in a romantic sense, like Hemingway fighting in the Spanish Civil War. He thought if you went you had to fight with your guts, that you could not be uninvolved. This turned out to be part of the picture he had altogether of intense involvement as a course that could cost your life.

Hugh enjoyed Dick, found him stimulating, and drew back from him precisely because of this. He saw him as damaged by the intensity of his commitments. By remaining aloof Hugh set limits on his life. He forced Dick to take the initiative in calling him by never calling him back and spoke of his friend as an intruder on his time.

He admitted that he has always seen people this way and often only realized he missed them after they had been out of his life for six or seven months.

Hugh met Holly when he was fifteen. He said they were both closed off from other people and they allowed each other to enter their respective worlds. He said they shared the same "philos and ethos" which set them apart from other people. Holly went off to college and Hugh implied he would not have seen her anymore but "she learned that there was a bus from her school to New York," and since then she came to see him every other weekend and he went out there on alternate weekends. They also called each other on alternate nights on her insistence that she did not want the whole phone bill. He said he saw Holly as a sanctuary and Dick as a stimulus; despite the fact that he felt he got a good deal from both relationships and said he was in love with Holly, he made clear he would not take any initiative in either relationship. He would not call Holly, he said, unless she called him, and she evidently was able only to get him to call her by insisting that he call on alternate nights because of the cost.

When I asked about his lack of initiative and passivity in the relationships he claimed to enjoy, he smiled with pleasure. He said he created his characters from himself, that when he saw some trait in himself he observed it with amusement from a distance. He felt his writing was his way of dealing with a very chaotic world, and that his relationship with Holly permitted both of them to withstand the disorder of life. Making Dick and Holly call him added to his sense of control. It was, he said, when he thought about it, a strange trait.

Hugh told me a dream that he had recently about Holly. The dream had followed an evening when she had come in to see him, and he had bought her a birthday present of a chess set, which she opened that night, and they played. It was also a particularly special day to them because they first had sexual relations one year earlier on her birthday. That night Hugh dreamed that he and Holly were living in some kind of house in the suburbs where their backyard faced another backyard. There was a man up on a balcony in a red house in the yard across from Holly. Holly was in her backyard figuring out chess problems, and this man asked several times if she would like to play chess with him and she refused.

The dream led to his discussing his relationship with Holly. He saw her as social, gregarious, and far more passionate sexually than he, and said he rarely felt lust for Holly or other women. The night of the dream they had had sexual relations which had not been that exciting. He felt the house in the suburbs indicated he and Holly were married, which, he said, they would be as soon as he earned some money. He was puzzled by the man in the red house in the dream, commenting that he associated the redness of the house with sexual passion. He repeated his denial of lust and remarked he rarely gets excited about anything. As an example of one of his rare moments of strong feeling, he told me about hearing the news of Nixon's refusal to release tapes and his desire to smash the television set. He saw no reason to be jealous of Holly, since he knew that Holly was faithful to him and had heard from other people that she had turned down other men who expressed an interest in her.

The very calmness and coolness of Hugh's dream of sexual temptation reflected his way of dealing with life. While the chess game suggested to Hugh that the man in the red house was himself, he withdrew from this recognition by saying that he did not think of himself as being in red. He laughed because he happened to be wearing a red shirt that day. He said that Holly was actually very responsive to him, which made more striking his need to represent her as unresponsive. The dream seemed to be an effort on Hugh's part to cool any passion, to curb it, to keep it under control, to keep his relationship with Holly like a game of chess. In not accepting the passionate side of himself and by making sex into a chess game he made it something that he could also have control over.

Hugh went from facts of his life to his work, his friends, and his girlfriend with equanimity and coherence. When he spoke of himself, the orderliness of his discourse broke. With a good deal of intensity, he said that he avoided passion because passion is the road to madness. He said he has been close to insanity on several occasions. At such times he felt everything was out of control, and he sat enraged and alone in his room wanting to smash the walls. He had a great deal of difficulty in describing these feelings and made clear he thought it was not wise to look at them too closely because they could only stir up what he feared. He told me this is what happened when he was fourteen and his family moved to Texas and he was upset at moving again since his family had moved to Louisiana only three years earlier.

He recalled becoming angry with a pastor who was going to be responsible for confirming him and was rigid in his view of God and religion. His anger translated itself into a hatred of Martin Luther, and a crisis that was precipitated by his rejection of Luther and the church which left him unsatisfied and apprehensive at life without the church and God and without a rationale for death. He felt that such questions led only to madness, and said he had once for a period of months felt out of control and going mad. Somehow writing about things in an ironical way was of some help.

Hugh went on to talk of physical sensations he associated with his entering puberty and "encountering the life force." He became involved with what he called black arts, perhaps, he said, to attempt to control through ritual whatever mysterious forces he was experiencing. He and several friends were interested in a particular girl who thought she was a witch. He would read books on incantations and wrote chants in his notebook. They had a party once in which they took candles and went to a graveyard and tried to evoke some ghosts. Their incantations were concerned with communicating with the dead, with the life force, with killing people, with turning into a raven, with freeing the soul from the body—all the things, he said, that witchcrafters were concerned with. They were very much "into the Celtic god of death and rebirth."

Hugh made no friends in Texas except for a motorcycle group he joined. There were six of them, and they were in an accident where three of the boys in the group died, and two of the other boys died in motorcycle crashes in the next six months. Hugh was sure one was a suicide because they had been talking about death and the meaning of life before the boy left his house and drove off a bridge. Hugh felt questioning the meaning of life might make you kill yourself. He decided it was more important to survive than to ask such questions.

It was not easy for Hugh to describe his family or his childhood or the events that led him to the view of life that he had. He stressed that his father had to move the family to wherever there was work. Hugh described his family by saying that it was the kind of family where everybody went their own separate ways. His father was not home from work till 11:30 at night, often worked weekends, and Hugh saw him perhaps Sunday for breakfast. Hugh stressed how little contact he had with him. He did go on to indicate that he learned carpentry and electric circuitry because of his father's interest in them. His father stimulated him to build a very elaborate three-level tree house with walkways and windows in five big hickory trees in his backyard when he was ten. He saw their relationship, however, as restricted to the kind of work project they did together.

Hugh said his mother was "a perfect person, the one perfect person." He said she was, however, something of an elitist who thought education was good in general but that "really the better schools were for the select few." He said that his mother considered herself well-read, but she was not and he was contemptuous of her in their literary discussions.

Hugh initially insisted he had no specific memory of his mother and father prior to the age of fourteen. Most of what he said at first was limited to recent years, to defiance of his parents by his brother, to disappointment that the father was not more firm with the brother. On the other hand Hugh admired his youngest brother, whom he considered "really a genius about everything," as someone who "does not need other kids that much and goes his own way" much in the manner that Hugh does.

Hugh also claimed to know nothing about the relationship between his parents. He said he just did not see what was going on, and in fact he claimed to have very little perception about life till he started writing at fourteen. He seemed to see writing as a rebirth and seemed to see himself as having been dead prior to that, although he also described writing as a kind of crucifixion. When I asked if his mother was bothered by the father being away so much he said she never complained. He went on to relate, however, that he and his brothers would always be playing in a mud hole and coming home dirty, and his mother would say they must not and that she would not clean them up anymore, but they kept doing it and she kept cleaning them up. He seemed to suggest that he felt his mother got a dirty deal with the father as well.

When Hugh eventually did begin to discuss his childhood, he said he was tyrannical with other children, unwilling to share, and selfish. He was defiant of teachers and had to see a school psychologist when in the third grade. His description of himself suggested an angry, unhappy child. When I asked him about this, he told me of an incident in kindergarten when everybody brought in things to talk about in class. He brought in a model Nike Ajax missile that he had assembled and which had been given to him by his father. He recalled feeling contemptuous of the other kids who were presenting egg shells or milk cartons and feeling that he really had something special and they were just taking away from his time. He got up to talk and he saw that they had the same contempt for what he was presenting. He felt this meant that there was no real truth in any position and no authority to decide whose project was more interesting; and this was the beginning of his awareness that there was no logic or order in anything. He went on to recall coming upon Gödel's theorem that in every logical system there was an unproved assumption and said this upset him very much. The sense of inconsistency in the universe was deeply troubling to him. He was not aware of how profoundly this anxiety reflected his sense of his family as a series of atoms bouncing off each other without pattern or connection.

When questioned, Hugh said he realized that being so troubled by inconsistency did suggest difficulty in his relationship with his parents, but reiterated that he had no memory of them before fourteen. He told me, however, that when he was in kindergarten he had a tonsillectomy and was bleeding in the hospital. His father was out of town and his mother came to the hospital several hours late because she had been caught up in traffic. The memory stimulated him to recall similar memories and a dream that he had when he was about seven or eight. In the dream he was having a good time playing and his mother insisted that he stop to take a nap although he was not tired. He finally realized that he would have to comply but he figured he would not sleep, he would just lie in bed for an hour. He lay in bed and got out of bed to go back to play when one hour on the clock had elapsed. His mother, however, insisted that he had only been in bed five minutes and made him do it all over again.

He was aware in the dream of being angry and also had a sense of the lack of synchronization between the two of them, of her not being in touch with his needs or wishes or impulses. She wanted him to sleep when he was not tired, which also suggested wanting him quiescent and out of the way. There was also the feeling of her being so into her own time clock that she was out of touch with him.

Discussing this dream further stirred up Hugh's childhood memories. He recalled at six coming home from school and finding his mother was very upset. She rushed him onto a plane. Her father had died but she did not tell him that. She was crying all during the trip but never told him what it was about. When they arrived at her parents' home, she went into one room and was crying and then an aunt whom he hardly knew undressed him and bathed him in the sink, which bothered him no end. He said he was a modest person and the whole thing was sort of incomprehensible. The idea of his mother being so into her own grief that she could not see or think about what was happening to him was characteristic of many of the things he related. There was no sense of acute anger when he described this, but a terrible sense of misconnection, of being out of tune, just as in his dream.

Hugh than recalled that when he was two or three he would get up in the middle of the night and roam around the house doing destructive things. Once he carved up a coffee table, once he spilled a bottle of ink accidentally onto a nice chair, another time he opened up the door to the basement where the staircase had just been painted and had been locked so that the wet paint would not be walked on, and walked up and down and around the house tramping paint on the carpet and everywhere. He remembered at one point having done something that bothered his mother and she was in another room crying to his father that she did not know what she was going to do because of him. He recalled being very impressed by that and said that that kind of behavior on his part stopped in response to realizing how hurt she was. Hugh and his parents shared an image of him as destructive if he was not quiescent, as someone who had to be in tight control or else he would do damaging things.

Hugh's own sense of being damaged by forces he could not control slid into a belief that he must control his own feelings, that they too would shatter him if unleashed. The destructive potential of people who have been "innocent victims" themselves loomed large in his vision of the absurdity of life. To give me an example of the absurd he told me a story about a boy who called the police and said his cobra had gotten loose. All kinds of disasters happened to the town while the police chased the cobra. It turned out to be a garter snake that had been sold as a cobra to the boy. He told me of an incident that happened in Taiwan where a town went berserk over a fear of ghosts and an old lady was beaten to death by someone who thought she was a ghost. Then the man who was punished was not the actual man who killed her. He felt the only protection against the absurdity of life was to shut off the stimuli by spending most of your time in your room studying and working.

He returned to the theme of the dangers of passion and of being so angry that you would smash the television set, and said if you put your fist through a television set you could be electrocuted, re-emphasizing his sense that strong passion meant a lack of control which would be destructive or fatal. He kept repeating that if one acted on every impulse one would be dead. He also related it to suicidal impulses, saying that if he had killed himself every time he felt like doing so, he would have been dead a thousand times, except that it only took once for it to be final.

Hugh had reached a control of his passions that enabled him to avoid feeling or knowing the pain and disappointment of his childhood and permitted him to describe his mother as a "perfect person." His stories were mysterious, poetic, beautifully written renditions of his life: tales of people who had been victimized by parents or parent surrogates, but who with great effort put their pain out of their minds and decided not to seek vengeance. For Hugh turning his emotions into quantities manipulable as chess pieces was a way of structuring his life and achieving mastery over it. To drain feeling from his life was Hugh's particular "achievement." Yet such skill in the forcible dislocation of self from emotion was yearned for by most of the young men I saw.

To keep life from spilling off the board, out of control, out of the containing structure of the chess game, the tennis game, the con game, or the straight-and-narrow path to graduate school was the hope of most male students. Maleness was experienced by these young men as an isolating tension, the constant demand for dominance and self-control, the threat of humiliation and collapse into anger and frustration if mastery was not achieved.

Camaraderie between young men was largely based on shared anxiety, the similarity of problems with their parents, with competition, and their common uneasiness about women. All can talk about women more comfortably than they can be with them. All can knock the competitive wars at school more easily than they can extricate themselves from them. Their friendships survive longest when there is no direct competition with each other involved and each is on a relatively stable emotional course. In moments when one young man requires his friend's particular understanding, the friendship often collapses because one person lets the other down. The students I saw invariably had no one to turn to when they were most in need. They came to try to need no one at all.

The flight from emotion often began for these young men in the flight of their parents from them. Their fathers had rarely made time for them and seemed unable to manage the combined pressure of wives, children, and work. Their mothers were not able to see them as people.

Often both parents arranged their lives so as not to include their children's needs. Strained relations between parents often resulted in a father's emotional abandonment of his children. Peter's father was typical of those men who won their "freedom" from their wives by giving up their children and leaving them to occupy the woman they did not want to be around. He preserved his capacity for enjoyment by withdrawing from his controlling, dour wife and sacrificing Peter. Jules's father preserved a stimulating marriage by enjoying his wife's intelligence and charm and permitting both of them to avoid daily involvement with their children. In both situations the marriage survived at the expense of the children. The young men I saw had been profoundly frustrated in their wish to be close to their fathers and to find in them protection, warmth, and the trust that would help them deal with their fears about themselves.

Fathers who did become involved with their sons often did so in a way that cemented them in competitive, anxiety-ridden situations, or undermined their ability to become independent. The competitive work situations that constituted the major bond between such fathers and sons served to create models for the sons' future relations with men. It is not surprising that many students seek a withdrawal from competitive war, or feel excessively wounded by its demands. For most it signifies the kind of manhood they saw embodied in fathers who left little room in their lives for tenderness, affection, or fatherhood.

The fathers' investment in competition often left the students with inhibitions about outdoing them. They frequently dreamed of their fathers as senile, pathetic, and ready to die. This was countered in waking life by a refusal to acknowledge their fathers' decline or defects. Tom's need not to criticize his father's salesmanship despite what he had seen was typical; many students insisted their fathers could beat them regularly at sports in which they had long since surpassed them. Even Fred, whose anger toward his father was conscious, let his father win because he was "too pathetic" when he lost. The message these students get from their fathers is that their manhood will be their fathers' downfall.

Coolness, estrangement, frustration, and loss were often the primary experiences of these young men with their mothers. If their fathers had often used work to escape from their wives, the mothers of most of these young men were unable to find any more satisfaction or fulfillment in their children than they had in their husbands. Many of the students I saw felt their mothers were so uninvolved with them that nothing they said or did could bridge the gap between them or prevent their mothers' detachment. Fred's mother was impervious to both her husband's outbursts of fury and to her son's successes in tennis. She seems to have disengaged her emotions from her family—perhaps to survive with so violent a husband —but in the process she provoked greater and greater anger from her husband and son because of her withdrawal. Peter's mother had a devouring, controlling concern for his professional success, but had so little concern for his happiness that he believed no relationship was possible with her if he did not get into medical school. Hugh saw his mother as always more involved in her unhappiness than in him. Many students saw their mothers as incapable of involvement with them through their personal depression or their need to belittle and control. Not surprisingly these young men feel enormous resentment toward their mothers for not caring how they felt, for being unconcerned with their happiness while, at the same time, often demanding that they reflect well on them by great achievement at school.

The conception that closeness with a woman would unleash rage was widespread among the students I saw. Fred, who feared he would beat any woman he got involved with, and who had already slapped a girl he knew in high school, only dramatized feelings that many students had. He and Bob pulled back from close sexual involvements, fearing their own potential to do harm. Often this kind of withdrawal marks a stage of initial inhibition over abusing women which is eroded by time and sexual need. It is the sense of anger at the core that shapes the methods students use to deal with women.

Scoring, the casual sexual encounter, seems to most young men the means of dealing with the problems intimacy might arouse and the way to express anger toward women without getting too involved with them. Men like Peter, Fred, and Bob who have no expectations of tenderness, friendship, or understanding from women, and who have never felt loved by their mothers, do not seek any real affection or friendship from women. Nor could they accept tenderness or concern if they were offered them.

Many young men believe they want a romantic attachment to a woman but immediately begin tearing her down, belittling, or abusing her as soon as they get involved. Such men will generally treat women with whatever cruelty it takes to drive them away, often unaware that the woman is guilty of nothing more than being a woman who cares for them. Such students invariably remain unaware of the source of their anger and believe their criticisms are well-founded. They keep alive the belief in their capacity for love by being drawn to hopeless situations in which a woman is perfect but unattainable. Often the woman they have been belittling figuratively steps onto their pedestal after she leaves or withdraws from the relationship.

Other students who find themselves helpless in the face of their own anger toward women move further into passivity to protect themselves and their girlfriends against their anger. The degree to which retreat from anger has increasingly become a problem for the young is underlined by the fact that impotence is now one of the most frequent symptoms bringing students today to seek help (see chapter 10). Several of the nonpatient students were also impotent, but were not seeking help and preferred to maintain nonsexual relations with women. Removing sex from life, eliminating physical passion was their way of draining the emotion out of their connection to women. What they feared was that sexual release would loosen the brakes on their anger.

Other young men struggle to quench the rage in themselves while at the same time forming a sexual, emotional, and intellectual closeness to a woman. Such men often establish relationships in which their impulses are checked by the woman. Young men who come from situations where they have been controlled themselves often handle their anger by finding a woman who will control them. Their own retaliatory impulses to control the woman often keep such relationships on a seesaw of submission and dominance in which each uses the other to control their aggression. This alternation often marks the painful attempt to find a point of equilibrium.

Relationships based on mutual insecurity and mutual reassurance often serve to keep anger in check. Yet as

Jules's situation makes clear, insecurity is not sufficient to keep anger in check for long. Like many students he was finding the burden of providing reassurance in the hope of insuring a similar return too great.

Many young men had given up on living a life that coincided with their feelings and involved any emotional depth. They felt that life would work out for them if they could learn to cool their anger or deal with it adroitly. Not being bothered by an absence of feeling or caring was the mark of their refusal to be grossly upset by anything. As the impotent students claimed they were not disturbed by their impotence and believed they would marry a girl who was not bothered by it either, so most of the young men I saw did not see their constriction as a problem.

Joylessness marks the lives of most young men today. The image of freewheeling scorers projected in the men's magazines, the Pepsi ads for the generation that lives thoroughly, enjoying the moment appeals as the fantasy of life that is unavailable in actual terms. Joyous, capable of pleasure in small things in a new and intense way is what these young men are not. Competitive sports, which Erich Fromm once referred to as the last unalienated activity, have become intolerable in college for many young men who played actively throughout their boyhood and adolescence. The strain of competition, the sense of winning being responsible for another person's humiliation, or of losing being responsible for their own, is fatal to their enjoyment.

Pleasure in work, thought, and study is eroded for many young men by the sense that their achievement is something accomplished for someone else, for the gratification of the parents they feel have let them down. Sniping at each other in class for grades greatly diminishes the pleasure of discussion, which becomes another extension of the grind. One result of the joylessness of work is the wish to use it as a means to escape work, the desire for an affluence that would minimize time spent at a particular field and maximize leisure. The attempt to win the prize without competing in any field was another sign of the same distaste. Yet some young men deal with the same pressures by reacting against the rip-off, materialistic, me-first mentality around them. Like Jules, who was outraged at people who stole from the library or cut in on line, and who wanted to work in public law improving the lot of the poor, some young men want to eliminate what they see as the disease of self-interest. Becoming activists in law, medicine, or other fields on behalf of the consumer, the poor, the sick, the unprotected, they often wage their fights with a grimness and solitariness that is the mark of having been scarred by the rip-off mentality they hate. Often their only available means of expressing what they feel is through the screen of a worthwhile cause.

Most of the young men I saw could not acknowledge they felt *they* were a worthwhile cause. They have been accustomed to not being seen, to being coerced into following paths that did not lead to their own interests or fulfill their own needs. Putting their emotions on center stage, permitting themselves to see exactly what they felt, and to express it on their own behalf aroused such anxiety because it was inextricable from the rage they felt at having been denied for a lifetime. The anger connected with being—or wanting to be—seen or noticed makes it a frightening experience.

The need to fight on behalf of someone else at the expense of one's own life and the need to rip off society, women, and friends for personal gratification are two sides of the coin of emotional constriction. Both are designed to minimize involvement in a deep and personal way. Nothing distinguishes this generation of young men more than the degree to which they are irresistibly drawn to killing feeling as a means of survival. Working at making life not matter may be intended simply to remove the depressions, the hurts, the angers that afflict, leaving only the better emotions. Yet the habit of detachment, once acquired, leads inevitably to a general numbing in the face of all experience. Belittling people to cut down their importance, attempting to control the flow of experience, concentrating only on one's personal gratification without concern for anyone else's are defensive maneuvers that inescapably squeeze the juice out of life.

4

The New Homosexual

MAYORS BOASTING in news stories of their towns' Gay Pride week, college officials who speak with satisfaction of increasing attendance in gay groups on campus, and glittering articles on bisexual chic are marks of a changing cultural attitude toward homosexuality. What does that change say about homosexuals and us?

It is hard to grow up to be either a man or woman in this culture today. Given the pitch of anger between the sexes and the modishness of sexual experimentation, it does not come as a surprise that what makes news are alternatives to heterosexuality. Surely one thing helping to liberate homosexuals is the extent to which marriage and family life are becoming so full of tension that people who are not homosexual are less willing to defend them or to insist that heterosexuality is intrinsically better than anything else.

Militant homosexuals often exploit the prevailing heterosexual morass by presenting themselves as the avant-garde of the sexual revolution. They have had great success in a society in which one of the few unchallenged values is the good of experiencing all. Many militants, however, are not satisfied by mere acceptance or tolerance. They want to be seen with different eyes. Some of their most notable battles in gaining a different image have been with psychiatry. In 1974 the American Psychiatric Association removed homosexuality from its list of illnesses largely under pressure from gay liberation groups who maintained that psychiatrists have only seen the sick and disturbed among them, and that there are innumerable happy, well-adjusted homosexuals who do not seek treatment. Their implication was that society, reinforced by psychiatric classification, has judged as a sickness what was merely an alternative.

The politics of liberation relies on the portrait of the happy, contented homosexual advanced by the militant groups. The truth is that neither militants nor psychiatrists have yet given us an accurate picture of the inner lives of the nonpatient homosexual. Militants are helped by the cultural trend toward politicization of feeling. The tendency is for individuals to make their problems collective, to find others with similar problems, and to see the beliefs of all others as the problem. Anguish becomes converted into a series of rallying cries: If growing up in your family has been a horror, do away with families! If intimacy is frightening, let us have open marriage! If children seem like a curse, let everyone stop having them. What were once personal choices are now causes proselytized and offered as the wave of the future.

People and the actual feelings of the individual get lost in the collective personality movements adopt. One purpose of movements is often to do precisely that—to depersonalize emotion and reduce its force and charge. One can ignore what life is like for the young homosexual who is neither an extreme militant nor dissatisfied with homosexuality. Yet he is crucial to the militants' argument and the culture's acceptance of homosexuality as an alternate choice. Is he as contented with his homosexuality as he says or as the militants insist?

As part of the study of nonpatient students selected at random, I saw homosexuals who were not patients and who said they were satisfied with their lives. They referred me to other students who also felt they were happy in their homosexuality. These young men had grown up during the sexual revolution and had come to a leading college long after the gay life had been institutionalized on campus. All the young men I saw were open about being homosexual, all more or less accepted it. Some were active in gay liberation groups, but most were contemptuous of men who made their homosexuality their entire life. All were sympathetic to the goals of the movement and many shared its mistrust of psychiatrists as being basically opposed to their life-style. They were bright, personable, and many were quite successful in their work. How did they feel about their lives?

Hal, a tall, handsome junior of twenty, was typical of students who said they had never had conflict over their homosexuality. He disparaged homosexuals who did not accept their sexuality and struggled against it. But he experienced homosexuality as painful and full of rejection. His only love affair had been in high school, when he became interested in Craig, a good-looking, athletic boy he pursued into friendship and then persuaded into a sexual involvement with him. When their relationship began to deteriorate, Hal arranged a summer for them in Europe to recapture Craig's interest. The trip was a failure, Craig was always reluctant sexually, and when they did have sex, he would always blame Hal afterward and leave him feeling humiliated. Craig subsequently married. None of Hal's homosexual experiences since that first affair have meant much to him.

A feature in the *Village Voice* on the Gay Activist Alliance's bars introduced him to the gay life when he came to college in New York. When he was "coming out" he answered an ad placed by a gay counseling group, which further involved him in the homosexual scene. His first experience was with a fellow he met at a bar who brought him home to his roommate and all three of them became sexually involved. Hal felt afterward that they were just using him to put some excitement into their relationship. During the time I saw him he went with some homosexual friends to a bar. They did not meet anybody and they all went out to eat afterward. Someone at an adjoining table vomited, and Hal came home feeling a kind of disgust with the whole experience, as though the man vomiting next to him symbolized everything that had gone on. He still felt "compelled" to go to gay bars, but always found the experience humiliating, whether he met someone and made out or not.

Hal's feelings about his sexual life filled a recent nightmare in which he was on an Arctic expedition trudging through the lacerating cold when he was crushed by a serpent. He spoke ironically of the serpent as "merely a phallic symbol," but he spoke with feeling of his sense of being painfully crushed in homosexual relations. He thought he partly crushed himself since he became subservient when he really cared for a man and wanted to do everything to please him.

Rejection and disappointment characterized Hal's sexual life. He says he would like to know someone who shared his background and interests, but he has rebuffed several students he met on campus. He seems to be drawn into becoming the pursuer who does not know whether the other person will accept him.

Rejection is for Hal a painfully familiar bond to other people. He described his mother as an "efficient machine with no heart or warmth," who had "more feeling for her cocker spaniel than for anyone else." He spoke of his parents as cool and removed and frequently dreamed of his home and family in an Arctic wasteland setting. His mother habitually put down his father in a cruel way and he would be on her side. He felt she was possessive of him and jealous the few times in high school when he had been interested in a girl. She often implied she was bored with her sexual life. Hal felt his father was unconcerned with his feelings or opinions on matters of importance but was an "obsessive, orderly person who filled his life with small things."

Whatever closeness Hal seemed to have had with his mother came primarily through his complicity in her contempt for his father. He saw her as a hard-driving woman whose ambition and success at work had totally absorbed her life. He felt she had only been concerned with his performance at school and he had felt pressured by her as long as he could remember, a situation which always made the school year a long bout of tension, insecurity, and anxiety. The summer brought no relief because he was always sent away to some sort of educational camp. In the climate of iciness and rejection he felt with his mother, rejecting his father and taking her side had been virtually the only warmth he had known.

Since he thought that neither of his parents had much interest in his feelings, Hal never discussed his homosexuality with them. He made no great attempt to conceal his

activities, but had never felt they called for an open statement. He dealt with his parents' indifference by pretending
not to care about it. He adopted a self-protective abusiveness toward homosexuals who confide in their families,
claiming such people tell their parents as a way of asking
for help to change or because they need their parents to
accept them as they are. He said he did not need his parents' blessing or their help.

Rejecting and belittling homosexuals who handled their
lives differently than he was part of a larger incapacity to
feel compassion. Hal said his lack of sympathy was a trait
he got from his mother, who dealt with problems like a
captain in the army. Rather than exposing himself to a
painful rebuff, Hal preferred to mock people who exposed
their vulnerability or their problems. He spoke of his acceptance of his homosexuality as part of a general tendency he had to accept all situations and not to fight them.
He saw himself as more resigned than self-accepting.

Hal feared that any close relationship would prove destructive and painful. His fear had been borne out in his
relation with Craig, which he thought had lost its warmth
and friendship with the onset of overt sexual experience.
He hoped for "a long relationship with a man," but his
ambivalence was expressed when he quickly added the pro-
viso, "so long as it did not interfere with my work." He
wanted an equal balance in an affair "where everybody is
willing to do everything, not one lover or one beloved or
any role playing," but he found himself attracted to men
who would reject him and uninterested in those who cared.
He retreated from his conflicts by resignation to a life of
casual contacts that were so meaningless that they could
not deeply hurt him.

Hal has learned how to use the Arctic mentality of his
mother as a way of warding off the intense pain and deg-

radation he experienced in a sexual life colored by emotion. His fear was allayed by the shallowness of most of his contacts. He did not want to change his life, but was resigned to the inevitability of humiliation and unhappiness in any relation that meant something. Insisting that he had no conflicts about his life, his mocking derisiveness of homosexuals who felt otherwise reinforced and cemented him in a coolness and denial in which he could bury his sense of rejection.

Other homosexuals cannot find relief by freezing themselves to their own emotions. They coincide with the full force of their anger and pain. Barry, a well-built junior of nineteen, spoke very seriously, and almost without stopping, of the pleasure he took in his work and earnestly reported that his music teacher had called him the "best composer of his generation." He said that he accepted homosexuality as a life-style, but that it was "messing up his life."

Barry saw homosexuality as degrading and connected it with his own feelings of inadequacy since he was a child. He said he was never a good athlete and never liked his body, remarking that he had a weight problem when he was younger and felt fat, ugly, and feminine. He had gone through boyhood and early adolescence feeling unattractive to everyone. He felt humiliated by both boys and girls in his first efforts to approach girls when he was at camp between the ages of eleven and thirteen. He recalled with particular embarrassment that he thought he had breasts like a girl, and he remembered feeling humiliated when kids at camp sang a song about queers that he felt was specifically directed at him. Male and female were constantly on his mind as expressions of self-confidence and hideousness.

Barry felt his mother had discouraged his masculinity

when he was little in ways ranging from preventing him from playing with other boys to dressing him as a girl for a costume party to which his younger brother went as a pirate. Barry envied his brother's athletic ability, his self-confidence, and his relationship with their father. His mother, however, had encouraged him to feel his father and brother were not as sensitive, creative, or intelligent as she and Barry. Later she became concerned over Barry's feminine behavior and disparaged him for it.

Barry hated the submissive, insecure aspect of himself and was drawn toward men he felt were masculine in an attempt to draw on their strength and incorporate it. How much his rage and humiliation shaped his homosexuality was dramatized in a dream in which he was defecating on a student in his history class whom he found attractive. His dream reflects his vision of relationships as a struggle to determine who degrades and befouls and who is degraded and befouled. While in his dream he expresses his wish to be the one who degrades, in reality he is invariably the one who is "messed up."

Barry is in touch with the raw, humiliating aspects of an attempt to achieve masculinity. He finds in acceptance of homosexuality as a life-style on the intellectual level, no relief from personal torment. He fantasizes a future relationship with a woman as saving him from the degradation he feels with men. But there were students who had found a way out of the pain of both rejection and degradation through their ability to deny who they are having sex with, and to make distinctions between male and female relatively unimportant.

In the new sexual mythology bisexuals are presumably the freest, most open people, who have simply "doubled their pleasure." Yet for homosexuals who envision bisexuality as a permanent life-style, the relation to men and women has a rather different significance. Carl, a tall, thin student with long hair, was typical of those who had found in bisexuality a compromise that permitted an escape from the pain and degradation of the homosexual world. Carl had sustained homosexual affairs all through high school and college, but was now living with a woman and had been for his entire junior year. He continued to have occasional homosexual experiences and his girlfriend was willing to accept these, provided he did not have any sustained or continuing affair with a man. Although Carl had sexual relations with Stella several times a week, during intercourse he would always fantasize that he was having sex with a man.

Carl seemed to hope that by dividing himself between men and women he would be protected from both. He did not hide his homosexuality, but had been profoundly hurt and disillusioned in intense love relationships with men. He believed his pleasure, spontaneity, and relaxation were greater with a man than a woman, but regarded Stella as his best friend and a refuge from the intense turmoil bound up for him in homosexual relations. Carl's inability to become deeply involved with her served to neutralize the emotional charge of all his sexual activity. He had avoided the pain he felt would come from involvement with either sex by becoming involved with both in a way that prevented his loving either.

Carl's sense of being trapped between two destructive unsatisfying alternatives had a long history. He had been a casualty in the war between his parents, remembering his childhood in terms of hearing his parents arguing nightly after he went to bed. He dreams he and his brother are caught in the crossfire of an underground battle between the Mafia and the blacks. Carl had tried to bury his sense of being the victim of the war in his family. His family is in fact divided into two camps with his brother and father in one and Carl and his mother in the other.

Carl was typical of homosexual students in having been his mother's accomplice and confidant. After allowing his grandparents to raise him until he was 2½, Carl's mother later attempted to bind him to her by confiding her dissatisfaction with his father, her boredom with her life. He said there was no physical warmth between his parents or between them and him. His mother told Carl that if he had to have sex, he should not have it with a nice girl. Carl's father worked seven days a week and came home tired, able to watch TV for a while and go to sleep. Carl felt his mother was really too good for him. In a current dream he saw himself in England visiting the queen. At one point some man stood up and said, "God save the king." Carl was glad the queen stood up and said, "No, it's God save the queen." Everyone then sang "God Save the Queen."

Carl clearly feels his mother is as removed from him and as important to him as a queen. He spoke of her as completely unaware of his loneliness as a child. She professed to be surprised when he told her at sixteen that he was homosexual. He said his father was totally inattentive and out of touch with him and that he had no respect for him and had never known any affection from him. His father had reacted to the news of his homosexuality by smacking him with his fist in the face.

Carl has moved toward adopting his mother's coolness and detachment. He dreamed of himself as the comet Kohoutek, an astral image that suggests how burnt out and remote he feels. By spacing out, he manages to maintain his bisexuality, avoid involvement with either sex, and maintain the primacy of his attachment to a mother whose early abandonment of him so terrified him that he is willing to pay the price of feeling to maintain his connection to her.

Fragmentation of sexual experience was the defense of other bisexual students like Carl who used each sex against the other as a way of avoiding involvement in either. Overriding sex is despair over the possibilities of life with men or women. Bisexuality became a way of splitting even erotic attachment so that neither sex becomes an indispensable pleasure source. The so-called bisexuality of homosexual students like Carl served to strip sex of sensation by divorcing it from its object.

Carl, Hal, and Barry were typical of the young homosexuals I saw in their openness about their homosexuality and their assertions of self-acceptance. The homosexual revolution has made it easier for young men like Hal to deny how painful their life is. It has encouraged students like Barry to accept homosexuality as a life-style and believe that only his disgust is the problem, and it permits others like Carl to think of themselves as part of the new wave. Nevertheless the pain and humiliation they experience makes their personal lives a nightmare.

The homosexual world is exerting taboos of its own. Young men are now not only faced with the traditional forces that encourage homosexuals to hate themselves, but also must contend with a strong counterpressure to deny even to themselves whatever conflict, pain, or anguish they feel. Many young men who are uncertain which way they will commit their sexual lives are under extraordinary pressure from what is becoming the institutional structure of homosexuality—the organizations ranging from sanctioned gay lounges to sensitivity sessions—in which people are encouraged to think of their conflicts as merely socially induced inhibitions over being what they are. Openness and politicization of homosexuality may overcome a sense of isolation, but for many they substitute the tension of denial.

Are homosexuals right in attributing their painful lives to oppression and in comparing themselves to blacks as an oppressed minority? Certainly the pain and suffering experienced by homosexuals is partly the outgrowth of social disapproval, repression, and discrimination. And just as the black militants' assertion that black is beautiful did not succeed in making black people feel beautiful, so now the homosexuals' assertion of happiness, the new myth of conflict-free homosexuality, and assertions of gay pride do not make homosexuals feel happy. Nor can psychiatric declarations, even though motivated by sympathy for the social and legal situation of homosexuals, create by fiat a diminished sense of self-hatred.

The analogy between discrimination against homosexuals and the oppression of blacks fails us for other reasons. There is fairly unanimous agreement, at least among social scientists, that racial oppression is a socially disruptive, harmful force. The social treatment of homosexuals, while unfair and unwarranted, is not in the same category if only because of the substantial evidence that homosexuality is itself socially disruptive and a sign of social breakdown. Obviously it is not a problem to be dealt with by repression; obviously society does not gain by making life uncomfortable for homosexuals. But society does have a stake in heterosexuality. As long as it does, homosexuality will be regarded as a socially less desirable alternative. As long as it is, homosexuals will grow up in a culture that to some degree disparages homosexuality. The prohibition against it is still so strong that it takes a great deal of unhappiness and sexual confusion to push someone in a homosexual direction.

More than social disapproval seems involved in the pain, suffering, and degradation of homosexual relations. The same disastrous early experiences of homosexuals that have led them to a homosexual adaptation operate to insure that pain, rejection, humiliation, and degradation are an integral part of their relationships.

Homosexuality must be seen in the context of the forces that are pulling people apart, the sexual anger that fills families with tension. Many of the mothers of the homosexual students had confided their unhappiness with their husbands to their sons and had made them their confidants in ways that were reminiscent of the mothers of many of the women students I saw. The boy derives whatever self-esteem he can from his narcissistic identification with a mother who remains through his life a queen.

We have long been aware that in no group is the absence of a relationship with the father more striking than with homosexuals. Bieber et al. in their comprehensive study of male homosexuality underlined this point by stating that "a constructive, supportive, warmly related father precludes the possibility of a homosexual son," protecting him from a homosexual resolution of any difficulties with his mother. Yet the father's absence is less causal in itself than it is a measure of difficulties between the parents. Even when the father was available, the mothers of these boys discouraged a relationship with their fathers and made these sons their own, while often leaving another son to become the father's child. Studies of identical twins have shown the pairing of one son with a mother and another with a father is significant in the one becoming homosexual while the other does not.

While one can agree with Bieber that with an involved and constructive father no boy would become homosexual, no matter what kind of mother he had, it is worth noting that boys raised with no father at all usually grow up without becoming homosexual. It seems at least as true that in the presence of a mother who enjoys and encourages the maleness of her son, no boy becomes homosexual whether he has a father or not. In most situations it seems to take both parents to make a homosexual. In the lives of young homosexuals the withdrawal of men from their wives and children and the anger of women toward their husbands leave their mark with a particularly cruel force.

Increasing mistrust between the sexes and the cultural trend toward prizing experience over all encourages some young men to think they should try anything once. Not all the students I saw who had homosexual experience while at college were homosexual in their interest and arousal patterns. Some students who are clearly heterosexual have homosexual experience in periods of severe depression often following heterosexual rejection. Fragmentation —the sense of life as a series of isolated experiences—can permit such students to envisage homosexual relations as simply another experience. But afterward the student usually feels depressed, humiliated, and anxious about his masculinity. Such experience was comparable to the casual sexual activity in a mood of desperation following rejection that one sees in female students. Fragmentation and detachment may serve in both cases to cut the student off from awareness of what has made him or her so profoundly upset.

What makes it increasingly harder to accept assertions of happiness or distress as providing any adequate picture of emotional life is the degree to which denial of feeling and even estrangement from acute turmoil have become widespread. The several impotent young men I saw among the nonpatient students expected to marry and hoped their wives would accept their impotence as they did. Their hopes, their lack of interest in help, do not signify they have no problem, but reflect their way of dealing with a situation they expected to persist for a lifetime.

This is a society that is increasingly denying its impotence by calling it tolerance, preaching resignation, and naming all this progress. Homosexuality is only one sign of existing disruption in the family, of its failure to be what society needs it to be: a force for stability, affection, and love. While oppression and intolerance of the individual homosexual is both cruel and foolish, the notion that social approval is a way of dealing with the question is equally destructive and mindless. Substituting approval for understanding is to confuse acceptance of social distress with controlling it. The more we approve of or institutionalize symptoms of disruption, the more we distract ourselves from the individual tragedies involved and the less chance we have to reverse the forces that tear the sexes apart and encourage homosexuality.

PART THREE

The
Drug
Degree

No more dramatic expression of the dissatisfaction students feel with themselves can be found than students abusing drugs. Students often become drug abusers, that is, heavy and habitual users, in an attempt to alter their emotional lives, to transform themselves into the people they wish they could be, but feel they never could be without drugs. What they crave is to restructure their own emotions, not to be themselves, but to live as some "other." What this "other" is like and how it can be achieved cut to the center of the changing American psyche.

The turmoil over performance, achievement, and success, the increasing terror of becoming "too" involved with anyone; the attempt to find in fragmentation the means of effecting a pervasive change in one's total relation to life—all these are everywhere prevalent on campus. Students abusing drugs are often attempting to cure themselves of the malaise they see everywhere around them and in themselves.

Why do some students take LSD or heroin while others

take marijuana or amphetamines? Why do still others take anything and everything? Students who are intrigued by drugs can learn through trial and error and from other students to find and favor the drugs which most satisfy their particular emotional needs. They rapidly become expert psychopharmacologists, able to locate the specific drug cure for what disturbs them. One student who by seventeen had tried just about everything and had become a daily, intravenous heroin user, had rejected LSD early in his drug career, explaining, "I can't see what anyone gets out of it. It just sort of makes you schizy—quiet one minute and freaked out the next."

Some students were initially drawn to the "cops-and-robbers" quality of drug abuse. While they were clearly out to defy their parents and the whole structure of authority, they were often unaware that their abuse had anything to do with their families, so profoundly had they pushed their rage at them out of their consciousness. Such students were invariably unable to deal with their parents directly and were bound in a need to defy them and a simultaneous need to punish themselves for their rebellion.

Drugs provided these students with both crime and punishment, while removing their defiance out of the direct presence of their parents. One student would "let his mind float away" and concentrate on music he liked whenever his father berated him. Afterward he went out and took whatever drugs he could buy. While he never connected his drug abuse with his anger toward his father, he often dreamed of it as a crime for which he would be punished. He had a dream in which a riot was going on in another part of town while he was shooting heroin. He was afraid that somehow he would be arrested along with the rioters. Drugs were clearly his way of rioting, of diverting the crime of rebellion to the crime of drug abuse and focusing his destructive potential on himself. The expectation this student had that he would be arrested was typical, and revelatory of the appeal of drugs for him. Jail signified to such students a concrete way of locking up their rage. Drugs permitted them to both contain their rage and to express it in a way that gave them a sense of defiance, however self-damaging that defiance may be. Often, students who are most in trouble with the police over drugs are those for whom the need for crime and punishment was more significant than the need for drugs.

For most of the students who abused them, drugs also provided the illusion of pleasurable connection to other people while serving to detach them from the emotions real involvement would arouse. Drugs were, for these students, the best available means of social relations. Heroin abusers found in the junkie underworld a sense of security, belonging, and acceptance derived from the acknowledgment and the shared need for heroin. LSD abusers felt their most intimate experiences involved tripping with another person. Marijuana abusers felt that drugs "took the edge off their personality" enough to permit them to be gentle and to empathize with other people. Amphetamine abusers were pushed into the social round on amphetamine energy, often being enabled to go through sexual experience they would otherwise have found unendurable.

For many students drug abuse is the means to a life without drugs. Such students take drugs to support the adaptation they are struggling to make. Once it is established, they are often able to maintain it without drugs. The period of heavy drug abuse often marks the crisis in their lives when they are trying to establish a tolerable relation to the world and themselves. Appealing, tumultuous, sometimes frighteningly empty, the lives of students who turn to drugs are an intense, dramatic revelation of the way students feel today, what they are forced to grapple with not only in the culture, but in themselves.

5

Marionettes on Amphetamine Strings

CONFLICTS OVER performance, competition, and achievement have traditionally been associated with men. Yet nothing more clearly suggests what has changed in this culture than the psychodynamics of amphetamine abuse and the fact that the overwhelming majority of student abusers are women. When Thomas Pynchon wrote in V. about an eternal woman who had conquered her vulnerability to hate, love, and death by becoming a virtual automaton, he captured the dream of many young women. If marijuana was the drug of choice for men who sought in drugs reinforcement for withdrawal from parental demands for achievement and from competition, so amphetamines were the drug chosen by women who were determined to push themselves, despite their feelings, toward goals which had been set for them by others. For some this meant career success, for others marriage, for still others a combination of both. But all these young women used amphetamines to drive themselves toward ways of life they did not desire, but felt they had to pursue.

The women on amphetamines I saw learned early in their relationship with their families that their needs would not be met or even acknowledged. They have been taught to ignore their own feelings and to handle their frustration by pleasing someone else and by sacrificing themselves to obey their parents' needs. This self-destructive compliance pervaded every area of their lives, their relation to men, to other women, and to their work. Amphetamines were the fuel that permitted them to disown their own frustration, to control their rebellious impulses, and to make them function to fulfill their parents' expectations like automatons.

Alison was a twenty-two-year-old senior in college when she was referred to me because of her enormous use of amphetamines. An attractive, fair-haired woman with a nice figure, she dressed in the most dramatic clothes, long flowing dresses, striking slacks, the latest in fashion—all of which she wore like theatrical costumes designed to set her apart from the other women who dress more casually.

Alison speaks of her life as a series of dramatic events in which she appears as a gifted or dangerous and destructive heroine. She says that as a child she gave concerts with prominent orchestras and had her paintings exhibited in major museums. Coupled with these exaggerations are frequent mentions of what Alison calls "pranks." She claims to have interfered with the generator supplying power to the town where she went to boarding school so there would be no light service and no final exams. She says she once put mescaline in the principal's tea. She says a man who was hassling her jumped on the hood of her car and to punish him she drove him twelve miles at high speed then stopped quickly, went into reverse, threw him off, and left him stranded.

She says she was on the verge of having her friends kidnap her former psychiatrist, who wanted to hospitalize her, with a view to leaving him tied up in the grounds of a state mental hospital. She claims to have been adopted by all fourteen boys in a local fraternity chapter, who treat her in a protective nonsexual way, from helping her with exams to advising her on her personal life. Alison's tales of recognition for her talents, her pranks, and her story of adoption all seemed designed to conceal how lonely and empty she feels about her life.

Since her first year in college, Alison has dealt with her dissatisfactions by taking amphetamines. She said she had wanted to go to a less pressured school, but her family had not permitted her to do so. She feels that she was brought up to be both successful at school and to get married; with the aid of amphetamines she hopes to do both. She says she puts all her "emotional problems into the garbage" and does not look at them, but "every once in a while they catch up with her" and she feels "unable to cope with anything." She sees amphetamines as pushing her toward functioning without regard to her feelings. She treads a precarious tightrope between nonfunctioning because of unhappiness and nonfunctioning because of mounting amphetamine doses (close to 200 mgs daily) that produce a drug-induced state of terror.

Alison's sense of having been programmed has a long history and finds explicit expression in her referring to herself ironically as "it" and speaking of herself as a machine running on automatic. Her detachment extends to a lifelessness of voice, a habit of relating tormenting situations with extreme blandness. She said her parents both treated her as a commodity and gave her lessons in everything—tennis, swimming, riding, piano, art. She felt her parents did not consider her feelings in any of these things. She described her father as a prominent businessman who mechanically and impersonally manufactured her to be a "successful commodity." He told her that "the merchandise is going off to school to be processed." She saw him as extremely strict, tyrannical, and prone to get upset at almost anything she did. He died when she was fourteen.

Despite her description of her father, it was clear that Alison had been involved with him. She avoids current involvements because she feels she will be hurt, as she was hurt by her father, or because she fears her relationships will be shortlived, a belief she connects with her father being sick with leukemia years prior to his death. She felt, however, that at least he wanted her, while her mother told her she was an unwelcome accident. She saw both of her parents as continually dissatisfied with each other and with her and felt that nothing she could do would ever please them although she clearly had not given up trying to do so.

Alison has an ongoing, ambivalent relationship with her mother, whom she calls regularly and who continually angers her by her lack of interest or concern for her. When Alison was twelve her mother told her that she did not care and did not want to know what she did as long as she did well in school, and she told her to handle any personal difficulty by herself. Since her father's death, her mother has sent her away to school and has been very stingy with her. Alison said her mother had ulcerative colitis, which would be aggravated when she was upset with her, and did not want her around the house. Alison claimed that when she was ten she replaced, with her father's approval, her mother's medication with talcum powder. While this capsule substitution seemed to be Alison's fantasy, it upset her so greatly to relate it that she started to choke and had to excuse herself to get a glass of water.

Alison found looking at herself distasteful because of all the destructiveness she harbors inside her and which she handles by self-destructive behavior. She is beginning to relate her anger more and more to her mother's lack of interest in her and insists that the only reason she does not show her anger is her fear that if she were to express it, she would go all the way and kill her mother. She uses the image of herself as somebody who is without restraint as a justification for living a life in opposition to her feelings. That she still feels she needs her mother is perhaps hardest of all for her to accept.

Welded in fear, need, and fury to her parents, Alison experienced these emotions in all her relationships. In coming to see me she continually feared that I would try to hospitalize her (other psychiatrists had at times wanted to), or disapprove of her friends and forcibly try to change her life-style. The theme of people attempting to manage her life (although by a kind of helpless portrayal of herself she invited it) and her resentment of these attempts was a frequent one. The relation of her fear of me to her relationship with her father became clear in nightmares that Alison had soon after starting to see me.

In the dreams, her father returns and is alive, but it means her funeral. He invites Alison, her mother, and her friends to visit, but the place they visit was filled with gas chambers, and they were all going to be gassed to death. She was trying to lead the escape. In one scene the rooms were like penny arcades, in another they went on trolley cars, but the trollies were always going to end up in the gas chambers. Her father was laughing at the whole scene.

Her father used to take her to penny arcades, which he liked but which she hated because there was something sordid about the atmosphere. His taking her there presumably for her sake but with no regard for her real feelings seemed to epitomize their relationship. His concern was suffocating. She was clearly afraid that my effect on her would be similar.

A nightmare that Alison had early in treatment shed some light on her insistence that I would think she was mad and would want to hospitalize her: The faculty had been irradiated, and they were going around killing everyone. The only way they would not kill you is if you were mad, and her friends in the fraternity were trying to get her former psychiatrist to declare them all mad as a means of protecting them.

Alison talked about her anger with the school faculty who had pressured her about her program and went on to describe a plan for destroying some school property. She began to open up her feeling of harming others through her hostility (irradiation of the faculty), and her fear of retaliation for her hostility and anger. She says if she were mad, she would not have to get married or get a degree, both of which goals are accompanied by enormous suppression of anger. While she said she feared that I wished to hospitalize her, clearly she had some wish to be hospitalized to protect herself and others from her destructiveness. She tries to avoid being in touch with her anger and makes great efforts to avoid knowing about it. Indeed after talking about the dream, she began to wonder whether there was any sense in coming to see me since it did not make her feel very comfortable.

To detach herself from awareness of her anger, Alison intensified her determination to be a good daughter by performing well at school. She exaggerated the importance of going to law school until it became the one worthwhile thing she could do. She did well on her law boards and was eventually accepted at an outstanding law school. However, she had to push herself with amphetamines to graduate from college, take her law boards, and show up for interviews. She did all this feeling she was going no place, that she was just a machine she was trying to overload and destroy, and that there would be some relief in death.

In the spirit of "overloading the machine" Alison had some months earlier become engaged to one of the fourteen fraternity men who have "adopted" her. She said since she had decided to marry, it might as well be one of them, and it did not much matter which one. She decided on Wayne because he was bright, ambitious, and cared for her. Now she feels she will harm people if she gets involved with them, that she "cuts people up" when she allows herself to say what she feels. She is afraid that sooner or later she will do this with Wayne. She handled her awareness of anger and discontent with Wayne by increasing her determination to marry him and taking more amphetamines. She was having increasing difficulty with Wayne because she cannot stand to have him touch her sexually. She revealed that she had been involved sexually twice in her life, both times very unpleasantly, and both times under the influence of drugs. She once smacked a boy at a dance when he tried to embrace her. To get back at a boy who pestered her to go to bed with him she thought of having sexual relations with him so she could stab him in the jugular vein with a hypodermic. She feels that with amphetamines she can go through with her marriage to Wayne, although the prospect increasingly depressed her. Eventually, despite all the amphetamines, she saw relief only through breaking her engagement and she did so.

After the relationship with Wayne ended, Alison related the following dream: She was with a lame man who took her to his room. There were dead chickens lying around the room and at one point the man proceeded to wring her neck and kill her. Then she was with somebody else crossing a river. She was feeling exhilarated and when the man asked, "What about the dead person?" she replied that has nothing to do with her, that she is free. The next scene involved a time machine, and she was riding with the Mongols through Russia, hacking off the heads of everybody in sight.

Alison's dream dramatizes her current situation. The fear and anger aroused by her engagement is powerfully reflected in the image of the lame man wringing the chicken's neck. Alison alternated between seeing herself and Wayne as the lame man and the chicken. She sees me as the man who is helping her cross the river, and putting her in touch with her history and her rage, reflected in the dream by the time machine that joins her with a band of marauders. Looking back into her own past and the sources of her pain arouses both destructive and self-destructive impulses. The dream crystallizes how much she alternates between hurting herself and wishing to hurt others and how powerfully the prospect of closeness with either Wayne or me arouses both fear and rage.

Alison's difficulties were increasingly expressing themselves in her relationship with me. She tried to deal with her anger at Wayne and me by behaving self-destructively. She agreed to marry someone else, she registered for an excessive course load which would necessitate her taking even higher doses of amphetamines, she spent three hundred dollars that she needed for tuition on a shopping spree, and she tripped three times in three days on psilocybin. She wanted me to worry about her and pointed out that as a child when she did anything self-destructive it reassured her that she existed and forced her parents to pay attention to her. She seemed to feel my interest in her was contingent upon her having one catastrophe after another. She wanted to put me in a supportive, accepting, protective role, to do her bidding in her behalf, and she would be furious when she felt this was not happening.

Alison related a dream she has had several times recently: She is on a frightening bus trip and the bus driver wants to turn onto the Tappan Zee Bridge in the direction of the psychiatrist whom she had seen before. She says no, pulls on the bell string, the bus turns over, and all the other passengers are killed. The police are then pursuing her across the bridge in the direction where the psychiatrist lives. The road she wants to take originally is the road toward Professor Z., an older teacher she knows who accepts her life-style and does not try to change it.

Alison sees me as interfering with her life-style, as the bus driver who will not take her where she wants to go. I have now replaced her father as the driver of the vehicle in which she is a reluctant passenger. She would like to pull the strings in our relationship, to control its direction, and to control her own feelings, and with the distance possible between a bus driver and passenger. While she would like to pull the strings to make me take the supportive "road" of Professor Z., her mounting anger at me is reflected in her pulling them to kill me instead. This seemed to be her warning to me of what would happen if I did not fulfill her wishes.

Alison expressed an awareness of a growing attachment and need for me while being furious with me for allowing this to develop. She fears caring about me or anyone will only lead to pain, and dates the start of her fear to the loss of a Swedish maid who had raised her. She was very fond of her, but when she was four, her family went to South America and fired the woman. She remembers the trip to South America as being one in which she was given some games and a doll to play with and locked up in the cabin while her parents evidently went off elsewhere. She recalls being perpetually frightened until she was nine, when she made a friend of another rather isolated girl.

To run from me and her anxiety Alison took impulsive trips by plane or car to visit friends in distant cities or to be alone in the mountains. Such trips were a longstanding way she had of dealing with her anxiety over closeness in any relationship. She would seldom stay any place long enough to enjoy herself, but rather needed the continual sense of rapid motion she would generate. In a way traveling was a way of speeding without speed and served the same purpose of keeping her away from herself through activity.

Alison insists that the only feelings I could have toward her are scientific interest and compassion. When I challenged this, Alison said that the whole question of people being involved made her panicky. It made her feel like "a fish out of water and it wasn't even her own water." She called several times after this session, saying she felt she was going to kill herself, was unable to study, and wanted to smash things. While she has been upset and depressed when she felt I do not care about her, she was even more upset and frightened by the thought that I did care. My interest makes her feel more alive on one hand and arouses her fear, anger, and destructiveness on the other.

Alison complained that she had functioned on either automatic or delete, and that since I was making the automatic impossible, she would have to delete or do something destructive. She gave me a copy of an Yves Tanguy drawing on a postcard. It was cold and bleak and showed several isolated figures. She said the postcard was really of a cemetery and since she had written on it, "Wish you were here," she felt the postcard had expressed her wish that I would die. She feels the only safe relationships that are possible are between dead people. She said she was furious with me for not letting her be a machine.

Alison was afraid that being upset about her feelings toward me would interfere with her ability to take final exams. She feared "that the machine would run down." She temporarily returned to amphetamines to force herself through. She dreamed of herself as Samson, as she saw him at the opera, tired of being at the grindstone and beginning to pull down the pillars of the building. In another dream the dean was running after her to give her a diploma and she did not want it. In still another she was near the top of a mountain and the only way to get off was to fall off. In another she was looking for a building on campus to jump off.

Passing her exams, graduating, and going to law school inevitably meant ending her sessions with me. Alison wanted me to attend her graduation and was quite furious and disappointed that I could not, saying she felt she would not have graduated without me. She dreamed that I was dressed in a top hat and tails and white gloves and yet was calmly proceeding to massacre everyone on the street. She was one of my victims. She feels, on the other hand, she "would have walked off a roof" if it had not been for me."

Alison was very reluctant to deal with the pain she was feeling at our sessions coming to an end. She considered her sense of loss a humiliating weakness. She preferred to think I would be relieved to not be seeing her. She could not admit to herself that I cared about her and that I too would feel a sense of loss. With her parents and with me Alison is moved toward a relationship by need and dependency, is made furious by the possibility of being frustrated, and anxious by the degree to which any closeness unleashes her destructiveness.

Alison maintained a relationship with me through regular letters and phone calls while away at law school and came in to see me several times. She refused my suggestion that she get regular therapy and continued to try to involve me in her life while keeping me at a distance. She became involved with a young man who was willing to accept their having a nonsexual relationship. He was very wealthy and appeared to be taking care of her. Alison called me just after her wedding. She wanted me to go out with her and Wesley as a way of establishing my approval of the marriage. She had persuaded herself that she might be able to accept a sexual relationship after they were married.

Alison came to see me a week after she was married to speak of the impulse to hurt her husband and walk out of the marriage. Sex between them had been an ordeal for her. She told me a dream she has had several times in the last few nights in which she is out in the cold and she goes into some kind of boutique and there is a girl there who has just been married, and is doing very well in school. She is telling her how happy she is, and then Alison leaves the boutique and goes out into the cold again.

Alison has fulfilled her "programming." She has married "well" and is doing well at law school. She has done all the "right things." She is clearly both the girl in the boutique and the "real" Alison, the unhappy, lonely woman behind the apparently successful automaton, the woman who is out in the cold. Her dream reflects all the misery and emptiness she endures, all the awareness that she tries to remove from her waking life with amphetamines, and the full recognition that the success she has achieved is only a sham.

Like her mother, who earned a Ph.D. in English and was not sufficiently interested to pursue her field, Alison regards her law studies primarily as a letter to be won. Her wealthy husband has also been acquired for show. The fact that everything Alison has makes Alison miserable is of no concern to her mother, and Alison has done her best to render her own emotions unimportant to herself.

Pushing toward achievement in school or in marriage against an inner reluctance was not always the issue. Emily, a college senior whose academic achievements in the face of painful parental opposition had been a great source of satisfaction to her, was using amphetamines daily to move toward a marriage that she saw as meaning the relinquishment of all her accomplishments, hopes, and pleasure. She was pushing herself toward failure in the process of fulfilling her parents' wishes for her.

Emily was twenty-one, an excellent student who enjoyed her work and was likely to be accepted in any graduate school in her field. She had chosen not to apply, however, because she was planning to go to work to support a young man she intended to marry in a few months. Her fiancé, also a college senior, needed some strong family influence to get into any law school. He took for granted Emily's giving up school and indeed Emily considered any reluctance she had to do so as pure selfishness.

Emily and Seth had been going together for three years and living together for three months. At times she describes him as boring, at times as confused, but never with any enthusiasm. He had been hospitalized for an acute psychotic episode nine months earlier. Emily's guidance counselor had urged her at that time to break her engagement but she felt Seth needed her all the more. She clearly sees him as a burden she has decided to carry. Despite the fact that her depression coincided with their living together, despite the fact that sex became intolerable for her during this period, despite the fact that she had become hysterical when someone else took over her old dormitory room, further cementing her to the relation with Seth, Emily insisted that her feelings about her relation with Seth had nothing to do with her depression.

Emily's ability not to see what she did not want to see was striking. After a few sessions she told me that she realized if she saw me on the street she would not recognize me since she never really "saw" me during the hour. Her not seeing me was very much in keeping with her strenuous efforts not to see or know her feelings toward Seth.

It was also in keeping with her tendency to deal with her own anxiety by becoming protective toward others, that the first time she said anything personal to me, it was in the nature of a solicitous inquiry as to whether I had a cold.

Emily's parents opposed her relationship with Seth, but they always opposed her relationships with men and are particularly troubled by the idea of her being sexually involved with anyone. She sees them as moralistic and puritanical. Their opposition gave Emily the illusion that her relation with Seth constitutes independence. In fact she has fulfilled their conception of what a relationship ought to be in the quality of her life with Seth. After sex with him she dreams they have taken heroin, with all the connotations of crime and guilt.

Emily's parents opposed her academic ambitions, feeling that work was not important for a woman. Her mother, who had not gone to college, felt she had martyred herself to earn money to help her father in his business. She is envious and resentful of Emily's success and becomes tearful and leaves the room if the family is discussing college. In an act of total indifference to Emily's feelings, her parents prevented her from making the valedictory speech she was scheduled to make in high school by moving a few weeks before graduation. Emily made a suicide attempt at the time. On some level she senses that giving up what promises to be an excellent career in mathematics would also be a kind of suicide.

Emily clearly feels guilty about achieving more in life than her mother. While complaining of her own life, Emily's mother behaved in ways to ensure that Emily follow in her footsteps. For example, her mother was always troubled by being painfully shy. To make sure that Emily would not be, she would punish and humiliate her for any signs of shyness or hesitancy. As a result, even answering the telephone was painful for Emily. While Emily says she does not want to be "another martyr," she clearly needs to repeat what she sees are her mother's mistakes. She insists that marriage will get her away from her family and make her feel less "inferior," although giving up plans for graduate school and making plans for her marriage make her feel worse and worse. For a few weeks when Emily was under the strain of mistakenly believing she was pregnant, her anger and resentment of Seth were less under control. She spoke of hating to be a woman and told Seth she hated sex. She dreamed of running from an exploding bomb. And in reality she ran from her rage, increased her use of amphetamines to control it, and continued to pursue plans for a marriage that she saw as an emotional death.

Unable to get through the day without amphetamines, unable to endure the night without sleeping pills, Emily used drugs to program her waking and sleeping life so they would never coincide with her actual feelings. For, despite the veneer of rebellion involved in her relationship with Seth, she is dooming herself to fulfilling her mother's goals of self-sacrifice and renunciation of ambition and pleasure.

At stake in Laura's amphetamine use was not merely work or marriage but a total and pervasive vision that affected every relation to life. Laura took amphetamines to construct a personality she admired but felt she could never achieve. A tall, thin graduate student of twenty-two, Laura had begun to use amphetamines in high school when they were prescribed for overweight. I saw her after she had been hospitalized for an extreme toxic reaction in which she experienced intense fears and delusions and which followed several months of massive doses of amphetamines.

Laura felt amphetamines helped her be giving and supportive to other people. She encourages friendships in which people tell her their problems so she can provide help and encouragement. She began her sessions by saying she knew I was studying students with drug problems and she would be glad to come and help me, and was repeatedly concerned over whether she was too "egocentric" or whether I was "getting enough" from seeing her. She feels if she were honest with her friends—particularly with Grace, whom she sees most—she would tell them, "Fuck it, who wants to listen to your problems? I got enough of my own." She feels considerable anxiety about seeing Grace since she has taken no amphetamines since her discharge from the hospital and feels unable to conceal her own irritability and need. She feels there is no alternative to amphetamines but ostracism and abandonment to her own lonely anger.

Laura related her recent high dosage (she had reached 180 mgs per day) to her need to control her increasing fear and anger toward her boyfriend, who was heavily involved with heroin, and whom she had felt compassion for. After she stopped living with Ned, he was "busted" and is in jail. She said she felt comfortable with people like Ned, whom she sees as underdogs, and reproaches herself as selfish for not wanting to visit him in jail or wait for his release. She similarly reproaches herself for not waiting out the night with another friend who was going to be sentenced and wanted company. She spoke of feeling ill at ease with the men in graduate school because they seem so in control of their lives. She told of another boy who was a friend of her brother and on whom she became dependent. He left her, and she implies that if she becomes involved with someone who seems in control of his life, she will become dependent on him and drive him away. Feeling people let her down, needing to bury her rage and to become supportive instead arouse enormous rage. But Laura sees no alternative to being either supportive and protective (without need) or to being abandoned because of her own need.

Laura feels amphetamines enable her to control her anger, to be with other people, and to be the only way she feels they will accept her. She "loves amphetamines because they give her energy, make her sexually responsive," and enable her to breathe by clearing her nasal passages. She feels that in fighting the impulse to return to them, she is depriving herself of life itself.

That the life amphetamines conferred upon her is simulated and mechanical is reflected in a recurrent dream Laura had in which everyone is a marionette dangling from strings. Laura saw herself as a marionette; she saw amphetamines as the strings with which she controlled her actions and which permitted her to do whatever she wished regardless of what she felt. The image of the marionette with amphetamine strings powerfully reflects Laura's sense of being an inanimate object, and how much she longs to be a mock-human, a puppet whose performance she can control herself.

Laura felt her fear of being herself, or saying what she feels, has to do with her parents. Her father always belittled or ridiculed her for crying over a film or novel that had moved her, and would say, "Why aren't you tougher like your friends?" While her father treated her like "his little darling" when she was very small, later he always found fault with her and always made negative comparisons of her with other children. He had started out as a science teacher, but because of the depression went into a neighborhood business. She feels he lost interest in everything as the years went by, and he became more and more disparaging of her.

Laura felt her mother was never very honest with her or herself about her own feelings. She describes her mother as always feeling she had to "give to people," but as being forced and unnatural in her concern. Her unnaturalness seemed to have centered about food. Her mother weighed two hundred pounds and battled constantly with Laura over Laura's weight. "Other kids went home for chocolate milk and I got skimmed milk, which I hated," Laura said. She recalls that for years her mother would give her orange juice every morning. Laura would drop the glass, and her mother would smack her, and they would both cry and make up. Laura describes this as a "sick thing" that went on between them for years.

When she was three, Laura was sent to live with an aunt because her mother had a "nervous breakdown." Her mother frequently gave her and her brother to neighbors for a day or two because she could not stand to spend much time with them. During the course of our sessions, Laura asked her mother about this. Her mother revealed that she had given Laura to her mother for three months when she was ten days old. She said Laura was a very "demanding, pesty baby who would not let her alone or let her out of her sight." The mother felt she had to have some relief. Laura was, of course, hurt and angered by this conversation; she kept trying, however, to reassure her mother that she did not want her to feel bad. At the same time the conversation gave her some insight into her conviction that she will be rejected by people if she lets her demands be known.

When she was younger, Laura says she was afraid to let her parents out of her sight because she thought they would desert her. She recalls being afraid to go to school in the morning and occasionally throwing up when she got there. When she was fifteen her mother took her to a doctor because she was overweight and she was put on amphetamines. She lost weight, but feared she would regain it when she stopped. Instead she dieted and went down to ninety-five pounds. She enjoyed the attention she got for not eating.

Laura had a dream that expressed more of her feeling toward her family, and indeed toward people, than she openly showed. The dream followed a call from her mother during which Laura offered to give her brother a suitcase that she thought he wanted. Laura was in a house with her mother, father, and brother. She was promising her brother something very good to eat in the kitchen and then she did not give it to him. He was very disappointed, and she could feel his disappointment. Then she was eating some cookies in animal shapes from a plastic bag in front of her whole family, and conscious about how they must feel about the fact that she was just feeding herself and not offering them any.

Laura says she is fond of her brother, who is four years older than she and very "stable." In the dream she seems to represent the conflict that pervades her life. She promises good things she does not want to deliver. The plastic bag in the dream suggested to her the plastic capsules of amphetamines she took. The dream strips aside the role she plays in waking life as the giver, and it reveals her own need and the fact that she is actually more concerned with feeding herself than giving. She disappoints and frustrates her family as she feels they have disappointed and frustrated her. If she offers to feed them as she would like them to feed her, she settles for feeding herself amphetamines.

Laura fears her appetite for food, the dependent longings that seem to her immense, and the specter of her two-hundred-pound mother. If she began taking amphetamines to control her weight, she went on to use them to control every aspect of her life, every kind of physical and emotional craving. Unable to breathe, to regulate her sleep, her sexual feelings, and her appetites, Laura uses amphetamines to control all these and to play the role she has chosen. They permit her to ignore her rage and frustration at never being fed herself. Laura's vision of herself as a mass of angry, demanding, frustrated appetites now corresponds to the picture her mother had of her as a "pesty, demanding baby."

No group of students resist more strongly trying to see what they feel toward themselves or other people than the students on amphetamines. They fear that if in touch with their feelings they will, like Alison, destroy others with their rage or, like Laura, be overwhelmed by their needs and appetites, or, like Emily, disobey their parents out of sheer enthusiasm for their work. Amphetamines give them both the energy and detachment to control their feelings and function efficiently. Amphetamines permit an active compliance with goals their parents have set for them and permit them to ignore their own frustration and their rage toward their parents. But succeeding at their parents' goals inevitably means, for these students, losing at their own.

Emily, taught to sacrifice her own aspirations by an envious mother who sacrificed hers and a father indifferent to her success, ministers to a crippled, dependent man who exploits her. Amphetamines permit her to ignore her real aspirations, her rage at her fiancé, and to submit.

Laura, browbeaten by her mother to stay thin, to be more in control of herself than she was, tries to play a supportive role with both men and women without acknowledging how needful and dependent she feels. She feeds herself amphetamines instead of food and uses the drug to blot out her own emotional hunger.

Alison retreats into fantasies of retaliation while she fulfills all her parents expected of her. Ignoring the pain and anguish she feels in human contacts, beginning with her parents, she has achieved a career and a marriage. The fact that these achievements were possible only with massive doses of amphetamines, the fact that they leave her miserable is, to her, beside the point.

All these students grade themselves on how successful they are at self-denial, self-sacrifice, and the destruction of their own enthusiasm. They rate themselves on their performance in human relations even more than in school, virtually shrinking life to a performance and achievement test. Amphetamines enable them to perform for their parents and to earn high marks.

Committed to ignoring how they feel, even in treatment these students want drugs that will give symptomatic relief to their anger without touching its emotional core. They see relations with people as ideally geared toward helping them to achieve particular goals. Alison attempted to make me an extension of herself that will help her function. She dreams of being able to pull the strings in our relationship so that I must help her in the direction she wants to go.

To function but not to feel, to perform well in painful situations, to succeed at goals they have not chosen and do not want to achieve is the ideal these students imagine. They speak of themselves as machines they will not permit to run down. The language of amphetamines— "speed," "flying"—does. not merely describe the sense of energy or elevation amphetamines provide. It also suggests how much these students seek a life in which they are moving too quickly to think about what they are doing or how they feel.

The preoccupation with success, performance, and emotional control has traditionally been considered a male style. But overwhelmingly the students who abused amphetamines were women. The drug of choice for men attempting to deal with conflicts over success and ambition is marijuana, which helps them to reduce the competitive, combative urge their parents had established for them, and to replace this with a more passive, introspective style (see chapter 6). Women, in contrast, are using a drug that enables them to work harder and program themselves more rigorously toward achieving the goals their parents had set and they themselves had internalized. The pattern of men "dropping out" of the male stereotype and of women stepping into an achievement-oriented, driving life-style was apparent.

A concern with living up to other people's expectations, an attempt to minister to others' needs and sacrifice one's own have been traditional adaptive modes for women. For many young women, traditional demands have now been coupled with the imperative to career success. It is not surprising that many use old methods to deal with new demands, or that success at careers or relationships they themselves do not want only accentuates their self-denial, cements them in living against their own grain, making misery and frustration inevitable. But many college women do not resist or revise the expectations that torment them. Dreaming of themselves as machines, as automatons, or puppets, they take more amphetamines and try to fulfill them.

6 | Marijuana and the American Way

THE CONTROVERSY OVER marijuana has always been waged in the shadow of the work ethic. Behind the great curiosity and apprehension expressed by parents, by school authorities, and others has been a pervasive concern that excessive use of marijuana would produce changes in personality that would turn an "achiever" into something else. Central even to the formal study of marijuana has been the researcher's attitude toward the intense, competitive quality of American life and his answer to the question of whether Horatio Alger is a model worth preserving.

Psychiatric work on marijuana has been shaped by either the fear or the hope that achievement and success would disappear as American faiths. In an overview of the problem, McGlothlin and West saw regular marijuana use as changing personality by contributing to the development of more "passive, inward-turning amotivational personality characteristics. For numerous middle-class students, the subtly progressive change from conforming, achievement-oriented behavior to a state of

relaxed and careless drifting had followed their use of significant amounts of marijuana."

Grinspoon, arguing against marijuana's power to
change personality, stated that heavy marijuana use is just
a manifestation of a change in life-style. Like long hair,
Grinspoon maintains, marijuana is but a mark of a
change in behavior quite distinct from personality. "This
type of change," writes Grinspoon, "may be likened to
that which a girl who decides to join a convent may un-
dergo; she certainly appears different with respect to her
values, goals, behavior and so forth, but beneath her habit,
the same pre-convent personality resides. Similarly it
seems more than likely that behind the hirsuteness and
the hip patinas are personalities which have not under-
gone significant and basic change."

Is excessive use of marijuana the cause of a change in
attitude toward achievement, ambition, and competition? If so, what motivates the excessive use? Or is it
merely one of the features that accompany a change in
values and life-styles, much in the way that long hair does?
If so, what motivates the change in life-style? In not confronting the motivation for excessive use of marijuana on
the one hand or the motivation for a change in life-style
on the other, both views are themselves, in a sense,
"amotivational." Certainly the sharp differences in views
of marijuana reflect the deep ambivalence in the culture
over the meaning of work, success, and achievement, an
ambivalence crystallized in the lives of heavy marijuana
users.

Detailed psychological study of heavy marijuana users
makes clear that marijuana is neither causative of changing attitudes toward ambition and success nor simply an
incidental concomitant of a changing life-style. Yet mari-

juana does play a specific role in the students' attempt to resolve conflicts over competition, aggressiveness, and achievement. Heavy habitual users of marijuana dramatize the forces that move students toward the drug and have made marijuana appeal to the culture as a whole. Typical were Dave and Ted, who are "stoned" every evening and part of every day. They illustrate how marijuana functions in the lives of heavy users and the impact it has on their conflicts.

Dave, a freshman with a pleasant, intelligent face, came in for the first time wearing what was a typical outfit for him: brown boots over blue jeans, and a khaki shirt worn outside his jeans. He vividly described his confusion over what he wants to do. He dislikes college and feels as though he is being turned out "like a product on some factory's assembly line." "Everybody," he said, "comes in, does the same things, goes on, and gets degrees."

Dave began to smoke marijuana during his last two or three years in high school, becoming heavily involved in his senior year. During the summer before coming to college he had "gotten into everything—ups, downs, cocaine, LSD, and mescaline." He has snorted heroin occasionally. At college he has been primarily involved with marijuana, smoking it every night and sometimes three or four times during the day. He says he thinks he will have to cut down a little because he has "just been getting too tired from it." He explained that he likes marijuana because it "takes the edge off [his] personality" and softens his competitiveness, aggressiveness, and combativeness, traits he would like to be rid of. He connects them with his family, which he described as very achievement oriented: his father is a bright, successful physician, his mother is getting her doctorate in psychology, he has a sister who already has a doctorate and a brother in graduate school. His family was much happier than he about his having been accepted at several Ivy League colleges.

Dave saw his father as autocratic and dominating at home, adding that his father had made him a good debater. He gave the impression that most of their conversations turned into competitive dialogues where the emphasis was more on making points and winning than on establishing any understanding or communication. Combativeness appears to loom large in his relations with his family, with much of it, since Dave was fifteen, centering on Dave's use of drugs. It was clear that using drugs has played a large part in Dave's attempts to resolve the difficulties he has with his family, and those aspects of his father that he so dislikes in himself.

Dave sees the competitive side of himself as "vicious." He says he admires people who are particularly gentle, calm, and introspective. He has a recurring fantasy of dropping everything and going off alone to the Canadian wilderness to hunt and fish and get away from everyone. He cannot even imagine a world with people in which he would not feel vicious. While he fantasizes peace in isolation and withdrawal, he nevertheless disparages his brother —who had been arrested for possession of drugs while in college, and who is now dealing in drugs while in graduate school—by saying that he has no ambition. Dave's contempt for his brother's lack of competitive drive and his contradictory admiration for those who do not compete, are but the surface indications of his own conflict over whether he should compete or withdraw.

The pervasiveness of Dave's conflict over competition was dramatized in the first dream he had after beginning our sessions. He dreamed he was in a gym class. The gym coach was telling him that somebody had a heart attack and that Dave should call his father's friend and tell him about it.

In discussing his dream, Dave explained that his father owned a tennis club, was an avid player, and competed intensely with Dave, even after Dave became so good that his father had no chance of winning unless Dave gave him a three-game handicap. The man he was supposed to call in his dream was a tennis partner of his father who had once been a top professional player, but with whom Dave now plays evenly. He maintained that his father was glad that he had become so good at the game. He nevertheless acknowledged that his father cannot stand losing in anything he does well, and becomes furious if Dave is winning one of their debates. Dave gave up playing tennis a year ago because "he didn't like being the boss's son at the club" and disliked "the way the men hung around after playing and drank." But it was clear that competing with his father in tennis and besting him had made tennis altogether distasteful to him. He has taken up bowling, in which he has no ability, and explains that he likes bowling because the game means so little to him that he does not care if he loses.

Dave feels that caring about what you are doing leads to a dangerous, cutthroat competition, and that competition unleashed the worst in him—the "viciousness" he referred to in earlier sessions. The heart attack of the dream suggests the disastrous consequences that can result from the competitive situations symbolized by the gym class. I am most likely the gym coach who is exposing him to this dangerous conflict. While his dream does not make clear whether the competition is going to be fatal to his father, himself, or to both of them, it dramatizes his sense that competition is a life-or-death struggle. And in his associations to it, he and his father emerge as primary antagonists.

Becoming aware of the competitive conflict between himself and his father and of the implications competition had for him in all his relations aroused considerable tension in Dave. He came into a session during the opening-up of this problem and told me he had been having an awful time. He had "gotten stoned" before going to a party and subsequently took muscular relaxants which would keep him stoned the next day as well. He then took "downs" and was about to go to sleep when his roommate persuaded him to take some acid.

Feeling terrible and unable to sleep during the night, Dave phoned a high school friend, Bob, who had gone to another college and from whom he had drifted apart over rivalry for a girl. On the phone, Bob told him he was planning to trip for the first time the coming weekend. Although the trip Dave was on was so unpleasant he had decided never to take LSD again, he said he wanted to share Bob's experience and told me he could not let Bob trip alone for the first time.

In moving so chaotically into drugs, in attempting to undo his former combativeness toward Bob by agreeing to trip with him, and by being protective toward him, Dave was clearly attempting to ward off his increasing knowledge of how violently competitive he was. Although he said that the weekend he spent tripping with Bob was "beautiful," two dreams he had at its end on Sunday night focused his essential conflict. Dave was Nelson Rockefeller walking the streets at night. It was dark and he had some black bodyguard to protect him against other black people who might attack him. One came at him with a knife and his bodyguard protected him with a hook. Dave was nevertheless cut on the arm.

Dave said the dream was triggered by his being stopped by a policeman for driving at 85 miles per hour on the way back to school Sunday night. His father had told him that if anything like that should happen he should mention the name of a police official who plays at their tennis club. Dave hesitated but as the policeman was writing out the ticket, he mentioned the name and the policeman changed the ticket to one for a headlight violation.

While Dave is Rockefeller in the dream, he also associates Rockefeller with his father, saying he admires the power of both men, but has contempt for them as people. He puts on his father's mantle in the dream, much as he did in reality with the policeman when he took his father's advice.

Dave saw himself as both blacks—either as the aggressive, attacking one, or the one who defends himself by trying to hook the aggressive one. Murderous assaultiveness or "being hooked" on drugs seem to be the alternatives Dave sees as solutions to his combativeness. And looming over his vision of himself as assaultive or hooked is the possibility of becoming like his father—able to succeed not through direct violence, but through hiring or manipulating other people to fight for him and retreating behind an invulnerability conferred by wealth and power.

In his second dream, Dave underscored the degree to which he hovers between drugs and assaultiveness. A sort of hip fellow Dave knew in high school was busting him. He had a lot of marijuana and just threw it away. Then he was holding this fellow in a pool and telling him that if he persisted in his desire to arrest him, he would hold his head under water until he drowned. The guy finally gave up.

In this dream it is clear that to be without drugs is to give free rein to a consuming, murderous rage. His associations alternated between seeing himself or seeing me as the hip fellow who was trying to stop his drug abuse. In either case, the dream suggests his rage and the degree to which marijuana is vital to containing it. This central core of combativeness, also reflected in the Rockefeller dream, seems to indicate that whether he is openly violent or verbally combative like his father, Dave is preoccupied by the need and desire to assault whenever he feels challenged.

While Dave described his father easily and vividly, he had more difficulty in giving a clear picture of his mother. He saw her as submissive and acquiescent to his father and did not condemn her for not coming to his defense more. All she will say during his debates with his father is "Maybe Dave has a point." There seemed to be little warmth between them. He described her as perpetually dampening his father's enthusiasm for things, putting down his excitement over parties, discussions, or sports. Although Dave made no mention of her doing this with him, he did describe her snooping through his things looking for condoms, and while she says nothing if she finds them, he is sure she is against his involvement with women. That Dave feels she has little interest in him as a person is evident in his comment that "she is determined to love [him] as her son who has gone to college and done well there."

Dave gravitates toward women who either thwart him or draw him into a competitive situation. He frequently becomes attracted to his friends' girlfriends and handles the situation by becoming verbally abusive to both the friend and the young woman. Long after he has alienated his friend, he continues to maintain a hostile relationship with the woman. An assaultive competitiveness and his inability to cope with it prevent him from knowing the woman who excites him and ultimately drive her away. He has been seeing a woman for some time who, like his mother, never gets too excited about anything. She has said she is not too attracted to him sexually and she rarely permits intercourse. There seems to be considerable emotional distance between them as well. But this very withdrawal from each other seems to have permitted the length and stability of their relationship.

Dave's admiration for gentle, compassionate, feeling people is understandable in the light of his experiences with his family. Equally understandable is his difficulty in being gentle himself, or in separating destructiveness and insensitivity from competition. But the degree to which combativeness controlled his life came as a revelation to Dave. He described one summer when he took a job as a camp counselor, hoping that he would be understanding and gentle with children. But he was disappointed to find himself becoming as authoritarian and insensitive as his father, and as concerned with controlling every situation.

Dave saw himself as a murderous competitor who could destroy his rivals in general and his father in particular. To care passionately—for a sport, a woman, a career—meant, for Dave, to be willing to assault anyone who challenged what he valued. To succeed inevitably meant to destroy. But to lose at anything he cared for, and to lose anyone he desired, was a source of limitless humiliation. How to avoid the murderousness of winning? The degradation of losing? Only by being leashed, checked, or dampened in all his interests did Dave mute his experience of life as war. He resolved his conflicts by giving up whatever he wanted or enjoyed—his tennis, an exciting woman, and even his involvement in school. He has abandoned his true interest, music, for French studies, because of what he sees as the vicious competition in the music world. He dreams of an absolute withdrawal into the Canadian wilderness to escape having to win or lose in human relations. And, in actuality, he takes marijuana in an effort to subdue his combativeness and anger.

Dave's struggles with his father had resulted in open friction between them, but Ted, who had similar conflicts, resolved them far more covertly:

A nice-looking, clean-cut senior, Ted came in following his arrest by police agents for dealing in drugs. He wore a blue shirt over blue jeans and white sneakers. He said he had recently cut his hair because he thought it would help him in his forthcoming court appearance. His parents wanted him to seek treatment when they learned of his arrest, and he gave this as a reason for coming to me. Although prior to his arrest he smoked marijuana all evening and several times during the day, he does not consider his own drug use a problem. He says he "isn't so foolish as to think he doesn't have other problems."

Ted described his most immediate problem as trying to decide what he is going to do when he graduates in a few months. His only plan is to get a job, live somewhere, and "get into reality." Eventually, he would like to get an M.F.A. so he can teach art, since the chances of earning a living by painting are not so great, a fact which his parents have stressed and used as a reason for opposing his interest in art. Ted considers without enthusiasm the possibility that he could earn a living doing cartoons. He says he "fritters" away most of his time and complained of feeling both listless and pressured. He explained that he got stoned to relax from the pressure of everyday life, and to escape a pervasive boredom.

Ted has used marijuana since his freshman year at college, increasing his use in the last year to smoking five or more times a day. He has been dealing in marijuana for the last two years and was busted when a fellow he knew came to his apartment with "two hippie-looking characters who wanted to buy." After the sale, the two "hippies" pulled out guns and arrested him. He stressed that he does not make a profit on marijuana, but merely makes enough to pay for what he uses. It was not clear whether this was an important distinction for him or whether he assumes it will be for me.

It was clear that much of Ted's behavior was designed to impress the adult world with his compliance. It was particularly important to him to be able to tell his parents that he was seeing a psychiatrist, and I was initially concerned about whether he would be motivated to continue his visits if the case against him were dropped. Putting on a good show for his parents and saying the right thing proved to be the pattern of Ted's life.

Ted grew up in Arkansas, his parents moving to Virginia some years ago. Ted described his father as "a big, tall man, about six feet three inches." His father manages a retail business. Ted spoke of him in a general tone of fear, mentioning that he holds over him the cost of his education and that he constantly belittles his mother, who has an M.A. in social work and works for the county. His mother endures this in silence. Both his parents are avid churchgoers, and Ted went to church for their sake until he came to college, although he stopped believing in God at an early age. He went so far as to become very active in the church and, in the twelfth grade, he actually preached a sermon on Youth Day, although by this time he neither believed in God nor in anything he preached. He also played little league baseball as a youngster because his father wanted him to. Ted felt he was very poor in baseball and disliked the game, although he eventually surprised everybody by learning how to hit. The same thing was true of his involvement with the Boy Scouts, which he hated, but in which he advanced to the rank of Eagle Scout. This pattern of shamming interest, of performing well despite a total lack of enthusiasm for what he is doing still persists. Without being at all involved in his work, Ted has done very well at college. He says he is sorry that he has not enjoyed baseball, the church, the Boy Scouts, or other things that his parents had wanted him to enjoy.

Ted's earliest memory sheds some light on how his parents responded to things that he did enjoy. When he was three or four years old, he had a white dog that he cared for very much. He remembers being in the kitchen and his parents telling him that they had given the dog away because he did not care for it properly. They justified this by telling him later that the dog had been away for several days before he noticed it was gone, which they used to prove that he did not miss it as much as he said.

Ted had become very much involved in his sessions, wanted them very much, and was clearly not simply going through the motions. He spent a good deal of time on his childhood and in discussing his anxieties about women, explaining that he gets involved with a woman, becomes critical of her, and wants to get out of the relationship rather soon. He never tells his family about his girlfriends because they would think it was immoral for him to be sexually involved. When his parents called his apartment and a young woman who was with another fellow answered, they were angry, thinking that Ted must have a woman with him too. Over Christmas vacation shortly after his arrest and before I began to see him, he went home to see his parents. He had several dreams during that visit which dramatize his way of dealing with them: Ted was in a pill box. He was attacked by someone whose throat he cut with a knife. He remembers it was hard to cut through.

He was about to marry a big, tall man. There was even the beginning of some sexual play between them, but he was very uncomfortable and unhappy about it, and he was relieved when he woke up and did not have to marry this man. At some point the man's father appeared in the dream.

He saw his father taking each of the other kids in the family through a door and beating them. He was very upset and angry, but did nothing but watch from a distance. He felt his father was beating down the kids in the family and that they were taking a lot of shit from him.

The idea of being forced to submit pervaded the last two dreams. All through the session in which he related his dreams, Ted's associations were about his father. It was clear that the man who might attack him and whom he feels so violently angry toward and afraid of, is his father. He does not confront his father about any of the issues that come up between them, preferring to deal with them through outward submission and compliance, and to avoid confronting his own anger. Yet it is clear that obeying his father against his own desires and trying to suppress his anger even from himself has eroded his sense of himself as a man and made him feel a little more diminished each time he complies.

Ted's dream of watching his father beat his brothers and sisters reflects both his feelings about how he has been treated and his defense against acknowledging how much "shit" he has taken from his father. In his dream he is a removed spectator, watching himself being beaten without defending himself or intervening on his own behalf.

In Ted's first dream, the rage engendered by his way of dealing with his father is clear. Although he has fortressed himself in a pill box, which he related to his drug use, and has boxed in his feelings, this defense breaks down under the pressure of his arrest and of being home for Christmas. His attacker (his father) is able to penetrate his defenses and unleashes Ted's rage. Boxed into a corner, Ted's anger proves murderous as he slits his attacker's throat.

In Ted's second dream he is marrying what he called, "a big, tall man." These are precisely the words he used earlier to describe his father. It appears that his actual submission and fear of his father have generated a good deal of homosexual anxiety and made him feel that he is not a man. In dreaming of his relation to his father as an unwanted marriage, he reflects his sense of being inextricably bound in a humiliating situation.

Ted crystallized the atmosphere of his dreams and associations during this hour in a parting joke about his possible imprisonment. He said he does not want to go to jail because he could be raped there. "Jail wouldn't be so bad," he commented, "but being raped every night would be." His "joke" reflects his sense of having been imprisoned by his father, of having further imprisoned his own feelings and interests, and of feeling that his obedience has been a kind of daily rape, a repeated violation of his integrity and of himself as a man.

Ted's childhood memories were filled with recollections of suppressed feelings, of things not said and not expressed. He recalls his father showing him some drawings he had done and feeling afraid to say that he thought he drew better. He described fearing bullies in his neighborhood, but being too frightened even to show his fear. He went on to call his father the first bully he knew. One incident Ted related from his childhood was particularly revelatory of the way he had handled his antagonism. When he was a child he would put on a Lone Ranger outfit with a mask, and his friend would mask himself as Zorro. The two of them would pick on children in the neighborhood. They were happy and surprised no one seemed to know who they were. Ted has expressed his anger secretively. And in masking his anger he has become as alone and unknown as a lone ranger.

In coming to college, Ted felt he would put his parents aside. But his parents continue to affect his life. Ted is particularly conscious of their disapproval of premarital sexual relations. Although he feels his father would also disapprove, he puts his concealment of his sexual involvements in terms of not wanting to hurt his mother. He describes his mother as a bright, but submissive woman. While he can give a very vivid picture of his father, Ted spoke of his mother as though she were a shadowy, disapproving figure. He clearly feels she does not want to respond to him as a person. When he was arrested for selling drugs, his mother never asked him about the cause and extent of his drug use. She merely said she hoped his therapy would give him some "moral sense." She appears to have focused on his behavior and conformity to her expectations without much interest in knowing what he feels. His father involved himself in Ted's current problems in an overbearing way that Ted resented.

Without consulting him, Ted's father went to see the dean on Ted's behalf and then came to see Ted unexpectedly. Ted was alone, but he remembers looking around the apartment nervously "to see if there were anything that his father should not see." "There were no drugs," he said ironically, "and no naked girls." He said that he was going to his girlfriend's house that weekend but that if he told his parents, they would question him about whether her parents were there and would be upset if he said no. He said that his friend's parents do not ask these questions because "they've been trained not to." Ted has clearly not trained his, but has rather played the role of a child, submitting and obeying outwardly and cloaking what he does in lies. This only further allows or encourages them to ask questions that are inappropriate to ask someone his age.

How profoundly Ted feels unable to keep his father out of his life was dramatized in a series of dreams: Ted was in bed with a girl undressed under the sheets when somebody knocked at the door. He reluctantly said, "Come in." With some difficulty a neighbor pushed the door open, entered the room, and began looking around. At this point the girl disappeared. Ted noticed a pile of shit in his bed. He went to clean it up, but somehow he could not get it all up with a towel—it was too much. Then he remembers it was as though it was all in his mouth and he was eating it. He was struck that he did not seem to mind eating it as much as he would have expected.

Ted's dream reflects his desire to keep his father out of his life, his inability to do this, and his sense that his inability spoils his pleasure and grossly humiliates him. In his dream it is the door that is presenting an obstacle and not his actions, a fact that reflects his wish that some thing or force will do what he cannot. As he does in his life, in his dream he goes against his strongest feelings and tells his father (the neighbor) he can come in. When he does, everything pleasurable turns to shit and Ted feels as though he is being made to eat it. Characteristically, he resorts to self-deception to deal even with this. He dreams that he does not really mind his humiliation.

The night after we discussed the above dream, Ted dreamed he was at a cocktail party with his family and me. His sister was giving me something to read, and I said, "Very nice," but in a rather sarcastic way, as a kind of put-down. He remembers being very angry.

Ted's dream reflects his sense that exposing his feelings will inevitably lead to his humiliation. The sister that has given me something to read is clearly a representation of him. Just as his dream of having to marry a big, tall man reflected his sense of humiliation and passivity, so this dream of himself as a sister who has, in effect, made her feelings an open book reflects his sense that even his therapy is a process of humiliating self-exposure that makes him feel that he is not a man at all. He experiences his parents' questions about his sexual life as a put-down; but he also experiences my challenging his way of dealing with his parents as a put-down. In his dream the feelings of anger that center around his father are directed at me. He is much freer to feel conscious anger toward me than his father. In this session he again referred to his previous dream while discussing his father by remarking that he was not as bothered by eating shit as he should be. But this is a meager defense against the destructive impact his submissiveness has had upon his life.

Frightened that his parents will abandon him if he is not acquiescent, terrified at the intensity of the anger that is increasingly coming to the surface, Ted was virtually impaled between his fear of the murderous rage he dreamed would make him able to cut his father's throat, and his humiliation at having so totally obeyed him. Marijuana was his way out of a situation to which he saw no exit. It permitted him to comply while muting his sense of degradation and provided the illusion that in the very act of taking it he was rebelling. Now considering other ways of dealing with his family makes him anxious. Discontinuing marijuana and becoming involved in his treatment only underlines the fact that far from having been the mark of change in his life or his values, marijuana was the force that had enabled him not to change at all.

Like the other heavy marijuana users I saw, Dave and Ted saw life as combat and found the pressures of work, sports, and human relations hard to bear. The one irresistibly drawn into competitive situations, the other perpetually acquiescent and disengaged from them, both were caught in the sense of living as a series of murderous or degrading situations. The appetitive, rapacious quality of middle-class life provided such students with a rationale for the intense pain they felt at having to compete at all. That so many people of their parents' generation were also ambivalent about the driving pace this culture exacts only served to focus their problems in a social rather than personal context. Had such students lost their ambition? Had they changed life-styles like Grinspoon's nun? Had they found in the counterculture some release from the rat race?

Faced by the culture's voracious competitiveness, aggressiveness, and pushed toward ruthless achievement, young men like Dave and Ted hoped that by changing their life-style they could free themselves from their conflicts and their parents' way of life. But such students already had life-styles that were quite different from their parents'. Yet even with the aid of marijuana, their changed values and life-styles did not help them escape the aggressiveness and combativeness at the center of themselves. Marijuana did not cause those problems, nor was it simply incidental to them. Marijuana was the tool they used to try to deal with them, to ward off the violence within themselves.

Heavy marijuana users experience reality as a life-or-death struggle in which the winner emerged as from a bloodbath and the loser felt psychically cut to bits. They could conceive of no competition that did not result in someone's annihilation. This sense of life as war seemed to have its origin in their relations with their fathers and pervaded every aspect of their lives. In Dave's gym dream, either he or his father must die. In Ted's dream, to survive as a person, to simply be himself he must literally cut his father's throat. Ted remarked that his father was the first bully he knew; Dave nicknamed his father the Old Warrior. But Dave and Ted, while bearing the brunt of their fathers' combativeness and while despising it, have been infected by it themselves. As a child Ted terrorized other children; as a camp counselor Dave found he treated the children no better than his father treated him. Both young men are in perpetual conflict over the way they are and the way they would like to be. To assert themselves makes them feel as vicious as their fathers. Not to do so invariably involves the sense of overwhelming failure. While they themselves were caught between the impulse to bully and the craving to be gentle, Dave and Ted alternated between rage at their fathers and fear of them. Despite their differences in style, neither student could assert himself easily with his father.

Fixed in their conflicts with their fathers, Dave and Ted saw them as the main source of difficulty in their lives. They saw their mothers as bright, but submissive, and unable to give them much warmth. Virtually all the heavy marijuana users saw their mothers as half-interested at best and impossible to involve in their emotional lives. In all cases the disappointment and injury suffered in their relations with their mothers seemed to make the students more vulnerable to competitive difficulties.

The need to escape the intense competitive charge any important human encounter aroused in them made heavy marijuana users withdraw from things which actually gave them pleasure. Ted considers abandoning a career in painting or art history in favor of drawing cartoons, which he cares nothing for and which for him literally involves turning a serious interest into a joke. Dave rules out a career in music and majors in French because of "vicious competition in the music world," and even gives up tennis for bowling. And in fantasy these students create worlds without people—Dave the Canadian wilderness, Ted a room where he can paint without anyone there to see or judge his work. While they withdraw from careers they want in the hope that they will thereby avoid the necessity to become either brutal or humiliated, they nevertheless can conceive of total relief only in isolation.

Ted said he took marijuana to relieve "the pressure and the boredom of everyday life"; Dave sought it to "take the edge off" his personality. In the course of his visits it became clear that the pressures that tormented Ted had their source in the increasing demands made upon him by life to assert himself, choose his life, and deal more directly with his father. For Dave marijuana was a means of subduing the anger of life experienced as a perpetual competitive struggle. Coming to college for Dave and graduating from college for Ted had clearly put enormous strains on the defenses of withdrawal and denial they had always employed.

Marijuana, the involvement in the drug culture, and a changed life-style gave students like Dave and Ted the illusion of defiance and of having escaped their fathers' combative world. But as their dreams and lives make clear, they continue to experience life as a perpetual struggle, they continue to alternate between the humiliating sense, so powerfully conveyed in Ted's dream, that they are being made to "eat shit," and the feeling that competing successfully will make them vicious and inhuman.

Dave, Ted, and many of their generation are increasingly unwilling or unable to tolerate the rage and rivalry, and combativeness that is generated in their families and is reinforced or reawakened by their social, school, or work experiences. Heavy users of marijuana only provide a radical portrait of the conflicts faced by all students and by the society as a whole. Even students who take marijuana only casually use it to provide surcease from competition. Typical was the senior who got "stoned several nights a week for relief from the premed rat race," or the sophomore football player who saw and dreamed of all relationships as a form of war, gave up football, and tried with marijuana to get away from the competitiveness within himself.

Among the student population, pleasurable, easy handling of competitive situations seems rare. The widespread use and appeal of marijuana in this culture suggests that more and more people see competition as a battle to the end of endurance. Such a struggle generates a good deal of rage and fear, which marijuana helps to subdue. If the "potheads" need marijuana constantly to relax and not feel vicious, society as a whole seems to share their need to an increasing degree.

7 | **Mother Heroin**

THE ANGUISH OF human relationships crystal-lizes in the lives of students who abuse heroin. This drug's use by college students and its advent into middle-class life provides a continuing revelation of the trouble between the sexes, between parents and children, and of the use of heroin as a tool for dealing with emotionally charged relations.

Some of the students I saw were heroin addicts. But many more used heroin in a pattern of mixed drug abuse, becoming addicted for short periods, or not becoming addicted at all. Because heroin abuse has shifted downward in age and prevented many users from ever getting to college, I saw students ranging from high school seniors to graduate students whose differences in age, backgrounds, and needs would provide a spectrum of the problems faced by students impelled toward heroin. For all their extremes, the lives of heroin abusers reflect the turmoil students generally experienced over intimacy.

The extraordinary passivity of heroin users is apparent to any observer. But this passivity has a complex function in the lives of heroin addicts, serving to mute their awareness of themselves and to conceal the forces that moved them toward the drug. That passivity could function as a powerful defense was clear in the life of Bart, a seventeen-year-old high school senior whose heroin addiction was discovered shortly before I saw him. His mother arranged for his appointment, not telling him about it until he was in the car on the way to see me. He seemed to feel that her handling him this way and his acceptance of it, were characteristic of their relationship.

Bart had been mainlining heroin for four months and had built up a twenty-dollar-a-day habit. Prior to that he had snorted heroin on and off for a year. He says that since he was ten he has been labeled by his mother and older brother as a "sort of half-assed person who is irresponsible and who doesn't do anything right." He described frequent quarrels with his mother which left him feeling "shitty."

While Bart saw himself as driven to heroin by his mother's criticisms, it became clear that heroin also tied him to her, partly because he was hooked on it in the same way that she had once been hooked on alcohol, and partly because the difficulties he got into with heroin gave her an opportunity to run his life. His heroin addiction reflected an attempt to deal with his anger toward his mother while keeping her involved with him, and coercing her into caring for him. His coercive self-destructiveness had a history that went back to his childhood. He told of having hidden in a tree as a child to worry his mother, who thought he was lost. He watched her search for him in the street and when he saw her give up and go back into the house, he fell out of the tree and broke his arm.

When Bart arranged to get caught taking heroin at school and was suspended, his mother tried to handle his readmission without him. During his suspension, Bart described himself as a straw in the wind to whom things were happening. He would pass the time hitchhiking just to see who would pick him up. When I pointed out that seemed to be what he was doing with his life, he laughed and said, "That's true but at least I had my thumb up."

When not seeing himself as angrily using heroin because of his mother's criticisms, Bart would attribute his use to the influence of companions. When he began taking less heroin he would attribute his diminished use to circumstance. In commenting on his unwillingness to see himself as in any way responsible for his fate, he says, "What's the difference? We all die anyhow." He is attracted to books like *Brave New World* or *Walden Two* in which people are brought up to have no will and no individuality. He spoke of his desire to be hit by a magic wand so he could change. He also related the magic wand to his use of heroin, a use that he had hoped would alter his way of being.

Soon after I began seeing Bart it became clear that his deepening involvement with heroin had started and grown along with his involvement with Lori, a girl of nineteen whom he had known for over a year and now saw virtually every day. Before knowing Lori he says, "I would try to get what I could from a girl I met within one week and that would be that. I left them before they could hurt me." Although he knows that Lori is not out to hurt him, Bart does not confide in her or reveal himself to her. He hid his heroin use from Lori, although he would get high before he saw her and if he could not, would excuse himself when with her and shoot heroin in the bathroom. He stressed that neither he nor Lori ever say anything that might hurt or anger the other. Although they had been through a lot together, Bart acted as if any strong emotion, particularly anger, would disrupt things. While such consideration was Bart's way of limiting his involvement with Lori, heroin played an even bigger role in his keeping his distance from her. This was dramatized by a series of dreams that dealt with their relationship.

Bart dreamed he was at the seashore with Lori and another fellow, and he and the other fellow were getting high on heroin. In discussing the dream, he began to reveal his fear of getting too high on Lori. He relates it to his fear of losing her and to his sexual insecurity. Initially he felt heroin helped him deal with anxiety about his sexual performance. However, after lovemaking he will question what Lori sees in him and accuse her of infidelity, although in reality Lori has remained faithful to him despite his provocations.

Discussing his need to avoid closeness with Lori was making Bart anxious. He dreamed he and Lori were someplace at an airport or terminal. They had rented a hotel room and they were in bed making love. But somehow the door was open and a well-dressed Negro came in. Lori hid in the bathroom. The Negro said, "What are you doing?" and Bart said they were making love. The Negro said, "Are you sure you're not performing an abortion?" There was a belt in the room, and the implication seemed to be that somehow the belt was used for that purpose.

Bart first related the dream to anxiety about Lori's period being late and his concern about a possible pregnancy. He then went on to say that he had not seen her the night before, but had spent some time with a black friend of his who had formerly supplied him with heroin. He associates blacks with heroin since this friend and his other suppliers are black. He also says that he has often used a belt as a tourniquet for taking heroin. The dream seemed to be a dramatic confirmation of how Bart uses heroin to put a stop to the excitement between himself and Lori, and how in effect he tries to abort the relationship.

Bart told me that heroin enables him to make love to Lori by prolonging his erection. Without it he would have an early ejaculation without satisfying her. While he feels it is important for her to be satisfied, he has little sexual desire for Lori. He derives his pleasure from heroin and joylessly performs for her. He had a dream in which he was in a grueling marathon race that seemed to reflect his image of lasting longer sexually without much pleasure. He has never told Lori of his feeling and never given her the choice of his trying sex without heroin, implicitly assuming that his performance is the only thing that matters to her.

Bart was becoming increasingly aware that his high constitutes a barrier between him and Lori. He can control and regulate the pleasure he gets from heroin. He is not dependent on Lori for satisfaction. In fact, he said, heroin made everything and everyone—school, family, and Lori—unimportant. Their unimportance to him seemed to make him feel as though he could not be hurt by them. With a good deal of pain and feeling he relates his need for invulnerability to the disappointment he felt as a child at the virtual loss of his mother and father. Friction between them had seemed to put a distance between him and them from the time he was very little, but when Bart was about eight, his father went abroad to work for a foreign branch of his company for about five years, and his mother was always up in her room drunk or else in a halfway house for alcoholics. One of his most vivid childhood memories is of hiding beer cans to prevent her from drinking so much.

While Bart recalls crying as a child for both his parents, he does not feel his situation has improved since his father returned and his mother stopped drinking. He sees his father, who is often away on business trips, as involved only with his work. His mother is now involved with Bart in ways which he both resents and encourages while both of them recognize the harm being done to him. His mother recently told him of a dream she had in which in order to keep him safe and secure she put him in a glass jar. When she came back to look at him he had died of suffocation. Bart saw this as reflecting her need to protect him, but hurting him in the process.

At times during his sessions Bart was quite friendly, at others he was even moved by insights into himself. But these feelings were always followed by a pulling back on his part. He would proceed to miss a session or become sullen and withdrawn. A similar pulling back would follow being close to Lori.

Bart now used heroin only occasionally, but he became sexually involved with different girls as another way of keeping a barrier between himself and Lori. He would confess his infidelity to Lori and wondered if he felt unable to end the relationship and was trying to drive Lori to do it. He talked with amused disinterest of these girls and treated them with contempt. He tried to deal with his coming to see me in the same removed, mildly derisive way. When I pointed this out to him, he agreed, but said this was the only way to deal with life: to be involved was to expose your vulnerability. He seemed to feel this was a reasonable position, since the world tries to screw you and if it sees you as hurt, will hurt you more.

If heroin kept Bart invulnerable, it also helped him to express his frustrated rage. He would frequently dream of heroin in the context of combat or war. In one such dream Bart is in a pool with a girl. She is making advances; he is aroused, and it's pleasant. Then Mr. S., the dean at school, says everyone has to get out of the pool. The scene changes and he is with four or five fellows by a river's edge. The girl is no longer there. Some guy comes up in a boat and begins firing darts from a dart gun at them. He and his friends have one dart gun among them and they fire back. The guy with the gun fires again and there are a lot of misses on both sides. Finally the guy does hit one of them, who dies because the darts contain a fatal poison.

Bart had missed the last session, feeling relieved that he did not have to discuss with me that he was "fucking everything up" and had used heroin. He sees me as thinking less of him because of his heroin use. He is sure that I am both the man interfering with his pleasure and with whom he is at war over his use of heroin. As in his earlier dream when his girl is locked away when his heroin supplier enters the room, in this dream the girl disappears when heroin enters the picture. That heroin is a powerful lethal weapon is indicated by the poisoned darts. He felt that it was characteristic of him that if he is angry it is he or one of his friends who gets hurt.

While Bart portrays me as interfering with a source of pleasure (heroin) it is clear that it is his deadness that is threatened by any challenge to his use of heroin. In his next session he reported the following dream: He was driving a car and passed two friends of his on the road; he went farther and thought they probably needed a lift. He started backing up, could not see where he was going, but could feel he was going onto the gravel and off the road, and somehow he was in the Sleepy Hollow Graveyard. He got out of the car to try to find his way out of the graveyard and some man said stop and was shining a flashlight in his eyes. He could not see the man and opened a gate to get out while a dog was rushing to attack him.

"Picking somebody up" or "getting a lift" suggested his drug use. Going backward with drugs does involve going into a graveyard and assuming a lifelessness he often adopted. Sleepy Hollow suggests the sleepiness he also often used as a kind of deadening device, as well as "being on the nod." He saw me as the man who shined the light and was attacking him for being in the graveyard, that is, for his deadness. When I asked what he felt he gains by his deadness he said he would like to be dead now because he would not have to ride home on the subway and he dreads his hassles with his parents. While death would put him beyond reach, heroin has provided him with the next best alternative.

Bart became acutely disturbed just before Lori left for a job in Europe, which he felt, probably correctly, she was taking partly to get away from him. He expressed his pain and rage through his own self-destructiveness. In our sessions, he would frequently burn himself with his cigarette ash. Bart's mood could often be read from his shoes and shoelaces. He generally came in, even when well-dressed, with torn shabby sneakers and long laces untied, trailing on the ground in a kind of invitation to trip himself up or to have someone else trip over them. When I questioned him about this, he tied them after a few minutes, saying it was easier to tie them than to think about why they were untied. When he came in once with one tied and the other untied, he laughed and said it reflected an in-between mood. On rare, happy occasions both laces would be tied. During the period of his pain over Lori's departure, he went barefoot, panhandling in Grand Central Station, enjoying coercing money from people and feeling contempt for those who gave it to him. After one such day, he came in to see me with his feet and ankles dramatically black from the city streets. This mood soon passed and without the pressure of the relationship with Lori, Bart found himself, for the time being, without the need for heroin.

Heroin served the double function of numbing Bart to the pain of his disappointments with his mother, and nevertheless keeping her involved in his life. However little she had been able to give Bart, she had clearly given him enough to arouse his expectations and to keep alive the possibility of love and concern.

Paul, the next young man, had little to do with his mother at present and had long ago given up on getting any affection from her. However, like Bart, his fear of closeness with anyone else both expresses his disappointment in his mother and keeps him tied to the buried pain of his early relationship with her. Like other black college students I saw who were addicts, Paul was from a ghetto background, where he had been exposed to heroin since childhood. But like most of these students, he only became addicted at college when his first serious involvement with a young woman triggered off an anxiety that drove him to heroin.

Paul, a handsome, well-dressed student, had sniffed heroin occasionally at his high school in a midwestern city, but he said that heroin had meant nothing to him then and he had not enjoyed the high. After two months at college he began sniffing it regularly, then skin popping it, and went on to intravenous use by the end of his freshman year. By the end of his sophomore year, he could no longer sustain his grades and took four incompletes. Over the past summer he had gone on to daily intravenous heroin use, although he had withdrawn from it shortly before I saw him, in an attempt to get ready for his junior year.

Paul described heroin as a crutch he needed because of a pervasive confusion about his life. He feels blocked and certain that he will never follow through on anything he starts. Initially enthusiastic about coming to college, he has not taken advantage of anything it has to offer and feels estranged from the other students, whom he sees as dishonest about themselves. "The nicest people," he says, "are on heroin. They don't pretend to be what they're not and they say what they feel." Paul felt at home and able to be himself in the heroin world, where "one person on drugs knows another, and you know what the main thing motivating you is." On heroin he escapes from his sense of paralyzing confusion. "Everything seems clear," he said, "I feel as though I understand everything and there are solutions to all problems." This sense only further estranges him from the other students who are not high: "The way they hassle each other all seems foolish and unnecessary." Despite the satisfaction he has derived from heroin, Paul has sickening nightmares in which he is looking for food and is surrounded by heroin instead. In one recurring dream, he is a child who sits down to eat some cereal and finds heroin in it.

Paul connected his starting to use heroin with his relationship with a young woman he saw during his first year at college, although he does not understand how or why women and heroin came into his life at the same time. That relationship ended and his heroin use subsided.

But his involvement over the past summer with another woman, Diane, has led him to shoot heroin in greater amounts than ever before. He is engaged to Diane and says he would like to marry her, but his ambivalence about getting close to her was reflected the first time he mentioned her, when he blocked and could not think of her name. Diane knew he was on heroin when they met, but he has hidden from her the extent of his involvement. He would lie about it to her in ways that reminded him of conversations between his father and mother about his father's drinking.

When I asked about his family, Paul began by saying he "didn't really have a hard time of things when he looked back on it. After all, when you're a kid, things are a lot of fun." He then proceeded to relate in a rather mild manner, without too much feeling, the story of his childhood and family. His story was so painful that his blandness about it seems to have been an attempt to deal with his pain.

Paul's parents fought constantly about his father's drinking and the family's lack of money. He described his mother, who worked in a hospital, as someone who had no time for understanding either her children or her husband. Paul laughingly said she was very mean and used to beat him frequently. His father, who worked as a presser in a dry cleaning store, also beat him but faded out of the picture after he began to drink heavily when Paul was about seven. Between the ages of one and eight Paul was sent south for varying periods of time to stay with his mother's parents.

While Paul initially says he had a good time at his grandmother's, his memories made clear that he had been miserable. He saw his grandmother as a strict and unaffectionate person who believed "the way to bring up a child is to beat it." His earliest memory in life is of learning to walk and of his grandmother beating him for not doing it properly. He recalls that while she would yell he would scratch his ears till they were sore, an early indication of his way of blotting out emotional pain by hurting himself. He quickly adds that in looking back on this, he did not really mind it. When he was fifteen Paul was offered a chance to go to an excellent eastern prep school as part of a special program for disadvantaged students. He felt his parents had no say over him once he was out of the house and he came home only when he had to.

Soon after I began to see Paul he developed fears of my getting close to him that paralleled his fears with Diane. He dreamed he came home and found Diane in bed with another guy. He was very angry with her. Somebody was chasing him and he jumped out of a second-story window and hurt himself a little, but he managed to keep running.

Paul said school was starting the next day and he did not know if he could continue coming to see me as often as he had been. My office, he noted, like the room in the dream, was on the second floor, so I was probably the person who was chasing him.

Although he has always had a problem feeling jealous about girls he sees, he knows Diane is not involved with anyone else. He thought the dream might have been set off because he has had no sexual desire since he stopped heroin. He thinks he has not recovered physically from his withdrawal. "When I was on heroin," he said, "I could make love all night without an orgasm. I could go on for hours." He did not find that frustrating because "when you're high you don't care about that." When not high, he would usually have premature ejaculations.

Paul says he is tired of always being the problem in their sexual relationship, and he thinks he should stay away from Diane until his desire comes back. However, when he was on heroin he felt he should stay away because of his problem with heroin. I raised the question of his inventing Diane's infidelity as a way of keeping a barrier between them, which led us to question whether he was afraid to get too close to anyone. This idea visibly upset him, while everything he then said made clear that this was the case. When he was with Diane and still taking heroin, he would excuse himself, say he had to go somewhere, go out, get high, and come back. Now he finds himself wanting to excuse himself to go somewhere, but he has no place to go since he is not taking drugs. He explained the feeling with some animation. "It feels like when I was a kid and my mother always made me stay inside to take care of my sister. They'd be away at work and I couldn't go outside until they came home, and I always wanted to be out on the streets. Even if there was nothing doing out there, I'd always want to be out on the streets, and I couldn't wait to get out. Somehow that's the feeling I have with Diane." Being on heroin created a barrier between them that made being with her more possible. He said he could be with Diane more when he took heroin because, as he put it, "he was only with her physically, mentally he was someplace else again." He began to have conscious fantasies of her being unfaithful and his breaking up over it, which would make closeness between them no problem.

Paul became increasingly uncomfortable in discussing his fear of closeness. He expressed the feeling that if people knew him, they would not want to be around him, that even apart from the heroin, he is somehow bad, although he finds it hard to define in what way. He asked what could make somebody afraid to be close. When told it usually had to do with having been hurt by those you needed most and then protecting yourself against ever being hurt again, Paul said this was his situation. He told of painful incidents going back to his grandmother's house and ending at fourteen or fifteen when he decided he would never ask his mother for anything again. When I pointed out that the way he had previously described his mother and his childhood indicated a need to hide his pain, he repeated several times, "Well, that's something else again. Somehow you don't want to show anybody that you're vulnerable, that you care, and that they can hurt you." He had always felt the need to show other people that he was strong and confident. Only in the drug world where he shared a weakness in common with others could he express the vulnerable side of himself.

When he talked to Diane about his need at times to withdraw and be alone, she responded with a good deal of understanding; he felt much closer to her after the discussion, and sex had been better between them. However, he frightened himself by this closeness and stopped seeing Diane and started seeing other young women. But not seeing Diane only made Paul depressed and upset. He said he felt like getting high. He continued that he "would like to smash himself in the face." The association of getting high with the image of smashing himself in the face suggests the self-destructiveness involved in his taking heroin. He talked about how someone with cancer would feel if he knew he had only three months to live. He said he feels like surrendering. In a dream Paul had after this session, he dramatized his sense of himself as doomed: Paul was being shown a movie. The reels were out of order, but the audience, rather than being impatient, was quiet, even though they had to wait a long time. The movie was *Rosemary's Baby*, except it was in black and white rather than color, and he remembers the feeling of horror he had in the dream at the reels being mixed up. He felt the same kind of horror the woman had when she saw her baby and saw something in its foot that told her it belonged to the devil.

Paul's dream vividly dramatized his feelings about showing me his life. Like the film, our sessions reflect his past out of sequence. I questioned the black and white reference of the dream, bringing up the fact that he never referred to race. He responded by saying he never lets anyone push him around, and that we were both aware of the race question. He said the black and white part might refer to the fact that when he was kicking heroin, everything seemed black and white, there was no color in anything. He associates heroin with blacks, since he has to go to Harlem to buy it. But he described his prime horror in the dream as looking "into the unpleasant things of the past." He seemed to mean by this both his childhood and his experiences on heroin.

"Heroin," Paul said, "is something of a devil that has you in its power and you become evil on it." He again mentioned his nightmares of being a child wanting cereal and being given heroin instead. The dream and Paul's associations to it powerfully connect his heroin use to his experience with a mother he dreams of as an evil demon. Paul is clearly the child of the devil heroin, the only devil strong enough to protect him from the pain he suffered at his mother's hands. In a sense, he has chosen to abandon his mother and to become heroin's child. But the price of heroin's protection is an addiction that makes it impossible for him to receive from anyone else any part of the care and affection he craves.

Paul dreams of himself as the passive spectator of his own actions. He sees his life as determined for him by fate and does not perceive anything he has done as being of his own choosing. His addiction, his withdrawal, and his subsequent lack of sexual desire, he uses to bolster his sense that other, alien forces are always in control. Yet it is clear that these devices reflect what he called the real horror of the dream—the fearful necessity of looking too closely at himself.

Both Bart and Paul have grown up with a guardedness, isolation, and mistrust that stem from a profound disappointment with their mothers. Bart's feelings are much more ambivalent than Paul's, for Bart is aware of both his anger at and his need for his mother. Paul's disappointment has caused him to expect nothing from his mother, and he is less in turmoil about his relationship with her. But both students expect pain and disappointment from all close relationships and use similar devices to protect themselves.

Paul and Bart have in common an identification with a parent—in Paul's case his father and in Bart's case his mother—who has been heavily involved with alcohol. About one-third of the students I have seen who have been heavily involved with heroin have one parent who has a problem with alcohol or drug abuse.

Both Paul and Bart insist that their girlfriends are unfaithful, although all evidence is to the contrary. Infidelity would justify their own inability to commit themselves and their enormous mistrust of women. Their girlfriends arouse hopes which reawaken fears they cannot tolerate. And while their girlfriends are not unfaithful, it is not surprising that Paul and Bart are unfaithful and become so in a driven attempt to put a barrier between them and their girlfriends.

Before becoming involved with heroin, Paul and Bart felt unable to shape their lives in directions they would like. Heroin permitted them to sustain a life-style of almost total passivity. Paul sees his fate as determined—he is the child of the devil; Bart wants a magic wand to change his feeling about life and at times thought heroin would be that wand. Passivity is part of the emotional deadness that both young men adopt to protect them from what they see as inevitable frustration and rage.

In the emotional isolation conferred by heroin, they insulate themselves from both satisfaction and disappointments and insure that their current experiences are no more satisfying than their earlier ones.

The frustrated rage generated by their mothers and the frustrated rage they feel with their girlfriends is, for the most part, expressed self-destructively. Heroin use itself was a most striking manifestation of this. Paul craves it while feeling a powerful impulse to smash himself in the face. Bart dreams of heroin as a weapon that will kill him in a war he cannot win.

While Bart and Paul hide their rage behind a passive façade, the next student openly revenges himself on women for the disappointments of his childhood. While heroin is his preferred drug, he has been equally involved with sedatives in the past year. At twenty-six he has become cemented in an adaptation to life that demands drugs.

I saw Gary after what was probably the most destructive

and self-destructive year of his life. He related a series of recent events that illustrate the profound degree to which he alternates between hurting himself and hurting other people.

Ten months earlier, in his last year of graduate school, Gary was caught taking graduate entrance exams for various college undergraduates and was not allowed to graduate himself. He had been doing this for a year for a fee of seven hundred dollars an exam and was proud of the good results he had obtained for his clients. Although his department had offered him another chance if he "redeemed himself," Gary's life since his suspension had been on an accelerating, downhill course.

When he was no longer in school, Gary began dealing in heroin while mainlining it daily in increasing amounts until, after several months, he had developed a fifty-dollar-a-day habit. At the same time, he introduced heroin to a series of women he became sexually involved with. After a group sex experience he "accidentally" broke the jaw of one of them, Fay, because she asked him to take her home. About two months before I saw him, Gary had helped and encouraged another woman, Susan, whom he had involved with heroin, in an attempt to kill herself. This episode is particularly revelatory of Gary's behavior with women.

Susan and Gary had been spending an evening together taking barbiturates and drinking. Susan said life was not worth living and Gary told her if she felt that way, why not end it by taking the thirty nembutals that were left. He told her she would have to pay thirty dollars for the pills, then persuaded her to make a check out for a hundred dollars, since she was not going to be alive and he could use the money. He watched her take the pills with ice cream and left.

Somewhat high himself, Gary went to sleep. He woke about eight hours later and persuaded some friends to go back with him to Susan's apartment, where they broke open the door and took her to the hospital. He never told his friends his part in her attempt, merely that he suspected that she had done something. She was comatose and had stopped breathing at one point shortly after she reached the hospital, but she lived. Although Gary seems to feel fortunate that she did live, he relates this episode, as he does everything, with blandness. He says he was more upset at feeling he had no control over his life or over how destructive he could be than of the particular consequences to Susan. In mentioning a psychiatrist who refused to let him see her when he visited her in the hospital, it is clear that Gary agrees he is a menace to women, and that he should be kept away from them for their sake because he himself cannot stop his destructiveness.

Gary feels the women he gets involved with are somehow destined to be part of his life. He elaborates whole systems of puns based on their names and his and is fascinated by numerological connections between their birthdays and his or the time of events. The first young woman he made pregnant was born on the same day of the same year as he was. Eve, the second woman, became pregnant just as the first was delivering. For Gary these are no mere accidents, nor events that are of his own choice. They are expressions of some destiny, some fatalistic force that he feels governs all his relationships.

Women and drugs were inseparably interwoven

through Gary's story. His involvement with both started in college, his first sexual relationships and his use of LSD and marijuana coinciding. He makes clear that he felt unable to communicate freely and was sexually anxious (he would have premature ejaculations) if he was with a woman and not high on something. By his senior year in college he had fathered two children and was a well-established dealer in marijuana and LSD. Eve, whom he married, was very much involved with speed and shared Gary's magical, mystical sense of life. Because Eve had a great fear of doctors, Gary delivered their baby.

Despite the fact that Gary seems to have cared for Eve, he did everything to destroy their relationship. He perpetually accused her of infidelity. But at one point he encouraged her to go to bed with his friend and watched. Gary was constantly unfaithful himself, saying he could not stand monogamy. Eventually Eve went off with someone else and, although Gary had clearly driven her away, he seems to have missed her and to have been deeply hurt by her leaving. When Eve left, she wrote a curse on Gary's sheets and stuck pins into a voodoo doll they had. He is only partially joking in linking the voodoo pins with the needles he began to use to mainline heroin shortly after she left.

Gary claims to have no regrets about his treatment of women. When I questioned his need to let Eve know she was not that important to him, he countered with some feeling, saying that he treats women that way because that is the way "modern, liberated women treat men." He says he feels no guilt over hooking women on heroin because he was hooked—"everyone is hooked by someone else, so in a certain sense, you're not too responsible. Anyway heroin is a disease, so it's not a matter of right or wrong."

When I asked Gary whether taking the entrance exams was tied up with needing money for heroin, he replied that it had more to do with a whole life-style that included heroin. He mentioned a scene in the movie *Super Fly* where "the guy wants to give up dealing and the other guy says, 'But you've got it made. You've got a color TV in every room and you can get heroin every day. That's supposed to be the American dream.'" He also regards taking the exams as extracting his revenge on "academia." He bitterly resented having been expelled in his last year of college for dealing in LSD and marijuana. He felt not merely justified in having sold those drugs, but as something of a crusader. "This corrupt society," he says, "floats on alcohol. The government wants the exploited to drown their sorrows in it; it's necessary for businessmen's lunches, for making sexual contact at cocktail parties. Marijuana and LSD open up a truer, more perceptive consciousness of what is going on and what is going wrong." He associates his activity with revenging himself on an establishment that is corrupt and has been, he feels, unfair to him.

Justifying his behavior on the basis of earlier injustices suffered by him inevitably led back to the injustices Gary felt he has suffered in childhood at the hands of his family. He clearly associated "beating the system" with defeating his highly competitive and successful father's expectations of him. When he was younger he thought he would try to outdo his father by being more successful. But eventually he felt it easier to beat him in a different way. He says his father used to adopt a bantering, belittling attitude toward him, but now treats him like a losing investment.

Unlike the first two students, Gary is not in touch with the pain and bitterness of his early disappointments with his mother. Nevertheless, he radiated a persistent, nagging sense that she had somehow betrayed him. He began his first session by saying: "I was born in January, 1948, and my sister was born in December of that same year." He feels they were like twins, but to avoid having them in the same grade, his parents pushed him ahead and he skipped kindergarten. He feels being pushed ahead and out of the way set a pattern for his entire life. It was clear that he felt he had been deprived of something, although he never understood what. He was sure his mother loved him because of the way she was concerned about his achievement at school, worried about his health, and would come into his room to tell him that he was her favorite, although he suspected that she did this with each of the children in turn.

During psychiatric treatment he received in college he was always complaining about his mother and recalling the times she let him down. His psychiatrist told him he was unfair; his sense that he had "gotten a raw deal" persisted. His mother recognized that she had not given him what he needed, but tried to attribute his anger to the fact that she only breast fed him for three months. Gary sees her now as a very driven person, more into her work, which she has lately resumed, than anything else.

Gary was unusual in having no memory of the first six years of his life. The one story his family tells about him is suggestive of his future behavior toward girls. When he was about two he took a scissors and cut off all his sister's hair. However, Gary does recall at thirteen trying to undress her while she slept. But what emerges most powerfully is Gary's sense of his problems originating in his birthdate and his sister's, in the earliest facts and circumstances of his existence. When he describes his feeling that all his relationships are fated, are magically linked, he is reflecting the psychological truth that they are all interconnected, for in each relationship he has behaved so as to insure the same, recognizable early situation of deprivation and loss. His girlfriends are always changing, but always seem to be used by him as replicas of his mother and sister. In his fantasies throughout his childhood and adolescence, Gary makes clear how longstanding are his pain and rage.

While going to sleep as a child and adolescent, Gary would often fantasize that two rocks were rubbing against each other without making any noise. They were cold and hard on the outside, soft and hot on the inside—like volcanic rocks. There was the expectation that they would crumble.

Gary had another fantasy when going to sleep of trying to picture the smallest thing possible. He would often picture "a cone that one would just cut and cut until it was down to something microscopic." I asked what he made of these fantasies. He at first said, "Well, in Freudian terms it could be that the rocks were genitals and the cone was a penis." He also saw himself as the rocks, hard and soft at the same time. Certainly he gives the image of someone who is relatively quiet on the outside, but who contains a fury turbulent and concealed as a dormant volcano's. When asked whether he felt he would crumble, he said that in many ways he already had. The rocks, he pointed out, are burned out on the inside, maintain the appearance of hardness, but are no more durable than ash.

Gary sees his sexual feelings as inevitably destructive or self-destructive. In a sense, obliterating his penis, burning himself out, or reducing himself to nothingness would seem to provide some peace if only the peace of death and dissolution. At present he has recurring sexual nightmares of falling, suggesting the way in which he sees sexual feelings as leading to his downfall.

Gary had a dream in the course of our sessions that further suggested the link between his feelings toward his mother and sister and his treatment of women. In the dream, Susan and her friend Andrea were sunning themselves on a high grass knoll at his parents' home.

In reality, Susan does not like to sunbathe. Her friend Andrea once came to a party dressed like her. Andrea and Gary got high and went to bed during the evening. The ambiguous identity of the two girls—one looks like another—is a theme that pervades Gary's life. Both women warm and high on the grass suggests both sexual excitement and turning them on to pot. In reality, Gary says he had been responsible for turning both of them on to heroin. The setting at his parents' home suggests a relationship between these two women and his mother and sister and implies a connection between what he does to the women and the raw deal he feels he got from his mother and sister.

Introducing women to heroin and taking money from them are recurring events in Gary's life. In the course of our sessions he saw Eve for the first time in many months. They fought all the time over a bottle of vodka. He had brought the first bottle and when it came to buying a second, which cost $1.25, he said she should give him 63¢

and he would pay 62¢. They quarreled over the odd penny until they ended up not buying it. Gary's relationship with Fay, whose jaw he had broken, ended when she left him because he charged her for heroin. And, of course, he charged Susan for the pills she had to take to kill herself. If Gary extracts money from women in place of the affection he feels he cannot get, he supplies them with poison in place of the affection he cannot give and makes them pay for it as well.

Taking barbiturates, quaaludes, and doriden helped free Gary to express his hostility without remorse or inhibition. He felt that the barbiturates he took enabled him to participate in Susan's suicide attempt without conflict. He feels these pills are in ways more harmful than heroin and because they do seem to permit him to be so destructive, they indeed are. He proved his point in the course of our sessions when, while drinking and taking quaaludes he went to bed with his friend's girlfriend while his friend watched. His friend became upset, left the bedroom, took twenty quaaludes in the kitchen, and told them about it. Gary was annoyed because his friend was so stupid and commented that if he had initially taken a little more quaalude, it would not have bothered him to watch. At one time such a triangle "would have added excitement," Gary remarked, "but even with that, nothing was so great last night." He had taken another quaalude that morning and I could see how animated, talkative, and expressive it made him.

Gary described his experiences with quaaludes as "being in a kind of sleepwalking state during the daytime. You can almost play-act any role. You learn to resist the initial sedative effect and then the drug comes to be like a stimulant. You get so you really have to have them to start the day; it helps you get through." Gary feels quaalude frees him because it cuts him off from his higher brain centers and makes it easier for him to talk. However, it is clear that what it releases are sexual and angry feelings that can be expressed in a detached, affectless way.

Gary does not permit himself to feel very much about anything or to acknowledge that he needs anything from other people. This was true of his relations with women and apparent in the manner he adopted with me. In his first session he used the bantering tone he said he once used with his father. He said he was curious to compare me with other psychiatrists he had been to. He would refer to the very limited dimensions of his mind that it would be possible for us to explore, commenting that conversation would be unnecessary in a century because people would use telepathy. He considered asking me for a prescription for sleeping pills to see if I could or would refuse. The day he came in high on quaaludes, he sat in the chair I usually used, and when I asked him about it, he said good naturedly he had wanted to do it before, the quaaludes made it easier, and its significance was up to me to figure out.

When I questioned how blandly he had spoken of his life, he admitted that he feels despair and futility over it. He had thoughts of suicide and he is preoccupied with the question of escaping or obliterating his identity. He was moved by his early experience with LSD, which helped him "pass through the dimension of Gary Burrell," and was excited at being someone else when he took graduate admission exams for other people. He cannot get over being asked who he really was when he was caught. He is intrigued by the idea of people being interchangeable when he goes to bed with Andrea, who looks and was dressed like Susan. In his fantasy of reducing the cone to nothingness, it is more than his sexuality he is wiping out—it is himself.

During the next to last time I saw him in what was a five-session evaluation, Gary came close to asking for help or admitting he needed some. He had referred to himself as a guinea pig in my drug research. When I questioned this, he said in fact he did not think I saw him that way. He had expected our sessions to be more impersonal, but their not being so had made it harder. We talked about how hard it was for him to ask for anything or to let people know they were important to him. With more feeling than he generally exhibited, he said it was a big mistake to let yourself need anyone.

Gary acts out the rage that Bart and Paul contain in a deadening passivity. The very disappointments Gary himself helps to produce—whether in school or with women—arouse an enormous rage. When he then takes large amounts of heroin, he is using it as a self-destructive rage and pain killer. When he "hooks" others on heroin, it serves as a murderous weapon of vengeance. Quaalude helps him express this vengeance in detached, destructive sexual behavior.

Despite the quality of his angry behavior, Gary has many similarities to Bart and Paul. He too needs heroin to have any sort of relationship. For him too it creates the barrier that makes a limited relationship possible. For all three students, heroin serves to relieve sexual anxiety and make orgasm irrelevant, permitting them to take pride merely in sustained erection. Their conception that a woman will only be concerned with their performance, not their pleasure, says everything about their expectations.

Gary, Paul, and Bart share a preoccupation with their girlfriends' fidelity. While needing to sleep with other women himself, Bart compulsively insists Lori will be unfaithful at just those moments when they have been closest. Paul fantasizes Diane's infidelity, which would provide him with the excuse he needs for anger and further distance from her. Gary arranges his wife's infidelity with his friend and watches it. "What meaning does it have?" he comments. "It's just skin touching skin." Watching his wife go to bed with another man and not caring is a way of proving to himself and making it clear to her how unimportant she is. Gary goes still further when he becomes an indifferent and encouraging partner to Susan's suicide attempt, only concerned with extracting the maximum money for his pills.

Gary's destructiveness does not conceal his passivity about his life. He attributes all the evils that befall him to a destiny outside of him and beyond his control. Intensely fatalistic, he marvels at the repetition of the problems of his life without seeing what he does to produce them.

Gary, like Paul and Bart, does everything to destroy his relationship with a woman and is then terribly hurt, depressed, and anguished when it ends. For all three becoming involved with a woman and losing her reawakens the pain and disappointment of their early relationships with their mothers. Not letting the woman become too great a source of pleasure protects them from that pain. But it protects them at the price of making it impossible for them to ever have an experience that would satisfy their needs.

Gary, Paul, and Bart were typical of other students who were involved with heroin. Some used the drug to soften

current disappointments while self-destructively expressing anger and frustration; others used it to restrict involvements that contained the possibility of hurt or
disappointment. For both groups heroin served to create
an illusion of invulnerability. The need for this sense of
imperviousness to pain was most striking in students who
had not used heroin at all, but who began to use it when
they became involved in what promised, or threatened, to
be a close relationship with a woman. Although these
young men would insist their anxiety about the relationship was due to a fear of losing the woman, when, with
the aid of heroin and other distancing devices, they managed to put a stop to the closeness, their anxiety and their
use of heroin stopped.

Heroin use had self-destructive implications for students who took it without becoming addicted. One student, who had used the drug only twice before, went into
an orgy of intravenous heroin abuse after the break-up of
his parents' marriage. In a few weeks he collapsed and a
short time later nearly killed himself in a car accident. He
now sees both his heroin orgy and his accident as suicide attempts. One young girl actually used heroin in a
conscious and serious suicide attempt when a relationship
which she had done everything to dampen eventually did
end. In such cases heroin comes close to its original medical use as a pain killer. But it is the pain of emotional
abandonment these students are trying to escape from,
and their use of heroin is accompanied by impotent and
self-damaging rage.

Heroin generates a powerful social mystique and, for
most of these students, becomes the medium of social relations, governing their friendships and their life-style.
Many students spoke of the common bond between junk-

ies, the tie of knowing "your friends all want the same thing" and no pretense is required. Bart, Gary, and many of the other heroin users were attracted by the excitement and illegality the drug world offered. Coming to life describing the excitement of petty crimes and illegal acts, they seemed to enjoy being outcasts from the comfortable, middle-class backgrounds many of them came from. Almost all of them did some dealing to support their habits.

Despite their enjoyment of the illicit, most of the student users were concerned over the practical problems of getting heroin and breaking the law. The same students who would rip off their friends, steal from their families, or deal would be shocked at the idea of a major theft or mugging to support their habit. They will not do absolutely anything to get heroin. If there is a diminution in the supply of heroin, they would rather turn to alcohol, massive amounts of marijuana, or sedatives.

Heroin is essentially a drug of despair. It has the effect of putting people—even oneself—in parentheses, of making everyone unimportant, of turning human involvements into an only ancillary experience. No group of students I have seen, with the exception of severely suicidal students, have been hurt so deeply and so early in life. Both students who do take heroin and students who do not see it as a lethal poison. Injecting it into the bloodstream, with such feelings and with all the risks it entails, expresses a profound misery, in which the twin themes of despair and invulnerability intertwine. If they inject heroin into themselves, feeling their lives do not matter very much, they also feel that their very lack of concern for their lives will render them invulnerable, even to the dangers of heroin.

In the despair of these heroin users is reflected an increasing fear and abrasiveness bound up in human relationships, a sense that to be free one must give up on the very possibility of closeness. Through heroin these students achieve the illusory freedom and illusory invulnerability of the isolated and the emotionally dead. This is the kind of freedom Janis Joplin, herself a heroin user who eventually died of an overdose, probably understood when she sang: "Freedom's just another word for nothin' left to lose."

8 | The End of the Psychedelic Road

ASKED IN AN interview by *Playboy* what LSD
has done for him, Timothy Leary replied, "I was thirty-
nine when I had my first psychedelic experience. At that
time I was a middle-aged man involved in a middle-aged
process of dying. My joy in life, my sensual openness, my
creativity were sliding downhill. Since that time, six years
ago, my life has been renewed in every dimension." In
The Politics of Ecstasy, Leary wrote: "Emotions are the
lowest form of consciousness. Emotional actions are the
most contracted, narrowing, dangerous form of behavior.
The romantic poetry and fiction of the last two hundred
years has quite blinded us to the fact that emotions are
an active and harmful form of stupor." How to explain
the contradiction between the pursuit of "creativity" and
"sensual openness" and the belief that passions are a
"form of stupor"? How to explain the simultaneous desires to feel alive and to have no feeling at all?

Among students who were heavy users of LSD and
other psychedelics, both the desire to feel alive and to go
beyond feeling were common. The conflicts and the

psychodynamic forces that produced these desires were central to an understanding of the psychology of psychedelic use and abuse. Students who habitually used psychedelics proved to be out of touch with much that is crucial in their emotional lives. Many of them spoke of being cut off from their inner feelings. Most had histories of loneliness, emotional withdrawal, and constriction extending back to childhood. Some students felt that LSD, mescaline, and psylocybin had helped them get in touch with themselves, with their real feelings about life. Some felt the sensory stimulation provided by the drug made them feel more alive. But others wanted to be taken beyond themselves. They had been so severely constricted that their emotional lives had been narrowed to feelings of tension, anxiety, and anger. They were unable to conceive of an emotion that was not constricting or unpleasant.

Even users of psychedelics who felt they had been helped by the drug consider tripping to be an overwhelming and shattering experience that they would not want to repeat too often. Most of the regular users were partially disenchanted because of the failure of psychedelics to carry enough liberating power into their daily lives. Most had had bad trips but went on taking psychedelics nonetheless. Advocates of the psychedelic drugs often discount the bad trip as merely an improperly induced trip, irrelevant to understanding psychedelics. But the bad trips of these students shed a good deal of light on their hopes as well as on the frustrations and anxieties produced by the drug. To ignore them would be as inappropriate as discarding an individual's nightmares in favor of his more pleasant dreams.

Alan, a tall, clean-cut, blond senior with a serious manner, used psychedelics regularly until a bad trip cut his efforts short. His description of what LSD did for him and the anxiety and nightmares produced by his bad trip combined to give a good picture of the psychological dilemma faced by student users. Since his bad trip a week earlier, Alan has had severe feelings of unreality and acute anxiety, and an intensification of his feeling that he cannot communicate with people, particularly women. His description of his LSD experience both reflected his sense of constriction and had a violent quality suggestive of his wish to blast free of himself.

Alan tried to describe his usual feelings while taking LSD by telling me that, were he to take it in my office, he might begin to see the office as a cube inside the larger cube of the hospital, which was inside the larger cube of the city. Or he could become conscious that we were two automatons, two conditioned animals in a Skinner box, and this vision might extend to everyone in the society. As the drug took more effect, he said he would feel an increasing sense of flight from the cube, of breaking out of his own personality.

For Alan, taking LSD or mescaline had the quality of a radical attempt to escape the box he felt he was in in his relations with everyone. His bad trip reflected a preoccupation with entrapment, but was made terrifying by the very process of escaping his own personality. He said he felt he was in a bubble. His face was not his face and nothing at all was real. He felt as though he were disintegrating within the bubble. Alan's bad trip reflects his fear of LSD's shattering power, his apprehension that in attempting to get out of himself, he may destroy himself entirely.

A dream Alan had the night after his bad trip suggests the sources of his need for the drug and his fear of it: He was in a house and there was some supernatural power that was telling him to do this or not to do the other thing, and he finally said, "Fuck you!" Then he was in the grip of another power that slammed him around, threw him against the walls and windows, cracking the walls and breaking the windows. He recalls taking some glass out of his arm.

Alan related this dream to nightmares he had as a child in which something was forcing him to eat an apple pie as big as a house, or to drink champagne from a glass as big as a house. He would lie awake at night wondering what it would be like to be hungry. But when he would tell his mother this, she would refuse to listen and once said, "I don't want a crazy child, if you're going to be crazy, you're not my son."

In Alan's associations to his dreams it was clear that he felt he had been tightly controlled all his life, that he had never been permitted to develop and satisfy appetites of his own. The sense of having been figuratively fed according to someone else's needs, and the feeling of being forced to consume what someone else thought was good pervade his life. His hunger fantasy as a child movingly expresses his wish to have been allowed to feel and gratify his own needs, and it dramatizes how profoundly and how early in life he had felt pained by having been forcibly alienated from himself.

In his current dream, Alan is ordered around by a supernatural power. He resists it and becomes caught up in another overpowering force that can magically hurl him where it will. His mother emerged as someone who was always telling him what to do and was always trying to rule every aspect of his life. The angry "Fuck you!" of his dream is the closest Alan had come to expressing the rage he feels toward her for controlling his life. Alan saw the second overpowering force, bound up with his rejection of the first, as drugs. In LSD Alan seems to have tried to find a force that would be sufficiently powerful and magical to counter the power he attributes to his mother. At the same time LSD arouses the anxiety that he is cracking the structure of his own personality beyond repair.

Alan's mother seems to have always refused to acknowledge any of his feelings that ran counter to her opinion of what he ought to feel. He told me that his real interest is in music, but that when he talked of majoring in it at college, his mother said she would not give him any money if he did and that he had no talent for music anyway. Although he says she knows nothing about music and is not qualified to judge whether or not he has talent, he feels that she told him he had no talent out of a concern for his welfare. While his father says that if Alan wants to major in music he has no objection, Alan sees him as someone who retreats into silence from everyone in the family and who avoids supporting him with his mother. Alan insists that it is very important for him to please his mother. Only in fantasy can he see himself accepted by her on his own terms—imagining himself, for example, coming home with a band and playing for her in the living room.

Alan's difficulties in communication with women are not hard to understand considering that he had a father who did not communicate and a mother who could only accept the kinds of communication and expression that she wanted to hear. Unfortunately for Alan he had absorbed his mother's wish to constrict him. He has great difficulty in caring for or getting to know women with whom he becomes sexually involved. He seems to get into relationships hoping that the woman will release his pas-

sion (much in the way he hopes that LSD will free him),
and when he becomes excited and involved with a woman,
he nevertheless needs to dampen his feeling by disparaging her or by rapidly becoming interested in someone
else. He feels he tends to try to impress women in the way
he tries to impress his mother. At times he treats them
like his mother has treated him, by being overly possessive and by trying to "keep them in a cage."

Alan began to see how his need to constrict women derived from his own emotional constriction and his relationship with his mother. He felt that he had identified
the problem, wondered how he could overcome it, and
unwittingly asked, "Is there some kind of pill?" As he said
this we both laughed because it was clear he had sought
the solution in a pill.

Frightened by the sense of disintegration that accompanied the feeling of breaking out of his personality,
Alan moved away from psychedelics. Other students were
willing to pay the price of fear for relief from themselves.

Disturbed by their own emotions, made anxious by anyone else's interest in them, these students seek experience
without emotion. Hating what they see as their too programmed, structured lives, they seek to be virtually torn
asunder by the chaotic effects of psychedelic drugs. They
turn their contacts with other people into a series of discrete events, converting all kinds of experiences into the
equivalent of a one-night stand. More than one pictured
himself as a wandering Odysseus, going from one encounter to another in a broken and fragmented life. It is
no accident that psychedelics have usually been the most
significant drugs in helping them to see their lives as a
succession of discrete, random moments.

The unpredictable quality of the psychedelic trip contributes to the sense of fragmentation it produces. Students who seem to take any and every drug without at times even knowing what, in a kind of psychopharmacological Russian roulette, usually find psychedelics the drugs of choice for extended periods. The use of psychedelics and/or the random use of other drugs permit the fragmentation of experience these students require.

Michael, a college freshman, began a heavy drug involvement with six months of continual LSD abuse. LSD permitted him to enter a succession of casual relationships that brought him temporary relief from an otherwise pervasive depression. His sessions were filled with parties he had been to, women he had been to bed with, drugs he had used, whistles he has stolen and blown to add a little excitement to life—a continual series of happenings after which he would return to his usual lifelessness. He would get stoned and see movies like *Night of the Living Dead*, because even the experience of strong fear and disgust were better than his usual numbness. In this film the dead come back to eat up the living. The fear of this happening to him persisted for several hours after the movie, and the image continued to haunt him. In fact the dead part of Michael did seem to be eating up the living, which he expressed in saying he felt "devoured by depression."

Michael attributed his depression to rejection by an aloof, withdrawn girl he had been involved with in his senior year in high school. Yet it soon became clear that this relationship had revived the trauma of his relationship with his mother, whom he saw as a chronically unhappy person who took out her dissatisfaction with his father and her life on her children. She would tell Michael he was rotten, that she did not like him, and would beat him in an enraged way for things that had nothing to do with him. He would pray for her to die or wait for the time he could be out of the house and free.

Michael saw himself as having been emotionally starved and having to work hard for the meager attention he got. He saw being eccentric, far out, and entertaining as a way of being liked, and feels drugs help him to achieve this goal. He said he is so hungry for affection that he "would go to bed with an octopus." But this image suggests his attempt to deny a pervasive terror of being held in an unbearable grip by closeness in any relationship. Casual "fuck them and forget them" relationships were only possible when he was stoned, loaded, or tripping. He is fond of the words of a B. B. King song, "It doesn't matter what I did last week 'cause it doesn't count when you're high."

When I saw Michael a year later he was far less depressed and his use of drugs had diminished considerably. Although he continued his pattern of casual sexual relationships while high almost nightly on beer (he had developed a little pot belly to prove it), he admitted that he considered his better mood very precarious. He was determined to avoid anything but the surface of experience and feeling. He felt that he had been helped by a recent interest in philosophy, which permitted him to look at universals rather than his own feelings. Most important, he carefully avoids any romantic attachments by immersing himself in beer and casual relationships. He said he felt at the edge of an abyss, sensing that if he were seriously involved with a girl, he would fall in. He told me of a dream he had of swimming happily in a pool, but then noticing parts of dead bodies beneath the surface.

Michael's dream powerfully represents his sense of depression beneath his surface equanimity, and his vision of himself as fragmented at bottom. While he has been attracted to chaotic behavior and to fragmenting himself as a way of avoiding the pain of close involvement, his dream reflects his considerable fear of this very fragmentation. In seeing himself as a dead, dismembered body, he reflects the fear that having split himself apart, he may be too far gone to get himself back together again. This dream of surface happiness, basic deadness, and fragmentation reflects Michael's underlying fear, depression, and defensive chaos. Through a combination of detachment and fragmentation, Michael can maintain an adaptation, tenuous as it is, with somewhat less help from drugs than before.

Some students alternate between random drug abuse and more or less exclusive concentration on LSD and mescaline. Both help them to achieve the fragmentation and detachment they seek. George began taking drugs after his junior year in high school while on a summer study program in Europe. He and a girl in the group smoked a lot of hash and tripped regularly on mescaline, feeling their drug taking brought them closer together. While he feels he initially tripped with LSD and mescaline to be close to her and to his friends, eventually he realized that he used the drugs to withdraw.

When he came back from Europe, George felt unable to accept the submissiveness and dependence that had characterized his relationship with his parents. He stayed out every night, getting involved with whatever drugs were available. He would take samples sent to psychiatrists from the mailroom of his building and swallow them indiscriminately. Despite his drug rebellion, he acquiesced in his parents' wish that he go to school in New York instead of the out-of-town college he had chosen. His mother said she had "visions of him lying dead in a lake if he went away." But at Columbia, George said, he has blown his mind more than ever before. He attributes his dropping out for a year to his increasing use of acid and mescaline. His trips brought on an increasingly "paranoid vision of things."

At one point, George felt torn asunder by the forces of good and evil which were struggling over him. Once when he was tripping he went into the West End bar and many students were leaving. He had the idea that "the bombs were about to fall, and everybody was seeking shelter and had someplace to go but him." But feeling isolated in an atomic war did not deter him from his acid trips. George wanted to get out of his mind, to be in contact with "ultimate knowledge," which appeared to be bound up with the experience of dissolution. Through LSD George hoped to achieve both the sensation of fragmentation and a detachment from it that would carry over into his daily life and make him able to endure its terrors more coolly. He was irresistibly drawn to films of violence like *El Topo* and *A Clockwork Orange*, but would get stoned before seeing them in order to make them more bearable. But his attempt to deal with life through a similar detachment has had the effect of crippling his ability to protect himself.

George had never taken any drug intravenously and never wanted to. On New Year's Eve a friend was shooting cocaine and wanted George to join him. Rather than admit to himself or his friend that he was reluctant or afraid, George told himself he would do it "to understand the feelings of his friends who took drugs intravenously." His friend shot it into his right arm; George was afraid to have it on the left side because it was closer to his heart.

Although he started coughing and felt he would die, he said he later became euphoric. But George deals with fear or anger with intellectual curiosity, amusement, or euphoria even without cocaine.

When robbed by two black youngsters with knives, George said he was not angry during or after the robbery. He said that "probably someone like me who is healthy and in good physical shape should have kicked their ass in so as to discourage them from approaching or attacking other people. Now they won't be discouraged." Telling himself that if he fought back it would only be for a socially useful purpose conveys George's way of dealing with anger. He behaves with a mixture of blandness and an air of invulnerability that make it hard for him to protect himself. Although George tries to insulate himself from his feelings, he had several dreams immediately after these incidents that indicate his emotional reactions were far from mere curiosity, euphoria, or amusement.

He was kneeling at the feet of a four-foot-tall black kid.

He was sharing a room with a fellow who started to make homosexual advances, and it was as though the fellow took over the room, and that it was not his anymore.

He was shot in the head. He had inadvertently been caught in the Irish rebellion. All kinds of people were shooting at each other. Some women took him to the hospital. They were all amazed he had survived with such a bad wound. George seemed bland about the whole thing.

These dreams all indicate the degree to which George felt humiliated, attacked, and forced to submit by both his friend and the pair who robbed him. But even in the last dream where what he described as the "jolt in the head" he got from cocaine appears as a murderous bullet in the brain, George attempts to deny; he may be dying, but he regards his situation blandly.

Shortly before I met him, George became involved with a married woman, Sue, in his first intense and romantic attachment. At the same time he started to snort heroin. He attributed his use to fear of losing her. But everything he did served to insure such a result. He would concern himself so exclusively with her needs, particularly sexually, that his own pleasure would disappear in the process. At the same time he was terribly afraid she would become too important to him. Although initially very moved and excited by her, George withdrew from his strong excitement into a more dampened state. This was dramatized in a dream he had during their early involvement: There were high cliffs over the sea. The cliffs split apart and some kind of monstrous serpent came out and rose toward the sky. It was almost like an atomic explosion. George was frightened and went back into the house.

George saw his involvement with Sue and his feeling for her as an earth-shattering revolution on his part. He is frightened and retreats to the house, that is, to the expectation garnered from his experience with his parents that everyone will expect him to ignore his feelings in favor of theirs.

George finds it hard to accept his passionate attachment to anything. A talented musician who plays several instruments including the guitar, sings well, and composes, George wanted to make a career out of music and was unrestrained in his enthusiasm for it. Yet he found this very interest in music so hard to accept he repeatedly consulted the I Ching oracle about it. The I Ching oracle gave him a high rating in enthusiasm for music until it finally told him that only a fool consults the oracle on the same issue several times. George deals with all strong feelings by an intellectualization and detachment from them. His girlfriend and his music excite him but generate a fear that if he gives in to his enthusiasm he will be engulfed by it and destroyed. A science fiction mystery George is writing says a great deal about his vision of relationships and his consequent fears of all kinds of involvement:

A couple has been alive since 1500 B.C. They survive by tapping someone's life energy every forty years. The story begins with the couple leaving the apartment of a man who died. Somehow the couple had massaged the man, given him drugs, and brought him to orgasm. The man died gloriously, but the couple had somehow tapped the man's life energy, enabling them to survive and stay young. The story becomes more involved but the theme persists: people live by draining the life from others.

George's sense of all human relations is dominated by this theme. He says of his story that after writing for six hours, he felt drained, as though "all his life was in the page and that it had become real and potent." He sees his parents as having sucked the life out of him. He describes his mother as somebody who feels a child must be exactly what she wants it to be, and gets very angry and upset if he questions her, going so far as to tell him that it was not up to him to think about college, he should merely accept her wishes and go. He sees his father, who is a successful behavioral scientist, as weak and ineffectual apart from his work, but also as egocentric, as someone who is "always right and never listens to others. He can pick up a newspaper while you are talking to him."

George's family considers his interest in music a "delusion," a word they use to describe any of his interests they do not share. George felt they would not object to his music if they could be sure it would succeed. As it was when he left school again, this time to pursue a musical career, his parents' attitude was that he had failed to fulfill a contract with them. His father constantly referred to his guitar case as "the shitbox of the devil."

As a child George had a recurring dream which vividly expresses his vision of his life and his attempt to deal with it: He would jump off the bridge near where he lived and dive underwater. When he reached bottom he found a school, very much like the private school he was going to, except that the teachers in the dream were all cannibals and were eating the children. They were really horrible; they would be fattening them and eating them. There were pieces of arms and legs on hooks. George's role was somehow to save the children that were still alive with his Boy Scout knife. He was a hero in these dreams.

The dream often took a strange twist. To escape the cannibal teachers himself, he had to go down a slide that went through a tunnel, and when he came out he was a jigsaw puzzle. He was stuck on the slide and his brother, who was horrified, slid down and released George, but then his brother was transformed into a jigsaw puzzle. This kept going on between them.

George feels he was used to serving his parents' needs, that they were fattening themselves on him, and that he was a choice piece of meat. In the dream, he fights back, as he almost never does directly. His older brother would fight with their parents but George either obeyed or did not, but never said what he felt. In reality, his rebellion has been through drugs.

To avoid the sense of emotional suffocation and the

rage and fear that rebellion against it entails, George attempts a fragmentation of his experience and himself—represented in this dream by the dismemberment of the children and by the jigsaw puzzle he becomes. Becoming a virtual jigsaw puzzle through drugs has been a reality for George. But in this vision, as in the image of dismembered children, there is the possibility of not being able to become whole again. In his dream either he or his brother remains on the slide, a disassembled puzzle. Even in this dream George reflects his sense that one person must be sacrificed so another may survive.

Drugs have been George's tunnel and slide, the means of going underground and remaining stuck in fragmentation, fixed in a chaotic state that is both desirable and frightening. Both he and Michael have similar, terrifying dreams of being dismembered under water. Surface calm and submerged death reflect their burial of their own emotions and their way of dealing with life through fragmentation of themselves. The films they are drawn to are often only pale reflections of their own dream images of cannibal teachers and institutions, of their own feelings of having been the victims of their parents' casual brutality, and of their own devouring deadness.

Many students said LSD opened new worlds to them. But what it revealed was, as one student said, "mostly lousy." The emotions it produces are often those of horror at perceiving that nothing is as it seems—schools are slaughterhouses, human relationships are all destructive and devouring. LSD and other psychedelics forced these students into an intense awareness of the horror of their own lives.

But the fragmentation produced by LSD—the state George described as becoming a jigsaw puzzle—also provided these students with an escape from themselves. Although they feared becoming Humpty Dumpties who could never be put together again, these students found in dismantling themselves a defense against all strong emotion, particularly against the depression and rage that mark their lives. In fragmentation they felt they were going beyond the human condition into a state of detached sensation. These students have gone beyond alienation, beyond despair over their estrangement from themselves. For estrangement is what they seek, enlivened by increased sensation and the chaotic, unpredictable effects of LSD.

Discontent with the "meaninglessness of life," "the search for meaning," have become so commonplace in the language of our time that it is hard to realize that these students share none of the lament for life lived in harmony with emotion that these phrases imply. These students rather strive for meaninglessness as a protection against what they see as the pain that will inevitably hit them if they become emotionally involved with anyone or anything. What conflict they have over living without meaning is expressed through their use of psychedelics and their attitude toward them. On the one hand they strive for the random, unpredictable effects of psychedelics and freedom from their all-too-predictable selves. On the other they search for the meaning of the randomness they create in astrology and the I Ching—both of which imply meaning is external and divorced from personal emotion.

The paradoxical pursuit of creativity and sensual openness and the belief that passions are a form of stupor is really a reflection of the basic conflict these students face. They have gone dead and sought meaninglessness to protect themselves from the awareness and experience of their own pain and rage. Yet they seek to feel alive and meaningful without having to connect with themselves emotionally and without having to expose themselves to anger and pain. In the random effects of LSD and the fragmentation it engenders they try to destroy their "programming," to experience pure sensation beyond emotion.

PART FOUR | **Students in Crisis**

Students in crisis, students chosen at random, and students who sought help for problems with drug abuse throw into sharp relief the problems faced by this generation. Students in crisis are those whose suffering has overpowered them, who are driven further and further into the behavior or symptoms that are their only resolution to their problems.

Students who are flunking out share with virtually all young men an intense anguish over the competitive strain in college. They live out the nightmare of many young men who see the rat race as the excruciating treadmill where they get nowhere. The rage between the sexes is clear and open in the lives of impotent students whose physical problem is the most concrete expression of conflicts shared by most young men today. In the intensity of their outrage against social injustice and the paucity of their belief in their own instincts and feelings as being of value, student revolutionaries then and now capture the flight from emotion, from personal and private value into the larger world.

The depressed and suicidal students are the most radically afflicted by the flight from emotion. They share with other students the tendency to ward off life with numbness, to pursue a detachment that carried to its ultimate expression is meant to sever them from life itself.

9

Growing Up Dead: Student Suicide

"How NICE—to feel nothing, and still get full credit for being alive," Kurt Vonnegut wrote in *Slaughterhouse-Five*. Thomas Pynchon's hero in *V.* is Benny Profane, who suspects he is inanimate. The trend is toward muted, diminished involvement in life. There is a rising tide of college students who try to blot out their pain, anger, and frustration with the ultimate numbness.

Suicide among young people and among college students in particular has been steadily and alarmingly rising during the past twenty years. Over 4,000 of the 25,000 suicides in the country each year are now in the fifteen to twenty-four age group. The suicide rate for this group has increased over 250 per cent in this period going from 4.2 in 1954 to 10.6 in 1973.* The most dramatic change is the increase in the suicide rate of young men fifteen to twenty-four, which has gone from 6.7 in 1954 to 17 in 1973. As these figures show, the suicide trend was evident through the quiet fifties, persisted through the political activism of

* Rates are calculated by the National Center for Health Statistics per 100,000 of the age group.

the sixties, through the many shifts in the drug culture, and continues on campus today. Why do increasing numbers of college students want to end their lives? What does their depression say about what is changing in American life?

The students I saw were drawn to death as a way of life. The most seriously suicidal were those whose absorption and preoccupation with their own extinction are an integral, ongoing part of their daily experience. These students see their relationships with their parents as dependent on their emotional if not physical death and become tied to their parents in a kind of death knot. Coming to college, graduating, becoming seriously involved with another person, and enjoying an independent existence have the power to free them. In fact the meaning of suicide and depression lies in their encounter with the forces that might unleash their own possibilities for freedom.

The question is often asked if the psychology of suicide can be determined from those who made attempts and survived. My own answer is emphatically, yes. The attempted suicide population contains the majority of the eventual suicide population in addition to many whose involvement with suicide will not be fatal. Some of the students I saw died from the consequences of injuries sustained in their attempts. Some, such as a student who survived a seven-story jump, survived by accident. This young woman had, and indeed a majority of actual suicides of all ages have, a history of prior attempts. Distinguishing the seriously suicidal from those whose attempts will not culminate in an actual suicide is not that difficult for any experienced clinician.

It is often said that suicidal students have been destroyed by the strain of competition and work and by parental pressure toward success. But far from being harmed by their work, many students used it as a barricade. "Work," as one student put it, was his "main defensive army." Nor were the parents of these students more achievement-oriented than most. Their own problems had led them to need their children to be quiet drones. They often opposed work their children found fascinating because they were unable to cope with pleasure and excitement. Dull, demanding mental labor was often the nexus of the suicidal students' existence. It did not have to lead to success or any pleasurable sense of achievement, but rather functioned as another link in the chain of emotional deadness that bound them to their parents.

It has been thought that the literal death or physical loss of a parent was crucial in producing suicidal people. Zilboorg, as far back as 1936, applied to the study of suicide Freud's observations on the importance of "ambivalent identification" with a "lost loved object" in causing depression. He called attention to the frequency of the actual death of a parent before or during the adolescence of suicidal patients. In my own work I found a significantly high proportion of seriously suicidal students had lost a parent. But what even these students made clear is that more than ambivalent identification with a dead parent is involved. What was crucial was the quality of feeling that flowed between the student and his parents. The bond of emotional death was as powerful in suicidal students who had not experienced the actual death of a parent as it was in those who had. Both groups were pulled toward their own death primarily by the bond that had defined their relationship with their parents while their parents lived, and continued to control their lives even if their parents died.

Leon had lost neither of his parents, although he could

be said never to have had them either. He had gotten along with them by burying himself alone in his room studying, listening to music, and having suicidal thoughts. At eighteen he had already been thinking of suicide for years and in high school had compiled a list of reasons why he should not kill himself. He enumerated them to me in the mechanical manner he usually adopted: First, things were so bad that they could only get better. Second, you had no right to take your life. Third, his parents had made a great investment in his education and it would cost a lot to bury him. Fourth, his parents would blame themselves. Fifth, they would be devastated and would miss him. Since he has been at college he has had a sixth reason —his friends would feel very bad if he did it. Leon had been able to resist his suicidal preoccupations during his lonely high school years, but after a few months at college in which he had grown close to his roommates, his need to kill himself became overwhelming. The challenge to his past isolation and deadness from his new friendships was finally pushing Leon toward suicide.

Leon wanted to hold on to his depression far more than he realized. He sees himself as always having been on "the losing side of the law of averages." He gave his dissatisfaction with his own average at college after studying hard all term as cause for his depression and sign of his bad luck. After a college mixer at which he met no one, he rode the subways and stood for a long time at one station in Harlem in a challenge to fate to see if he would be mugged. He considers it a bad omen that two of his favorite professional football teams lost on the day after he was admitted to the hospital. During the time I saw him, after his favorite team won its crucial game, he dreamed that in the last minute they lost.

Leon saw defeat as preferable to victory, but for the most part he sought an impregnability that prevented both. He had a recurring fantasy in which he was a medieval citadel under attack. He drew a map to illustrate the deployment of his protective armies. Areas were indicated in different colors to mark his social, academic, spiritual, and emotional defenses. Most of his forces were concentrated in the academic realm. Leon's map is a powerful symbol of his emotional state. He feels that he will survive only as long as his defenses hold.

Leon sees life as war and himself as the ultimate weapon. It is easier for him to see danger as an outside attack than to see his own destructiveness. After an incident in which his roommates had disappointed him, he dreamed that he was an executioner who had to decide whether people should live or die. He condemns them to death and "some kind of angel came and killed them all." Leon clearly sees himself as the Angel of Death. His suicidal preoccupations and his depression mask an image he has of himself as sitting on a time bomb that is "getting ready to explode." When I questioned him about the anger and destructiveness suggested in this image, he is quick to tell me that the most that would happen is that he would "quietly and nonviolently" kill himself.

Leon's need to hide his anger was bound up with his need not to blame his parents for his problems. He insisted that he had little relationship to them, liked them from afar, but was always irritated with them when at home. All the incidents that he related of his childhood cast his mother in the role of dampener of his or his father's pleasure or excitement. His father handled the situation by being away much of the time, leaving his mother to rule the house. Leon felt that he and his parents had never been able to talk about anything, but expressed no anger or bitterness over this. His suicide note conveys the quality of his family life.

Addressing his letter to both his parents, Leon wrote that by the time they read it he would be dead and that they were not responsible for his act. (In suicide notes, such statements specifically freeing particular people of any blame or responsibility are usually to be read psychologically as meaning the opposite.) He added that he was depressed and could see nothing coming out of his life. He went on to dispose of his possessions, leaving his tapes and tape recording equipment to his mother and requesting that his favorite tape be buried with him. From beginning to end, Leon's note is about communication from beyond life. He tells his parents that it is too late to reach him but goes on to leave them equipment which permits him to speak to them, like the Angel of Death he dreams he is, as a voice from beyond the grave. In asking to be buried with the tape of melancholy songs he played again and again as accompaniment to his suicidal thoughts, Leon is almost literally asking to be cemented for all eternity in his unhappy, isolated relation to his mother. It is not surprising that his TAT (Thematic Apperception Test) stories had the repetitive theme of a parent's affection for a dead son.

Although preoccupied with suicide for a long time, the next student only became overtly suicidal after the death of his mother. His story makes clear that his tie to her when she was alive required his own emotional death. He says with a flat, depressed intensity, "I don't think life should be lived if it isn't worth living for its own sake. No one should stay alive for anyone else's sake." It is clear that he feels he has lived or not lived for her sake, not his own.

Larry was a twenty-six-year-old graduate student referred for evaluation following a serious suicide attempt which he barely survived. He had been preoccupied with suicide since his sophomore year in college and had made three previous attempts. Neatly groomed and casually dressed, he seemed alternately fearful and lifeless. He says he tries to have the least possible contact with people, has only the few friends he made in high school, and spends most of his time studying in his room. While he shares an apartment with two other students, they merely live together and do not socialize. He protected himself against letting me know or reach him by attempting to stop any observation or interpretation of his behavior by quickly saying, "It is possible." Insisting on the futility of our talking and on the futility of his life, he said he could stand back and listen to our conversation and that it was like a grade Z movie. Standing back, listening while grading himself and others were characteristic ways in which he defended himself against involvement. He kept insisting that nothing can change his life to a degree that suggested a determination to see to it that nothing did.

Larry's one close relationship with a woman was shaped by his need to retain his deadness and estrangement. He lived with a woman named Jill for six months, which he describes as the liveliest, happiest, and most spontaneous time of his life. Nevertheless when the time came for Jill to leave for Europe, where she had planned to live, he made no attempt to persuade her to stay and did not seriously consider going with her.

When Larry met Jill, his mother was dying of cancer. When I asked him if the fact that his mother was dying made him more willing to be involved with Jill, he said he had wondered many times if that were the case. During the six months after his mother died and Jill had left, Larry made several suicide attempts. Although he felt they had more to do with Jill than his mother, he insisted that he was not bothered by missing Jill, but by his lack of control over the situation. The need to deny her importance to him and the pain of losing her were further expressions of Larry's general deadness.

Larry attributed the origins of his lifeless, isolated existence to being the only child of an overbearing mother and to having a father who was removed and out of things. One of his earliest memories vividly dramatizes his family situation. When he was about seven his father was away for a day and his mother was going to a shower. He does not recall what he was doing, but feels he must have "been playing in a way my mother didn't like." His mother screamed at him that she would not go to the shower because of him. Now he thinks she was looking for an excuse not to go. But the situation conveys not only her use of the role of martyr, but her message to Larry that if he is playful, mischievous, or alive, she will not live or enjoy anything.

Larry saw his mother as refusing to let him grow up. Until he moved into the dorms when a college sophomore, she refused to let him have a door on his room and insisted on her right to open his mail. She seemed to have been particularly fearful of his involvement with girls. Larry felt his mother tried to live her life through him. As he spoke, it was clear he felt he had performed at school and lived for his mother and not for himself. Yet he had felt lost and out of control in the unstructured life in the dorms and felt depressed and cut off without his mother while he attempted to bury himself in his studies. It was in this period that he first became preoccupied with thoughts of suicide.

Nothing outside of his family has much deep, living reality for Larry. In all his dreams he was back where he grew up with his parents. After our first session he dreamed of Jerry, a lively, outgoing boy he knew as a child and whom he associates with fun. He saw himself as rarely capable of having fun and enjoys himself only when he has had a couple of drinks or smoked pot. It is also clear that he associates fun with separating from his mother, which he is clearly afraid to do. He says, "What's the use of talking about her? She's dead and I'm alive." Psychologically speaking, the reverse seemed truer.

Larry dreamed he had a heart attack. In actuality, not he but his father had had a heart attack a few months earlier. His father had remarried a year before that and seems much happier than when Larry's mother was alive. Larry has been afraid, since the attack, that his father would die and leave him alone.

In dreaming that he and not his father had the attack, Larry feels he is saying, "Better me than you." This powerfully represents his feeling that one life can be sacrificed to keep another alive and that his "death" had been a way of keeping his mother alive. He acknowledged at times he had wished she would die, thinking her death might liberate him. He became tearful in talking of how her death had liberated his father but not him. When I pointed out that he seemed unable to bury her, he replied he would not know how to take the first step with the shovel. His numbness minimizes the distinction between living and dying and creates a middle state in which he figuratively does keep his mother alive through his own emotional death. Suicide is but the final dramatization of this process.

Larry's suicide attempt is not simply a journey toward reunion with a lost loved object. His whole life has been a death tie to an object both needed and hated. In not living he keeps his mother alive, atones for his rage toward her, and preserves their past relationship. What overwhelmed Larry is not simply her loss but the fact that her loss constituted an invitation to life—an invitation his father could accept but that he could not.

Maria "went dead" during her high school years and looked forward to college and a career to bring her to life. Yet she had great difficulty in going away to college, dropped out for a while, and became absorbed with suicide during the year before her graduation.

Slender, attractive, serious and intellectual in manner, Maria, a twenty-three-year-old senior, took thirty sleeping pills for what she insisted were work problems. She told of writing a paper for a history teacher who thought well of her, but of not having followed his suggestions for the direction the paper should take. She feels the paper has turned out badly and will lose her his good opinion. She told of her disappointment in her senior thesis when someone told her of a paper that presents good evidence against her point of view. She said she took a difficult course in math, knew she was doing poorly, but would not take a pass-fail because that was too easy and is now afraid she will get an "F," which will mar her record. Finally she says she is depressed because her adviser is unresponsive.

Maria's feelings about her work both reflected and disguised her feelings about her life and the problems which pervaded it on a far deeper level. Her sense that she will disappoint someone whose good opinion she wants if she follows her own inclinations, her difficulty in pursuing these inclinations in the face of opposition, and her need to make her performance in school a test of her worth were all evident in her family situation.

Maria's father has made a fortune in business despite a sixth-grade education. He still leads what she describes as a working-class life-style. Disappointed she is not a boy, he feels she could "at least marry an engineer who could fit into his firm." He has no interest in her education, ignores her considerable academic success, suggested that she study dressmaking, and offered to buy her a place at their local shopping center. Yet his opinion is important to her and she knows the life she wants and an academic career will only take her further away from him. Maria describes her mother as hysterical, unable to tolerate criticism or suggestions, and given to falling apart under pressure. She tells Maria to do whatever her father wants.

Since she was twelve or thirteen Maria felt she was just marking time to get away from her parents. She saw college as the means of shaping a new life for herself. Now she feels that her life in college is a sham, that her girlfriends do not know who she really is, that she has made a failure of her new life. She says she has no option but to go back home to the situation and the life she detests. She has had virtually no social life in the past year, commenting that she does not enjoy dating because she never wants anyone to see how depressed, weak, and unable to cope with life she really is. Not getting involved with anybody, of course, keeps her tied to her parents. She has really shrunk her life to her schoolwork, feeling that if she could do it well, it would give her the confidence to handle the rest of her life. In the process she seems to have made school into a life-or-death test of her worth.

Yet Maria has clearly been drawn to failure. On the verge of graduating, she sees herself as having lost out. Going on to graduate school would also represent a further break with her parents, and despite her excellent marks and the encouragement of her teachers, Maria had not applied. She now adopted the attitude that it was too late to even try. How hung up she felt in her emotional deadness was reflected in a dream she had shortly before her suicide attempt. She dreamed a dead cat was suspended by its hind paws from a clothesline. Her associations made clear that the cat was Maria.

Maria identified with her father's lack of emotional expression, sensitivity, or responsiveness. In her drive and ambition, Maria also seems to resemble him, but these are not qualities that win her his love or the support of her mother. Her mother's tendency to collapse under pressure has also been incorporated by Maria, although she fights against it.

Maria's suicide attempt was the radical expression of her fear that she would indeed be able to graduate well and might begin to make her own life. Her sense of failure, her feeling that she had nowhere to go but back to her family or to death express how much deadness constituted a persistent bond with her parents and a defense against life. Her attempt managed to fuse, in the act itself and in her perception of its motive, the ambition and emotional numbness of her father with her mother's habit of collapse.

Leon, Larry, and Maria were typical of suicidal students whose intense concentration on academic work was the means they used to deal with existence. The meaning they give to their work served to conceal their sense that they had no right to live. All these students had come from families in which the relationship between their parents and family life as a whole were essentially dead. They had an awareness that their parents required their lifelessness. Although they often appeared to be concerned over failure in school, they turned out to be more concerned with being working drones and not becoming too successful or finding too much pleasure in what they were doing. Like Leon, who saw his academic efforts as a defensive army, these students used the continued deployment of uninteresting and methodical work in the service of a withdrawal from either satisfaction or rage. Their withdrawal signified for them a holding on to the past and strengthened the tie of numbness they had forged in their relations with their family.

Many students continued in college to use contact with their parents to control their own enthusiasm and insure their lifelessness. Elated by a new relationship, excited by school, they would call their parents when they were feeling best, knowing that their parents' lack of response would kill their mood. When happiest, one student described having the impulse to throw herself in front of a train or call her mother, equating the death-dealing power of both with a wry seriousness. Being happy for these students meant giving up the past; giving up sadness meant relinquishing the most secure part of themselves.

When a parent actually died—as had Larry's mother—many suicidal students felt they had no right to continue to live or tried to keep the parent alive and preserve the relationship through their own death. But living independent lives was a stimulus to death whether or not a parent had actually died. Suicidal students were generally lifeless and outwardly compliant in manner. What lay beneath this compliant surface was an enormous fury. They dreamed of themselves as forces that can and do murder the people who let them down, or as people held in the grip of a rage beyond their own control. Suicide and suicidal preoccupation was for them a way of extinguishing their anger.

What overwhelms these students is not simply grief over separating from or losing a parent, but the fact that the separation or loss constitutes an invitation to freedom.* The long-observed phenomenon of depressed patients becoming more suicidal as they overcome their depression takes on new significance in this light. It is said that depression operates to paralyze action and that a lessening depression makes possible an overt, actual suicide attempt. But this is an inadequate explanation for what takes place with these students.

Depression is actually a form of protective deadness which can shield the individual and may even make suicide unnecessary for some. Larry, Maria, and Leon became acutely suicidal when life beckoned most and challenged their familiar depression. They broke down under the stress of probable pleasure, success, and independence. Suicide and suicidal longings are means of recapturing the depression that seems to be slipping away, the means these students used to cling to the deadness they see not merely as their best defense, but as the basic human bond.

---

* Depression in these students does not fit Bibring's description of "an incapacity to live up to . . . narcissistic aspirations" as much as it resembles the "essential" depression described by Weiss in which the individual is bound to a relationship he cannot relinquish.

Suicide for love, the wish to die when love and need are not requited, are traditionally causes of suicide attempts in the young. Moreover, suicide in response to rejection suggests a strong desire for love, life, and involvement and unbearable disappointment over the frustration of such needs. It would seem to be quite different from the deathly tie to parents and the resistance to involvement that has been described.

Yet relationships that lead to disappointment and suicide often have death, disappointment, and depression built into them. The "I won't live without you" message to an unwilling partner is a restatement of earlier disappointments relived with and through a lover who remains aloof. The suicidal often make conditions for life: if I don't succeed, I'll kill myself; if you don't want me, I won't live. Such conditions are not only self-fulfilling, they are meant to be. Just as conditions for love set by one individual on another are designed to kill affection, so are conditions for living designed to kill life, not to sustain it. Such conditions are for the suicidal invariably admissions reducible to the message "I can't love you or live with you, but through my death there can be an enduring bond between us."

Who attempts suicide over rejection? Women students, in response to the failure of a relationship, frequently made attempts which were not serious, but were rather designed to revive an affair that was ending. What was remarkable, however, were the many young women I saw who made serious suicide attempts in the throes of disappointment in love without being aware that they had been hurt by men, and without connecting their depression to the painful experiences they were having with men. Their attempts were more serious almost in proportion to the degree to which they were unaware of, or needed to deny, the source of their pain. That the actual pain of abandonment was greater than they felt able to cope with was clear in their stories.

Lisa was typical of the young women I saw whose anguish over rejection found no clear articulation. Her only expression of despair was intense menstrual pain, to which she attributed her depression and suicide attempt with fifty tranquilizing tablets. She told her story with only the most casual reference to her social life. When asked about it she said in a bland, emotionless voice that she had been infatuated with someone, but he had recently left her for her cousin. Only after her blandness was challenged did she express the pain, hurt, and anger of this experience and reveal she had made a suicide attempt two years earlier after a comparable rejection. Then too she had insisted her response was due to severe menstrual pain. She attributed her depression and suicide attempt to this pain, rather than face the emotional pain she felt so intensely she wanted to end her life to avoid and extinguish it.

Acknowledging physical pain and denying emotional pain were the norm in Lisa's family. Even after she became able to feel and acknowledge that her suicide attempt was precipitated by her boyfriend's rejection of her, her parents kept insisting that only her menstrual pains were responsible. Downgrading the impact of feeling, ignoring the importance of love or its loss, and trying to deal with life in a way that bottled up emotion were long-standing practices of both parents. When Lisa was twelve or thirteen she was terribly hurt by the death of a grandfather who had been close to her. Her mother tried to talk her out of her tears by telling her there was no reason to cry because her grandfather was old and had died without pain. She was unable to deal with Lisa's feelings or even to acknowledge their validity.

A brilliant linguistics student, Lisa had made her work her life and sought relationships that would result in her rejection. When she was not rejected, she withdrew, using her schoolwork as an excuse. Welded to her need to be apart is an impulse toward violence and self-destruction. She sees herself as potentially violent, feeling she could have killed a girl on the ward who pushed her around. When she drew a picture of a man during her psychological tests, she thought of him as her father and wanted to draw a knife sticking into him.

Shortly after her suicide attempt, Lisa had a dream that suggested the connection between her violence, her withdrawal, and her relationship with her father: She was in a ring, boxing against her father, and she won. Lisa revealed that her father, although a writer, had once been an amateur boxer. He and Lisa's mother quarreled continually. While Lisa was close to him as a little girl, when she was about twelve he withdrew from the family to avoid Lisa's mother, who scolded him perpetually. He would write for days at a time in a room in the basement referred to by the family as the "mole hole." Lisa saw her suicide attempt as outboxing her father at his own game, that is, withdrawal. Lisa sees withdrawing as easier for men. Her acute menstrual pains were clearly an expression of how painful she felt it was to be a woman. In late adolescence she developed epileptic attacks which, while controlled by dilantin, reoccurred after rejections such as her recent one. She saw these attacks as withdrawals she could initiate. Her suicide attempt and the partial death of an epileptic unconsciousness gave her the feeling that withdrawal or emotional death was under her control and could be used at will as a protection against pain. Withdrawal, suicide, and death were not merely an expression of her rage with men in general and her father in particular, they were also an identifying bond with a father who handled frustration and rage by withdrawal to his mole hole—a bond that served to block Lisa from awareness of the pain of rejection or abandonment.

Although not attributing her depression to physical causes, Kathy was even more startlingly than Lisa able to blot out her awareness of the source of her pain and depression.

A tall, attractive, friendly young woman, more poised than her nineteen years would suggest, Kathy had no idea why she made a suicide attempt with twenty-five sleeping pills after she had been drinking heavily at a party. She was talkative and vivacious and told me that she thinks of suicide when she feels life is boring. A dream provided the first indication of what was troubling her: Kathy was in a car with Ray, who was driving fast to elude a man who was pursuing them. They had to abandon their car because they had a flat and they started running. The man caught up with them and shot Kathy dead.

In speaking of her dream, Kathy described her relationship with Ray, a fellow of about thirty whom she has seen for a year and who she mentions is a dangerous driver. He had hurt her very deeply by his behavior, and the flat tire after the fast ride is clearly an image for her disappointment and depression. Ray had stood her up the previous New Year's Eve without explanation; all spring and summer he dated friends of hers and lied to her, telling her he had not seen anyone else. Kathy recalls being depressed during these months but did not connect her feeling to anything that had happened in her relationship with

Ray. She related an episode which occurred during this period when she was drinking very heavily at home while studying chemistry. Her book was open to a page on some medication she had in her medicine chest. She thought she might have taken some pills and was unable to determine whether or not she had without going to the medicine chest to see if the pills were still there. She did not connect this with her depression over Ray nor with the similar blackout of emotion that characterized her current attempt.

Kathy had hoped that after a reconciliation this fall, Ray would treat her better. This has not turned out to be the case and he had cancelled arrangements to spend a weekend with her that they had been planning right before her suicide attempt.

When I asked her why she had stayed in the relationship with Ray when it caused such pain, she said this was characteristic of her and told of a relationship she had in high school which lasted for two years although she felt there was something strange about the boy who once, in a minor argument, punched her in the face and started choking her. He stopped when she went limp to indicate her surrender. She nevertheless stayed in that relationship for some time afterward because she did not know how to get out of it.

Kathy's dream makes clear the ways in which she cuts herself off from awareness of her feelings. Her anger with Ray is not expressed directly—it is someone else who is out to get them and even then it is Kathy who gets hurt. It was clear that her attempt was bound up with her mood over the past year, which was related to the pain she felt and the need to cut herself off even from awareness of that pain. Suicidal attempts in the context of heavy drinking served to permit her to act on her despair without clearly or consciously recognizing it.

Kathy's family history documents her feeling that involvement with anyone would be painful. She remembers no affection between her parents and cannot recall ever kissing either of them. Her father worked in a factory, was quiet and "out of it" most of the time except when he was angry. Her parents fought a lot, her father drank heavily and would stop off at bars after work with his friends. He had never finished high school, was opposed to her pursuing an academic education, and wanted her to take a secretarial course instead. Despite her description of her father, Kathy has pleasant memories of him before he began to drink so heavily. None of Kathy's memories of her mother were happy. Her mother wanted her to do nothing but stay in and study, and always accused her of meeting fellows when she went out. At sixteen Kathy started to work full-time after school, earned her own money, and felt entitled to ignore her mother's restrictions.

While Kathy says she is in love with Ray, she insists she is not bothered by his not loving her, saying that she knows he is not the loving type. In fact she feels bitterly rejected by him and cannot confront herself or him with her feelings. Her heavy drinking, her suicide attempt and suicidal thoughts, and most of all her inability to know why she wants to die, powerfully reflect her attempt to ward off knowledge of her own emotions. Her belief that she wants to die because her life is boring is belied by her actual story—it is because her life has become so full of the possibility of intense pain and rejection that she clings to the sense of boredom, has the impulse to deaden her awareness with liquor and to end it with sleeping pills. In doing this, Kathy becomes a stranger to herself and cements herself into the role of perpetual outsider she occupied in her parents' house.

Both Kathy and Lisa share a tendency to become involved in painful, even masochistic relationships with men. To simply say they are reacting to rejection would be misleading since rejection and disappointment seem built into the situation that attracts them and since they make so little effort to protect or disengage themselves. They seem through such relationships to hold on to the dead past. Both young women at one time felt closer to their fathers and felt deeply disappointed by them. Withdrawal, rejection, and disappointment were deeply rooted family styles for both of them. In a sense their current involvements are a means of insuring withdrawal and of holding on to past disappointments.

For both Kathy and Lisa, withdrawal was a violent physical force. Lisa experienced epileptic blackouts, feeling she controlled them and thus her total disappearance from consciousness of what she felt. Kathy drank heavily and in her drinking would make suicide attempts, thus insuring that she would always remain distant from her moments of greatest despair. Suicide for them was the ultimate paradox, the simultaneous withdrawal beyond awareness and return to the dead, emotionless life they had known with their parents.

Although male suicide attempts over a woman were remarkably rare, acute despair over the loss of a male lover was frequent. A common and important factor in suicide attempts among college men is rejection by another man during a homosexual relationship. In no homosexual rejection (male or female) was the student unaware of the relationship of the rejection to his unhappiness. The problem was more the opposite—all the student's unhappiness was blamed on the rejection. Nevertheless it is clear that unhappiness and rejection are actively being sought. When these students are not being rejected in their homosexual relations, they are the ones doing the rejecting. This pattern may be seen among homosexual students who are not suicidal. Homosexual students who were suicidal, however, had death at the center of their adaptive history.

The life-or-death, "I can't live without you" quality suicidal homosexual students gave their relationships derived from their need to recapitulate and relive the intense unhappiness they had known with their parents, particularly with their mothers. Suicidal homosexual students did not turn out to be reacting to guilt over their homosexuality to the degree one might expect. I saw young men with great guilt but often they were nonpracticing homosexuals who were depressed at their isolation. The sense of a death bond with the mother seemed to be necessary to make the homosexual student suicidal. Homosexuality permitted him to have some separate life while not making a break with his mother—that is, he does not reject her for another woman and by identifying with her even sexually, he does not feel he gives her up.

Bill, a college senior who was homosexual, made a serious suicide attempt after a quarrel with Tom, a student with whom he was sexually involved. Quarrels, jealousy, and fault-finding had marked the several stormy months of their relationship. It was usually Bill who felt hurt and neglected by Tom. He is convinced that Tom had lost interest in him and felt he had been overly friendly with some other fellows at a New Year's Eve party. Nevertheless Bill came to life only when discussing the jealousy and arguments that persisted in his relationship with Tom.

In a depressed, inert manner, Bill told me that he had moved from New York to Virginia as a child when his father went there to sell antiques. His mother helped out in their shop. He described hating Virginia because he felt lonely and isolated, thought the other kids were mean, had no friends, and was not good in sports. He tried to discuss how lonely and uncared for he felt as a child without relating it to his mother. He does complain that his parents did not know or care what he felt, perhaps because his mother was "too busy with her own depression." In high school he appeared to have overcome his sadness and isolation for a few years. He was on the basketball team, active in social organizations, and became president of his class. At this time he actively hated his parents and defied his mother's strict, puritanical rules against staying out at night with his friends. Even during this period he would often react to the restrictions placed on him by locking himself in his room.

Bill dates his own chronic depression from the time his mother died of cancer when he was eighteen, the summer before he entered college. His sadness in relation to his mother clearly had a much longer history. He sees his mother as having been depressed all of her life. She did not complain in the last painful months when she knew she was dying and seemed to Bill "beautiful and sad." Bill feels he was closer to her during that period and became tearful when discussing this. Bill feared his father, who would, on occasion, drink and physically abuse his mother. He was told by one of his mother's friends that she would have left his father had it not been for the children.

Both Bill and his father drank heavily after his mother's death. His father eventually pulled himself together, remarried, and seems much happier than he was in his first marriage. Bill feels he has never recovered from her death and attributes to it his insecurity and uneasiness in all his relationships. Since he was sixteen he has been aware of being attracted to both boys and girls. His earliest sexual relationships were with girls. After his first year in college, he was involved with a young woman who became serious about him. Bill felt disturbed by his inability to love her and attributes a suicide attempt he made that summer to this. He first became sexually involved with a man after his sophomore year in college. While he fought it at first, he says he is now clear that he is and wants to be homosexual, feels no guilt, and is quite open about it.

Bill's dreams illustrate the object of his guilt and the source of his conflict: The night he took the sleeping pills, he dreamed he was in the home of a woman school-teacher whom he had in the first grade that he did not like. He was trying to destroy the evidence of something he had done, but was unable to do so. The woman called the police and people were running after him. Bill relates the evidence to the bottle of pills he took. To the schoolteacher he associates both his mother and the separation from her of starting school. When he made his suicide attempt he felt he just wanted to die, now he feels it was directed against Tom. The imagery of the dream, however, suggests that it was even more involved with his mother.

Bill's dreams are all permeated with the repressive unhappy presence of his mother, his anger toward her, and his awareness that he will not escape her, but will become her instead. He says he must identify with her since he predicts he will die at thirty-eight, which is when she died and when her mother died. Conscious of feeling guilty over never having loved her enough, Bill not surprisingly could not tolerate feeling a girl loved him and he could not respond in kind. The experience of female love seems bound up with his guilt over not being able to give his mother whatever it would have taken to bring her out of her chronic depression. In his brief open rebelliousness in high school, Bill found relief in unleashing his resentment at the damage he felt she had done to him. His earliest memory is of being burned by his mother at three or four when she accidentally dropped scalding water on him. The image is expressive of what he feels did occur in their relationship.

Just as Bill as a child dealt with his resentment of his mother by locking himself in his room, so does he deal with his current life in a self-punitive way. He had been an excellent student in high school, had one of the highest IQs of all the students tested, but has just drifted through college and stopped a few credits from graduating. He says he is attracted to Tom because of an aloof, rejecting quality about him. He tends to the domestic details of their life and chain-smokes in front of him when angry since he knows Tom disapproves of his smoking. Building rejection into his sexual life is part of a pattern of self-destructive behavior that maintains Bill's connection to his family, as it was when his mother was alive to keep him contained.

Female homosexuals were an important part of the student suicide problem. Like the homosexual young men, these students made their relationships a life-or-death matter. They were conscious of the pain of rejection, although not of their need to provoke it. Suicidal behavior and the threat of withdrawal often dominated their lives with each other. Typical was the relation between Sally and Ann, whose relationship had survived—perhaps because of—illness, respective suicide attempts, infidelity, and bisexual affairs.

Sally is a twenty-one-year-old senior at college who impulsively jumped seven stories from the window of a hospital where she had been admitted for a checkup. She shattered the bones of her legs, tore her liver, damaged her jaw, and loosened many of her teeth. When I saw her a few days after she jumped, despite her pain and immobility, she pleasantly and coherently told me what happened. She was insistent at first in maintaining she fell, but later said she went out on the ledge to jump, that as she did so she changed her mind and tried to catch a railing but she could not. She is afraid to admit any suicidal intent because of her fear that it will result in her not being allowed to continue at school.

She at first blamed her jumping on the fact that she has missed a lot of school because of illness. Her current hospitalization resulted when she was found unconscious by friends who knew she had an epileptic history. She has had occasional seizures since being at school, and since no disturbed EEG pattern was found she was told they were functional. She said she was upset and angry because she had just been reprimanded for missing so many classes and during her checkup the hospital had not permitted her to attend school.

As Sally spoke more of her life, it was clear that her difficulties in school were the least of the problems that made her feel "everything in her life was going downhill," a striking expression in view of her jumping. She began to speak of difficulties with her boyfriend, Mark, a twenty-nine-year-old man with whom she had spent most of the summer and who was the first man she had been involved with sexually. This fall he took a job which required that he travel extensively; he told her he was too busy to see her and that he "was avoiding her because he was in love with her and didn't want to be," using the fact of an earlier marriage at twenty as justification for this feeling. When Sally thought she was pregnant, he wanted to know nothing about it. Her pain over Mark's rejection of her was further complicated by facts she later revealed—Mark is actively homosexual, and she was introduced to him by Ann, her black, female lover who was also interested in Mark. A month before Sally jumped, Ann had become involved with another woman and Sally had become jealous over this.

Sally's relationship with Ann was central to her depression. On an earlier leave of absence from school, Sally spoke regularly with Ann on the telephone and became upset at the emotional distance she detected on Ann's part. She impulsively and severely cut her wrists, requiring extensive stitching. Ann had also made a suicide attempt because of Sally—in anger when Sally went off with friends for a weekend and left her. Sally's first epileptic seizure occurred while Ann was in the hospital following this suicide attempt. Sally felt guilty not only for Ann's attempt, but for remaining in school after Ann had flunked out. She was very concerned about losing Ann and her blackouts, like her suicide attempt, seemed to say she will not accept life or consciousness without her.

Sally had never thought about a lesbian affair before her relationship with Ann. She had been aware of less sexual interest in men than other girls, but attributed it to the strict, antisexual attitudes of her family. Her relationship with Ann was not sexual for a long time but became so. Ann, however, had been involved with girls before and now openly says she is a lesbian. Sally is not sure she is, feels she was in love with Ann and Mark at the same time, and wonders if she is bisexual.

Sally traced her vulnerability to a feeling she had in her family since childhood of being rejected. Her father and mother were never affectionate with each other or with the children. Her earliest and most powerful memory was of coming to the house when she was about three and feeling upset about something. She climbed into her mother's lap because she wished to be held. Her mother had started reading a magazine and pushed Sally away rather brusquely, saying she had no time for her. Sally recalls crying and leaving the room, feeling hurt particularly because all her mother was doing was reading a magazine. She feels this incident had enormous impact on her but as she talks about it, it is clear that it was a prototype of less dramatic repetitions of the same experience.

Sally also felt rejected at an early age by her father, who made no effort to conceal his disappointment that he did not have a son. In fact he treated both Sally and her sister like little boys, buying them guns, but refusing to get them dolls. She saw him as a rigid taskmaster who whipped them severely with the buckle end of a belt for any expression of disobedience or anger.

Sally describes herself as a shy child, frequently sick, and protected by her mother at least in this regard. Illness was one way she had of getting attention, and although robust in appearance, she continues to have an image of herself as sickly. She seemed surprised, however, that her father had flown in to see her in the hospital. When she told him she had not fallen, but jumped, he left the room, came back, and never referred to it again.

Sally feels she and Ann became friends because they shared a common misfortune: each had felt abandoned by her mother. Sally's mother died of cancer when Sally was fourteen and her father remarried two years later. Ann has been a devoted friend through all Sally's illnesses. Since her jump, Ann has been to see her every day. Sally was planning to live with her when she was discharged from the hospital. Nevertheless she still did not want to make a permanent commitment to the lesbian life. She dreamed she was living with Ann at Cape Cod and Mark and Victor were living nearby. Ethel, who was Ann's music teacher and a very successful singer, was singing at a party Sally was giving for everybody. The mood of the dream was very happy.

In actuality, Ann does not like Cape Cod and will not go there. Sally had lived there with Mark and several other couples. Victor, she said, was Mark's male lover. Sally revealed she had been involved sexually with several men in that house. In her dream Sally is not forced to choose between homosexuality and heterosexuality. She has both. Her involvement with both Ann and Mark, each of whom has impelled her toward suicidal thoughts and acts—suggests how much she has sought to maintain the link of rejection that prevailed with both her mother and her father. Depending so greatly on a woman when she does not want to commit herself to a lesbian life and falling in love with a man whose allegiance is strongly homosexual are dramatizations of the degree to which she expresses her need not to be fulfilled in any relationship at the same time that she believes she is pursuing affection.

Sally's Cape Cod dream also suggests the significance her seven-story jump had for her. She identifies with Ethel, the successful singer whom she has been told she resembles. Sally also sings and seems to feel her suicide attempt has brought her the kind of attention Ethel gets through her voice. Ethel is also someone Mark admires and was once involved with. If Sally's jumping epitomized her sense of going downhill, it also meant to her the opportunity and notoriety of a starring role at the opera. She had been willing to be dead to be noticed and Mark, Ann, and her father had responded—Ann most of all.

Both Sally and Ann had been deeply hurt by maternal rejection. In each other they found some extension of the tie of resentment and need that they had experienced with their mothers. It is no surprise that Sally speaks of their bond as one of shared misfortune. Each has used suicide coercively, to induce remorse or concern from the other. Whatever affection they have for each other, their respective attempts make clear their feeling that the only way anyone will care for them is if they are dead or about to die.

Suicidal lesbian students generally linked affection and death. Their relationships were marked by an alternation between hurting or feeling hurt similar to the seesaw between Sally and Ann. Many lesbian students use suicide attempts to arouse the concern of women they have been involved with and who are rejecting them. But if, after the attempt, they have succeeded in bringing back the woman, they frequently reject her. For such students rejecting or being rejected serve as necessary brakes on involvement. These students saw closeness as inevitably destructive. As one student put it: "All anyone really wants is that you should be dead. People like to have corpses around."

Suicidal male and female homosexual students generally had far more traumatic personal histories than nonsuicidal homosexuals. One does not see in them the overprotective seduction common to homosexual histories. Overt rejection or the loss of a parent through death, and the parental desire for a lifeless child predominate. Using another man or woman to relive their original sense of rejection, suicidal homosexual students remained true to the parent of the opposite sex in both their sexual and emotional lives. Crucial to reforging the bond with their pasts was a conception of themselves as dead.

The patterning of suicide over rejection reflects the tension between the sexes, the degree to which students now try to resist letting the opposite sex become too important to them. Male suicide attempts over women were uncommon. The most seriously suicidal women blotted out the awareness that what depressed them was the loss of a man. Homosexual men and women were not merely an important part of the college suicide population, but virtually the only group which consistently saw failure in sexual relationships as crucial to their suicide attempts. Yet virtually none of the students who became suicidal over rejection were aware of the extent to which rejection and death had been the cohesive forces in their lives.

What emerges from the lives of all the students whose suicide was over rejection by someone they loved and needed is the overwhelming sense that it was precisely rejection that they sought. Students whose suicide attempts were precipitated by rejection served to underline the degree to which deadness and detachment have become needs and are frequently pursued by the young.

Suicide is a way of life for the many students I saw who continually killed their enthusiasm, their hope, their freedom and finally attempted to kill themselves. It is the climax of the ongoing drama they play out with parents in which emotional death is seen as the price of domestic peace.

The method many students chose was not only their last message to their parents, but the climactic gesture that also expressed how they had lived and how they hope to resolve the conflicts that plagued them in life. One student who spent the night on the roof of his dorm thinking of jumping, spoke of it in terms of the tragic fame suicide had given Marilyn Monroe. He had the fantasy that he would call to tell his parents he was going to jump and while they were upset he would leave the receiver hanging and go up on the roof. They would call someone at school but it would be too late. The fantasy reflects the blocked communication that had always existed in his family and his wish to make his parents experience the frustration he had always endured in trying to reach them. He clenched and wrung his fists as he spoke of how much he wanted to strike back.

Perhaps most important is the meaning of his preoccupation with Marilyn Monroe's suicide—the grotesque, grim wish to make a splash by jumping to a notorious death. Sally, whose jump was spectacular, had wanted the attention that would come from it. But the need such students have for a dramatic, newsworthy attempt derives from the intense experience of having been passed over by their parents. "Do I have to die before you'll notice me?" "Do you have to read it in the news before you know I'm dead?" is the cry such students are making. And they are all too willing to die to be noticed.

Physical agony was a last resort for students whose parents never cared about their emotional problems, and only sometimes responded to them if they were literally hurt. Sandra, who severed an artery in a dramatic wrist-cutting suicide attempt, told of less severe wrist cutting in high school which had gone unnoticed by her parents. (Several students had similar experiences in which they never told their parents what they had done, but seemed disappointed their parents had not noticed their scars.) After her recent suicide attempt, Sandra dreamed that she had on dungarees streaming with blood and her mother watched her without saying a word. In discussing the dream she bitterly said her mother would never acknowledge she felt pain and was hurt. The vivid childhood memory of another suicidal student is of being unjustly punished by her mother and sent to her room. She spent an hour working loose a tooth that was not quite ready to come out so as to have an excuse to leave her room and be forgiven by her mother.

Many less seriously suicidal students used the threat of suicide or irreparable damage to themselves as means of reaching people they felt were unavailable. Some students used suicide threats or attempts to try to arouse guilt in a lover who was withdrawing or even to merely express how hurt they felt at the withdrawal. But the suicide attempt which is intended to try to bring back a lover or to sustain a relationship that may be about to end is often only a radical means of prolonging and maintaining the unhappiness and distance inherent in a collapsing affair.

None of the students described are heavily involved with drugs. But while some studies understandably emphasize that suicidal students do not get involved with drugs, drugs do play a part in the college suicide problem. Heroin abusers often have a "what's the difference, what's so special about life" attitude that translates into behavior so inimical to life as to suggest they are looking to kill themselves without wanting to acknowledge it. That many deaths from overdoses of heroin are even conscious suicide attempts is suggested by the many students who made suicide attempts with heroin and survive.

Suicide attempts were common among amphetamine abusers, who were similar to the suicidal students in their attempt to live in contradiction of their own most basic emotions. If suicidal students often turn themselves into drones seeing joyless work as the price of their existence, the amphetamine students drove themselves far harder. Having incorporated their parents' demands, they programmed themselves relentlessly, contained with amphetamines their self-hatred and anger, and at best achieved the living death of robots. But sometimes, as one amphetamine abuser put it, "the machine breaks down." Suicidal longing and suicide attempts often marked the failure of amphetamines to contain emotion.

The suicidal students who were the subjects of this study neither made drugs the main source of pleasure in their lives nor believed that by fulfilling their parents' expectations they could validate themselves. They were adept at turning their lives, their work, their relationships into a series of ordeals. They make conditions on life—often quite literally.

One student had shot himself in the heart—the bullet having grazed his heart, pierced his lung, and came to rest close to his spine. He came into treatment telling me that he would give me six months to make him less lonely, isolated, and depressed before killing himself. This kind of ultimatum, whether given to a therapist, a girlfriend, or to oneself is designed not merely to bring about the end, but to kill whatever relationship comes before it. This young man was treatable only by focusing on the way in which he tried to make our relationship one in which he could be dead and challenge or resist my efforts to bring him back to life. Life is not, as it seems, or as the patient often says, unbearable with depression, but is inconceivable to him without it.

Suicidal students destroy any possibility for pleasure, often believing they are searching for affection at the moment when they are killing it. Their inability to tolerate or find positive experiences reflects the extreme emotional hardships they have gone through in childhood. But the more severe conflicts of the families of suicidal students only dramatize the problems shared by the families of many students today. Pleasure and enjoyment are casualties in the modern war of the family. Too many children are growing up feeling that their mothers and fathers did not regard them as sources of pleasure. Young people today with diminished capacity for enjoyment, or diminished sense of their own ability to give pleasure have for the most part grown up feeling they gave little to their parents. Even in cases where the parents did the right thing, the sense of joyless duty was often communicated.

We tend to regard the capacity for pleasure as a biological fact in which experience determines only the particular sources of pleasure for the individual. But it is not. Children who see they are not a source of pleasure to their parents become unable to be a source of pleasure to themselves, and have few expectations of happiness with others. The unrelieved numbness of the depressed and suicidal students dramatizes how profoundly the lack of parental desire for an alive child can produce people who feel that emotional lifelessness is the price of any relationship with their parents and of survival itself. Unfortunately, we are gearing more and more people for numbness.

Society is fomenting depression in the trend toward the

devaluation of children and the family. The increasing emphasis on solitary gratification and immediate, tangible gain from all relationships only encourages an unwillingness in parents to give of themselves or tolerate the demands of small children. It is not surprising that the family emerges through the eyes of many students as a jail in which everyone is in solitary confinement, trapped within their own particular suffering. The frequent absence of intimacy, affection, warmth, or shared concern, the prevalence of families in which no one had found what he needed or wanted has had a profound impact on this generation.

Out of the most tragic disaffection has come a rising number of young people who are drawn to suicide because deadness has been their only security for a lifetime. Whenever the newness of coming to college, of graduating, of finding a person or a pursuit interferes with that security and threatens to break the bond of numbness that held them to their parents, these students are overwhelmed by suicidal longings. Certainly in their attempts at suicide these young people were moving toward becoming finally and forever what they felt they were meant to be.

10

Impotence:
The Heart
Is a Bullet

SEXUAL WAR has reached such an intense pitch
that sexual relations are often not even a sign of momentary truce, but the most violent arena for the forces
which drive people away from each other. The growing
body of clinical evidence indicating that impotence among
young men is increasing points toward the frequency with
which more and more men discover sex to be only another moment of withdrawal. The impotent students one
sees now are not simply sexually passive. They are usually
preoccupied with sex and actively engaged with women.
But they are men whose fantasies and desires toward
women are destructive and violent. Often they are men
who consciously want to hurt women, who rarely connect
their impotence with their hatred, but who know they regard women as enemies and sex as war.

Perhaps the mildest expression of sexual anger is the
vision impotent students share with many other young
men that sex is a competition in which the goal is to get

the woman and score. This converts relations with women into a game in which neither the woman nor the sensory experience has primacy, but only the sense of having broken down the woman's defenses. One impotent twenty-four-year-old graduate student was finally able to get a date with a young woman he had admired for a long time. He did everything he could to make sure the woman would never want to see him again, but boasted of his success in making the date. Afterward he dreamed he was a baseball player in a close game of the World Series. His team was doing better than predicted. They were down by two runs. He drove in a run. There were two outs. Then some "schlep" struck out and they lost. They still got attention from the press.

Sex for this student is the competitive struggle in which he is both the team doing better than he thought and the schlep who struck out. Turning a young woman into merely an object for self-validation is probably the most prevalent form of hostility among young men. But it reaches greater heights among the impotent. Typical was Steve, who graded all the women he met on a scale from one to ten on the basis of looks, personality, and intelligence. After a date with a woman to whom he gave a six rating, he had a dream that expressed what grading and being graded meant to him: One of his favorite teachers is outside a classroom busily marking papers. Steve is with him. They are so involved in the grading that they ignore a disturbance by radical students going on inside the class.

In his dream, his preoccupation with grading blots out his awareness of the rebellion. In his life, Steve converts sex into a performance which kills his awareness of his feelings toward women. To stop grading, to be potent, would unleash what he fears would be a violent revolution. Instead he reduces his human contacts to achievement tests in which he can give himself a poor mark for premature ejaculations.

Steve saw his life as having been governed by goals his parents had set for him without regard for his enthusiasms. He is currently avoiding rebelling against their wish he go to medical school and distancing himself from his real interest in botany. He wrote a letter of acceptance to a prestigious medical school, as his mother wished, but afterward dreamed he was at a reception at which somebody from medical school was to speak. He was served food, ate it, and became sick. At one point he indicated that he was not going to medical school and a tall man threw him out of the reception. Then he lost his wallet. He was not concerned about his money, but about losing his identity cards.

Steve saw the tall man as his father. He insists he will lose his identity if he does not go to medical school. Yet everything he says indicates that in going to medical school he has no independent identity but is, to use his phrase, "just an appendage of his parents." He clearly feels they will flunk him if he chooses botany; he sees abandoning his former role of fulfiller of his parents' expectations as an abandonment of self. Steve has spent his life achieving for an ambitious mother, whom he sees as never having been deeply involved with anyone, including him. In turning relationships with women into dreary tests, he kills any excitement and revenges himself on women by treating them as inhumanly as he feels he has been treated by his parents.

The image of sex as violence that dominates impotent students goes far beyond scoring. Dwight, a twenty-one-year-old senior, has had difficulty in sustaining an erection or in having an orgasm. A psychology major, he says that he relates to women by becoming a kind of therapist to them: "I get into a girl's problems, rip up the flooring of her mind, fuck her up a bit, and play therapist at the same time." Picking up women in a driven way in museums, subways, supermarkets, or wherever he can, Dwight sees himself as attractive to women because he is "a super-intellectual student and looks somewhat freaky." He sees his relationship with a woman as a trade-off between what they want and his interest in an exclusively sexual experience. He describes his encounters in terms of combat in which he "fires salvos" at women from a distance, keeping them "fenced in" while not revealing himself, and doing his best "to gain control over them." In no way does he recognize that his rage at women and his impotence are connected. In this he is typical of most impotent students, who feel fury and use impotence to control it.

Speaking in an obsessional intellectual way that discounts feeling, Dwight uses speech as a way of keeping his distance from people. He remarked that he often talks to women on the phone for hours in preference to seeing them. He perpetually analyzes the struggle for control that goes on in his relations and measures and evaluates how much interest to show in a woman, not in terms of what he actually feels, but as a stratagem in a game plan. He sees me as a kind of coach who will give him advice that will insure his success in seducing women.

Dwight relates his need to manipulate other people to something that went wrong in his family. He describes his mother and father as people who are never interested in what you feel. He recalls little affection from his mother, but has vivid memories of violent fights with her when he was between six and eleven—after that he withdrew to his room and avoided her. Once he had threatened her with a baseball bat. Another time he hid from her in a closet and when she opened the door he yelled to frighten her. This seems to be very much the way he treats women now— hiding on the one hand and frightening them on the other. Soon after I began seeing him, Dwight had a dream which reflected the connection between his sexual activity and his rage at his mother. He dreamed he had a propeller on his finger; the propeller started spinning and Dwight just took off and flew into outer space into a kind of total darkness or void where he could see the earth below—what he saw was a red-haired woman in a coffin.

The spinning propeller suggests the vertigo of his sexual feelings and the way in which they seem to space him out. The dead woman suggested to him his mother, who also had reddish hair. He has great difficulty in seeing her or acknowledging the pain of their relationship except in a distant, spaced-out way. In a paradoxical way, sex has been Dwight's way of detaching himself from his rage and expressing it at the same time. The few times he has had no difficulty with erection or ejaculation have been with women to whom he was completely indifferent and the pleasure he received sexually was minimal.

Dwight also uses sex to get back at his father. He brags to him about all the women he picked up and how available they are, believing that his father never had such opportunities and feeling that his father is very jealous. He sees his father as burning up with frustrated passions that will kill him. Dwight sees passion as killing both of his parents and actually fears it will kill him as well. It seems to be his anger that he fears will destroy him. When he begins to be sexually involved with a woman he gets tense. He will think of "wanting to fuck the shit out of her" as his anger and tension mount.

Impotent students are trapped in sexual rage and fear over their anger. They may speak with graphic hostility about women, insisting they want to "just grab a woman's crotch" or "fuck her eyes out." Their dreams reveal the violence they see as inevitable in sexual involvement. They recurrently dream of their penises as swords or knives, represent sex as a bloody mutilation, and have nightmares of retaliation.

In reality for many the most direct expression of anger is an emotional withholding of which sex is just a part. One student's violent fantasies were so frightening that he was unable to sustain an erection or have an ejaculation even through masturbation. But he avoided "following through" on anything. Although an excellent student, he had delayed for two years completing the work required to graduate. His need to "beat around the bush" (his favorite expression) in every aspect of his life was his form of striking back at everyone. His rage was expressed through not giving precisely what he thought his girl, his teachers, or I wanted. He would come into my office, announce that he had dreamed a lot, pause, and say that he did not remember any of his many dreams. This pattern of teasing and withholding pervaded his life.

Contrary to what most impotent students believe, sexual pleasure with a woman is not what they want. Nothing insures them better against the danger of involvement than its absence. Pleasure is not simply the casualty of the student's rage and concern with performing, but what he needs to avoid. The imagery that these young men use to describe their lives reflects how profoundly aiming at performance rather than pleasure is designed to prevent them from becoming too engrossed in any pursuit. One student related his story rapid-fire, as though trying to cover every detail of his life in his first hour. He says he has a tendency to try "to complete things without getting too much out of them." He describes his sexual life in these terms, saying he "really doesn't want a girl-friend, he only wants to get laid." His lack of enthusiasm for sex is even the analogue of his problem with studying, for he cannot get involved in reading because he perpetually looks ahead to see how many pages he has left.

The usual explanation for the increase in impotence is male fear of sexually free women. Young men do alternate between fear of sophisticated women who might compare them negatively to other men and the hope that such women will lead them smoothly into sexual experience. But a woman's desires only become a burdensome obligation to young men who already have difficulty in seeing her as a source of pleasure.

Impotent students shared with many potent students the feeling that it was more important to satisfy the woman who would judge their performance than it was to satisfy themselves. Such concerns exist long before actual sexual failure has occurred in their lives. These students, however, had less an interest in a woman's happiness or reaction to their performance than a fear that letting her become a source of pleasure and excitement would leave them too vulnerable. Some impotent students, patients and nonpatients, expected to marry the sort of woman who would not be bothered by their impotence as a way of dampening their own excitement and emotion for a lifetime. This underlies the degree to which they feared close human involvement so profoundly that they were willing to do without pleasure or enjoyment to avoid it.

A need to dampen both their own and their partner's passion is a common trend in today's students. While they can conceive of sexual pleasure achieved against women, or their own sacrificed for them, they find it hard to conceive of an involvement that could be mutually satisfying. Impotent students exaggerate this tendency to see themselves as mechanical people, one of them dreaming of his testicles as two metallic balls dangling from strings. This student wrote down his feelings on cards which he kept in an indexed file and dealt with his life with an obsessional intelligence designed to encapsulate his emotions.

While impotent students try to treat their problems as mechanical failures of their genital organs, their dreams reflect that it is their emotions that plague them. Norman, a twenty-year-old student who had been completely impotent in both casual and sustained contacts with women, dreamed he had a heart attack and became a cardiac cripple. He went to a rifle range in an amusement park. He fired an odd-shaped gun, and not a bullet but his heart came out. His heart bounced along and some doctors examined it and then put it back in his body.

Norman saw his heart as a murder weapon. While he tries to tell himself he is only involved in life as a game, and is in the amusement park of reality for fun, all involvements are far too serious for him to laugh at any of them. He associates all feeling with anger and all anger with murderous rage. His penis is a weapon in a war waged by a damaged heart. His sense that potency means destruction is too strong and too threatening for him to enjoy it. Impotence was, for him, a way of checking his anger and stopping the destructive force he feared. Many of the impotent students saw passion as lethal. One student dreamed of women as cats who go into heat as he approaches them, but who literally burn up from their own excitement and die. Whether their own or a woman's, these students feel passion could never be free of an overwhelming destructiveness.

Both potent and impotent students now try not to get too excited about anyone and aim for coolness as an emotional style. The quality of sexual relations inevitably reflects this abhorrence of involvement. To assume that the tension of impotent men is caused by women's new demands for satisfaction is to overlook the possibility that men who are bothered by women's desires may be generally bothered by women, upset by the intimacy intercourse suggests, and paralyzed by their own anger. What is crucial to impotent students is crucial to many of their generation who are not impotent: the need for emotional distance, for a separation of feeling and sex great enough to engulf the destructiveness they feel is inherent in any close relationship. In their vision of ideal sex as a virtuoso performance to be enacted with changeable, unimportant partners, impotent students reflect a widespread pessimism over the possibilities of affection, tenderness, and need.

11 | **Flunking Out**

YOUNG MEN ARE so avidly geared for cutthroat competition since their earliest years that it is usually taken for granted that all of them want to be winners. But there are students who consciously want success in school and in careers, who are more than intelligent enough to achieve it, yet who find themselves flunking out of school. Acutely bothered by their failure, such students are not dropouts whose distaste for establishment goals makes them choose not to finish college. Even when they complain of a lack of interest in school, they see their boredom as itself representing a failure on their part. But flunking out is for them the best available way out of competitive strife and off the treadmill of frustration where they pursue, with all their available energy, goals they invariably miss.

Why are some students irresistibly drawn to failure? The failure of bright students has often been regarded as a means of passive rebellion against the coercion of parents who demand success and achievement. But the students I saw were not flunking out in rebellion, nor in many cases were they the sons of parents with any ambition for them. The student's failure has been called the result of his identification with a father whom he consciously or unconsciously perceives as a failure. Some of the students who are flunking out do perceive their fathers as failures, but many see them as successful. What is crucial in insuring the student's failure is not rebellion or identification but the message he has received from his father and mother about his own independence and success.

Many of these students had parents who pushed them toward success with one hand while holding them back with the other. Sometimes one parent is pushing and the other pulling, and in some cases both are threatened by their son's growth and independence and are unambivalent in their opposition. In all these situations, students become tied into conflicts over their own success which hold them virtually in thrall.

Typical of students whose parents push them toward achievement while undermining their chances for success is Eddie, a tall junior with a serious manner, who came to see me in the throes of shame over his own helplessness. He told me that he is flunking out of school because he is unable to go to classes. He sleeps through most of the day and has this recurring dream: He is on a roof and is sliding off. He is afraid he will fall and then thinks that he will let himself slide, rather than try to stop. He does this and wakes. Eddie calls this a "cop-out" dream that reflects what he is doing with his life. He feels that he will not try to stop the way things are going in school, that he will hit bottom when he flunks out, and he fantasizes starting over in another country.

Eddie sees school and most of his life as a hassle that is forced on him. He spends most of his time alone, has few friends, drives a taxi on Saturday nights, and sees his family as little as possible. Yet he feels perpetually put upon. He finds himself walking on campus thinking with fury that if anyone tells him to do anything he does not want to do, he will say, "Fuck you! I'll do what I want to do." He is not clear who he is saying this to, but in his associations to this incident, he begins to trace the origin of these feelings to his parents.

In most of his stories of his parents there is a recurring theme of being controlled without regard to his pleasure or interests. His earliest memory is of being stopped from playing with other children by his mother, who came to take him home three hours before any of the other boys went in for supper. At home he had to play by himself until dinnertime. His father appears to be the controlling force in his current school situation. A scientist who went to Columbia and did well there, Eddie's father has always assumed that Eddie would go there too.

Eddie's father appears acutely competitive with his son and seems to pressure him into taking courses in which he cannot possibly do well since he has no interest or ability in them. Although interested in painting and art history, Eddie took and failed calculus because "you can't be educated without it," a remark he admitted simply reflected his father's opinion. His father demands so strongly that Eddie continue like this through college that Eddie feels "no relationship is possible with my father unless I graduate."

During our sessions it became clear that both of Eddie's parents had bound him up in their frustration with each other. When he was seven years old, his mother discovered that his father was unfaithful to her and there was talk of a divorce. Instead his parents bought a new house and car and appeared to settle down. But his father's lack of enthusiasm for his mother has always been evident, and his mother made a point of her discontent with his father, confiding in Eddie that she considers him a failure in his work. She expresses an excessive interest in Eddie's relationships with women, disapproving when she sees Eddie is strongly interested in anyone.

Since having to please his parents to his own detriment—whether socially or scholastically—arouses considerable resentment in Eddie, it would seem natural to assume that his flunking out of school is merely an expression of rebellious anger against parents who seem so little concerned with his needs. But his experience of life as a series of duties he must fulfill pervades everything he does and effectively blocks him from rebelling at all. When he chooses his own courses in subjects he likes, he sees any work expected of him as requiring an act of submission on his part. He tends to see all personal relationships, including his therapy, which he sought for himself, as obligations. He has little feeling that his own actions and decisions can improve his life. He has difficulty asserting himself in situations in which people are using him. He told of several squatters who had moved in to his apartment. One was a casual friend who came for a few days, never left, never paid rent, and brought in others. Despite his anger, Eddie felt unable to kick them out and resolved the problem by finding a new apartment for himself and moving out.

As Eddie's pessimism and passivity were challenged, there was improvement in his social and scholastic life. Over Christmas vacation he became involved with a woman for the first time in a year. When I saw him after vacation, he related a dream he had entitled "The Lion's Teeth."

A girl comes to his apartment, looking for someone else.

They make out and she leaves. He goes looking for her. A girl behind him says, "You shouldn't threaten me." When he turns around, she says, "I didn't mean you." He is walking around campus taking ten-foot strides. He is then in the lobby of the student center and his father is in the Lion's Den (a student cafeteria). Eddie is taking the teeth out of a lion's jawbone which is lying in a sand-filled ashtray. All of the teeth are decayed and dirty. The sand turns fluorescent purple and some girls who are helping him scream that he should cover it. He puts a clear plastic over it. He then sees a glass case containing the dead body of a hippie. As he throws the lion's teeth into the glass coffin, the corpse begins grimacing and reviving. Some policemen are there and Eddie backs out to avoid incriminating himself. He joins his father in the Lion's Den, where a film is in progress. A girl is with them and comments on the film, which seems to have something to do with his sexual activity. His father becomes furious and starts to throw glasses at the screen. Eddie is about to hit his father with a broom when the dream ends.

Eddie associates the lion (the Columbia symbol) with his father and himself. The dead hippie and the decayed lion's jaw seem to be representations of both of them, counterparts who are bound together in a common lifelessness. Images of sex appear in the dream against a background of death—the skeletal jaw, the decayed teeth, and the sand. But the teeth have magical power to revive the hippie's corpse, and to cause the sand to glow with vitality, images which vividly convey the quality and sense of Eddie's sexual resurrection.

Eddie sees any emergence into life, any sexual awakening as threatening to women. He feels that everyone—women in general, his mother in particular, and his father perhaps most of all—prefers that he be entombed in a shell, the glass case of the dream. Being a man has always led to conflict with his father, as it does in the dream. Even when Eddie expresses political opinions counter to his father's, he relates that his father becomes hysterically angry with him. In his associations he also saw the hippie as mass murderer Charles Manson, a connection which suggests how destructive and dangerous he believes his potency is.

Eddie assumed the girl in the dream was Linda, with whom he had become sexually involved during Christmas. He is not too enthusiastic about the relationship (he compares his feeling with his father's lack of enthusiasm for his mother) and says he does not want to be trapped. He says Linda was reluctant sexually and complained that she would not use a diaphragm and that he had to use a condom (the plastic of the dream). Nor does he connect her reluctance with the fact that Linda had said she feels he hates her. On some level her feeling is not unfounded. Eddie's behavior is full of hostility and rage, especially toward women, whom he believes all want to imprison him as he feels his mother does. He shows no interest in Linda as a person and thinks he should break off with her "because her breasts are too small." Although his relationship with her has made him feel better than he has felt for some time—as reflected in the image in his dream that he is virtually a giant who can take ten-foot strides—he is not able to express any positive feeling for her.

Eddie's need to deny his potency and to minimize the virility and strength he feels as a result of his sexual experience results in his dreaming that the girl was not really looking for him. Similarly, in the session after we had discussed his dream in terms of the dangerous conflict with his father his potency presented, Eddie retreated from this idea, saying that he could not conceive of his father as being threatened by him since his father did well at college and insists that he graduate too. But while he retreats to this defense, Eddie gives more and more evidence to contradict its validity. He recalled an incident where he handwrestled with his father. It was a stalemate. His father's hand was swollen and cut from trying so hard. Eddie, however, was satisfied with a draw and admits he probaby did not want to win. His need to present himself as a loser, or at least a nonwinner, carries over to all his relationships and activities. When he told stories of things that had happened to him, if they turned out well for him, he would leave the ending off.

It began to become clear to Eddie that his insistence that he is a loser and not even a potential threat to his father was part of his need to curb his effectiveness so as to avoid conflict with his family. While Eddie is unsure if he shares his mother's view of his father as unsuccessful at work, he does see him as unsuccessful in his marriage. He feels his father is "too straight and tight" to enjoy sex. He says he wishes his "parents would have an orgy somewhere and leave me alone"—implying that he sees their interference with him as a product of their frustration.

Eddie has been consistently undermined by his parents. Their lack of passion for each other appears to have caused them to crush any passion Eddie might feel, whether for work that interests him or for women. To compete but not to win, to pursue goals but to fail to achieve them seem to be the double message Eddie has been given by his family.

Unlike Eddie, Andrew is not under parental pressure in

his daily life at college, but his family situation has operated for years to tie him up and to insure his failure. Andrew's father is successful at work and found in his career freedom from the wife who constricted and controlled him at home. Andrew's mother had succeeded in restricting Andrew's freedom to be effective both socially and academically and had left open no exit from her control.

Andrew is a tall, slender nineteen-year-old with a sensitive face. A bright, articulate sophomore, he is nevertheless failing all his courses and has been put on probation. He came in upset at flunking and complained that he is unable to read or concentrate on his work. During his sessions, Andrew often sat on his hands or locked them under his arms. Nor did he restrain himself in his mannerisms alone.

Andrew consistently disparaged himself, turning his dreams, conversations, fantasies, humor, and behavior into targets for his contempt. He introduced his first dream by saying that it lacked imagination. He attributes his feeling of isolation from his roommates to being unable to participate in their bantering conversations. Although they find him funny when he joins them, he avoids them because he does not regard his wit as adequate. When it was pointed out to him that this self-disparagement leaves him with his hands tied in every situation and that his mannerisms seem to give concrete expression to a need to tie himself up, Andrew appeared very embarrassed and went on to reveal that the issue of being tied up even extended to his sexual life.

Andrew began to masturbate at thirteen and would tie his penis with a necktie and masturbate with masochistic fantasies of being tied up by girls. His fantasies can switch to his tying up girls and whipping them. His masturbation has always left him feeling ashamed and ugly. He said he fears the consequences of orgasm, which he describes as guilt and depression. He related that since he was thirteen, he has been "paranoid" about masturbation, fearing that even if his mother were in Europe, she would know what he was doing. In recent years it has left him feeling "depleted and rotten." He stopped masturbating a year ago.

Andrew's perception of life, like his sexual fantasies, reverberates with the sense of being tied up. Andrew said his mother has always infantilized him, never letting him play with other kids after school, but insisting that he come home immediately and wait around the kitchen all afternoon while she made dinner. She also blocked her husband's enjoyment in taking the family for walks in the woods, generally does not respond to his jokes, and disapproves of any remark he makes with sexual overtones. She consistently frustrates any direct dialogue with her and will not respond if Andrew tells her how he feels. She believes in "nothing in excess" and cautions Andrew not to drink too much if he is thirsty, or to dive too much for fear he will become so excited that he will forget to come up. She has blocked Andrew's relation to his father to the extent that when his father has had a good time skiing, he will not even mention the trip to Andrew. Andrew frequently made slips in which he referred to his father, whom he sees as a successful attorney, as his mother's son, implying that at home he sees him in precisely his own position. His greatest admiration is for his brother John, who he describes as the fun in the family and the only one who never let his mother interfere with anything he wanted to do. When John went away to a private boarding school, Andrew, then in the seventh grade, cried with disappointment.

Andrew related an incident from his childhood concerning three dogs his family had while he was growing up. The first was lively and free, fond of chasing Andrew and his brothers and of being chased by them. "We were on his side against my parents," Andrew said. One day he came home from school and his mother told him that the dog had been run over. She had taken it to a vet, who had put it away. He remembers the "hard, hollow feeling" he had when he learned the dog had died. He recalls feeling guilty, as though he were responsible for the dog's death. The next dog they had was a boxer who was friendly, but Andrew always pretended to be afraid of him. That dog died of natural causes. When they got a third dog, Andrew teased it, treated it cruelly, and frustrated it.

Andrew had identified with the freedom and liveliness of the first dog and seemed to have taken what happened to it as a warning of what would happen to him if he behaved as freely. Psychologically he moves from this position to hiding his enjoyment of the second dog. When he becomes the oppressor of the third dog and consistently frustrates it, in effect he is repeating the way his mother has treated him and the way he has treated himself and frustrated his own powers. Moreover, his treatment of the dog reflects the way he would like to treat other people.

Andrew's depression and constriction keep him tied to his mother and her way of dealing with life. He checks his sexual pleasure and his success at school out of fear that pleasure, release, and success will separate him from her. Flunking out of school appears infinitely more painful to him than to his mother, who has offered to take him with her on a trip to France if he is forced to leave college.

With treatment Andrew began to unwind. He started to read and study and made plans to move out of the suite he shared and find a single room in the dorm. By the end of the term, Andrew was elated at having done well in his courses and having found an especially large, desirable room. He occasionally became frightened of his liveliness and would need to check himself. He related wanting to call his mother when he discovered how well he had done in school, but he realized she would manage to dampen his pleasure. His increasing confidence in himself also made him more adventurous socially.

Andrew went to a party and met a young woman. His relationship with Carol reflects where he currently is psychologically. He appears suffused with excitement and expectation, yet he checks his feeling for her, saying that he is not in love with her, but merely wants to sleep with her. His obsessional need to define himself as being in or out of love effectively blocks any feeling from developing. He treats her as a prize, or an obligation, but does not seem to see her as a person. The first night they spent together, they had intercourse twice. After the first time, Andrew felt euphoric. But after the second, he began to fear that he had depleted himself in some way, and in our session recalled his mother's admonition "nothing in excess." Andrew had a dream in which he was being taken to prison for having violated a princess. Andrew said that as a boy he saw all women as princesses, and thinks of princesses as being sexually inviolate. Making Carol his princess and sleeping with her stirs up both incestual anxieties as well as feelings of infidelity toward his mother.

Andrew shies away from both crimes by continually blocking his feeling for Carol and disparaging her as less attractive or less intelligent than the other women in her dorm. He similarly tries to deny any relationship with me in this session by forgetting my name.

Andrew is now in a mood of rebelling against other people's feelings. He appeared to want to force an open confrontation with his family and, to do so, took Carol home with him for the weekend. He related that his mother was grief-stricken at his excitement and exhilaration and full of anxiety at the knowledge that he had a relationship with a woman. When Andrew playfully threw a piece of bread at his brother in violation of a family rule against playing with food at the table, he was startled to see his father coming toward him with clenched fists. Andrew was able to calm his father down, but was bewildered by his father's fury and unable to connect it with his father's reaction to seeing him with Carol. But Andrew's attempt to deal with his parents openly in no way helps him to escape their influence. He has adopted his mother's way of ignoring people's feelings and of seeing freedom and self-expression as hostile. He will push Carol physically if he does not like what she says. Andrew has escaped being tied by becoming the tier, which permits him to hold on to his mother by adopting her behavior.

Other students had placed even stronger restraints on their abilities in order to maintain relations with families. Both of Henry's parents were uncomfortable at his moving ahead scholastically. They preferred him home and working in their business. He had been pushed forward by his own brilliance and the encouragement of teachers, but he justifiably perceived his success and independence at college as destroying his relations with his parents and was prepared to give college up to avoid the conflict. When first seen, Henry had less awareness than Eddie or Andrew of the conflicts that were making college impossible for him. His need to blot out any such awareness turned out to be a reflection of how crippling and deadening his difficulties were.

Henry came in upset because he "has no interest in anything" and has become increasingly suspicious and withdrawn. He has been thinking of leaving school and returning to his home in Omaha, although on a recent visit there he felt estranged from his family and felt there is no home for him there anymore.

Henry said his parents are simple people who have had very little education. His father grew up on a farm and now runs a small business. When Henry is home, he helps him there. His mother is from the city and is a rather devout Lutheran and the main force for church-going in the family. Henry has had more education than anyone in the family and said that when he goes home he feels completely cut off from his parents and his two brothers. Nevertheless he feels that some rapport might be established if he dropped out of college and went to a school near home. It would be cheaper and he could help out in his father's business. His mother did not want him to go to a private prep school to which he had won a scholarship. He had been urged to go by a teacher. Similarly he was urged to come to Columbia by another teacher.

While it was clear that growing up, getting an education, and becoming involved with women are cutting Henry off from his family in very deep ways, Henry makes a point of saying they do not oppose him, that there is nothing to rebel against in his family, and that he likes them. But his dreams reflect how intensely at odds he is with them—a conflict he represents in one dream as a full-scale war: It was the Civil War, except it seemed to be taking place in some kind of family. There was a Confederate leader and a leader from the Union. Although Henry was not a participator, he somehow sensed that he identified with the Confederate leader. The Confederate leader had a weapon, some kind of gun, and he could win the war if he decided to use it. But he decided to wait a year before using it, and meanwhile the war was lost. Then there was a group of people who had deserted from the Confederate army, and the Confederate leader went and somehow faced them down.

Henry identified with the rebel leader and felt that he too had become an outcast by going away to college and getting an education. His dream suggests the way he has dealt with the conflict that his growing up and leaving has precipitated in his family. He goes off to war (school), but holds himself in check, not firing his gun, so to speak. Socially, sexually, and scholastically he holds himself in check.

Although Henry says he is tied to his parents because he is unable to make a home for himself away from them, the reverse seems to be true. Holding himself in check has resulted in his keeping his distance from people and withdrawing from any strong involvement with women or with school. He thinks of going home but feels that doing so would be giving up. This seems to be represented by the deserters of his dream. Henry does not want to desert, but he cannot let himself win the battle either. As a result, he perpetually paralyzes himself. Henry was able to begin to understand this, but clearly fears the conflict this knowledge will cause him. He attempted to deflect it with an easy acceptance, saying, "I guess we've reached the end now."

Feelings, personalities, his own reactions to any of the

events he had mentioned were entirely absent from Henry's account of his life. It is precisely this emotional emptiness that is his main association to his family. He had a dream in which he was lying in bed sick and his mother was asking the men in the family who were priests to perform the last rites. They did not want to do it. Henry's vision of the men in his family as celibate priests represents the extent to which he sees his mother as stopping sexual life. She strongly spoke out against his one sexual involvement in high school. In the nightmare it is she who is anxious to have death rites performed over him. Henry sees her as wanting him asexual and dead, and as being against his virility and education.

Students who are flunking out of school are often educated to fail. Constricted by their parents in their emotional, sexual, and academic lives, they feel unable to pursue either their own interests or those their parents have chosen for them and fall into a lassitude in which they literally flunk themselves out of life. The student does not see the role his parents have played in creating his situation. He tries to believe his family's explanation that they are only concerned for his welfare when, like Henry's parents, they want him to live at home and attend a community college, or, like Andrew's, they offer to take him on a European vacation if he flunks out of school, or, like Eddie's, they want to choose the life they "know" is best for him.

Students do not want to recognize parental envy. One student accepted at face value and without anger the idea that, as he put it, "my father doesn't give me or my brother any money to go to Columbia because he wanted us to go to MIT and study math." Another student whose father was an unskilled worker said his father put down both him and Columbia, saying on the one hand that Columbia was not a good school and on the other that Alex was too stupid to be there. Alex tells him he is probably right. He does not want to lose his relationship with him or to acknowledge the possibility of his father's envy and resentment.

To continue in ignorance of the harmful force their parents exert on them, students adopt a variety of devices. Some, like Henry, feel obliged to go dead. There is no question of confusing Henry's emotional depletion and failure in school with any attempt to rebel against his parents since failure for him comes so explicitly close to submission.

Instead of going dead, many students, like Andrew, adopt a defense that is active and obsessional. Andrew kept himself tied up through his own self-disparagement and his contempt for the woman who gets involved with him. Since this involvement brings Oedipal conflicts into the picture, it would be easy to say that the paralysis of Andrew (and of other students) is simply a defense against anxiety over incestual longings. To do so tells us nothing of what makes these young men different from thousands of other men at the same period in life. It is to confuse a problem in development with the reasons for the failure to resolve it.

Eddie, who dreamed of himself as contained in a glass sepulcher, was typical of the many students who had difficulty in identifying their parents as the source of their rage, but whose anger is close to the surface and who feel perpetually used. Far from flunking out in rebellion against his family, failure for Eddie is but another way of keeping himself encased.

But students who are flunking out do not rebel and are

failing in school partly because they do not do so. They try to push every feeling of their own strength, achievement, and mastery into the background. To avoid seeing their parents as too fragile or too threatened to deal with their life and success, they try to inflate their parents' potency at the expense of their own.

The need to curb themselves, to crush their own potency, and to be perpetual losers arouses an enormous rage in these students. But like Henry, Eddie, and Andrew, they repress their anger and thereby increase it until it is so great it dominates all their other feelings. This only reinforces their fear that being successful is being destructive. Any close human contact is bound to unleash their anger. Their sexual experience is consistently marked by hostility toward women and by the feeling that they must use women to avoid being used by them. These young men might seem to revenge themselves on their mothers in the way they abuse, dehumanize, and tie up their girlfriends. Yet nothing keeps them more effectively tied to their mothers and their parents' way of life than their inability to feel deeply for another woman. The passion that they all see as missing in their parents' marriages, and do not see was discouraged in them, is the last thing they can permit themselves.

Neither rebels against their parents, nor simply the sons of unsuccessful men who were determined to follow in their fathers' footsteps, students who were flunking out were in an abrasive bondage to their parents. Breaking out meant for them escaping the ethos of failure in which they had grown up. Flunking out for them was the state of paralysis—a middle state where they were held static in tension and frustration—in the nowhere between trying and not trying, winning and losing.

12 | Student Revolutionaries Then and Now

"Trashing is no use. We have to work for po-litical action and prepare with guns for real revolution."

"If Bobby Seale is convicted, it would be OK for us to kill a couple of police."

"The judge let me go after a talk on student problems. With fools like that running the system, how can the revolution help but succeed?"

A few years ago these voices were said to herald a movement that would transform America. Now it is said that the angry words that once reached and moved so many students meant little, and the wave of political violence that went so powerfully through the nation was only a passing fad. But anger is still widespread among students, and revolutionaries are still in evidence on campus. What has changed is that the violent few are no longer able to excite or politicize the anger of the many. As a consequence, revolutionary leaders find themselves talking to each other. Violence is now mainly wreaked by one radical group upon another. But from the heady activism of the late sixties to the political war of attrition waged by today's radicals, the people behind the politics have remained hidden in their many acts of violence—the building occupations, the bombings, the confrontations with police, the street fights for the movement in which they used their bodies as political tools. Who are student revolutionaries? Is there a difference between the violent radical then and now?

Sympathy or antipathy to the radical attack on American values and ethics so absorbed psychologists, psychiatrists, and social scientists that they reflected little more than sophisticated ways of disapproving or approving of the students' moral or political stance. Some dismissed revolutionary students as the products of overpermissive families who tacitly encouraged violence by never exerting control over their children so that the children never learned to control themselves. By contrast others held that radical students, violent in justifiable outrage at the social, cultural, and political vices of this society, were "healthier" than nonradicals, and said they came from close, supportive families who encouraged their individuality and with whom they are not in conflict.

Popularization of these views accustomed us to thinking of student revolutionaries as all of those who share a common political, social, and economic critique of society. But the heart of the revolutionary student movement was the translation of the critique into violent or potentially violent political action. Obviously the vast majority of students who may agree with the radical critique are not committed to such action, but for a while violent protest struck a responsive chord in them and they supported student revolutionaries if only by joining in a building occupation. For most students the commitment

to violence is not one they could or cared to sustain. But
the core of committed student revolutionaries radiate the
sense that political violence is their only available life, the
only vehicle for their emotions.

James, an intense and articulate young man, spoke ani-
matedly of the revolution he felt would come to America
through violence. He was sure it was inevitable, but was
uncertain whether it would take the form of a race war
or of a broad-based battle between all the oppressed and
all of those in power. He spent his first year at college
organizing in high schools, at the college, at army bases,
and becoming involved in the violent disruption of university life—all of which he saw as preparation for the revolution to come.

When I first saw him in the winter of 1970, James was
depressed and discouraged about the lack of progress of
the revolutionary movement during this his second year
at college. Political activity had been minimal on campus and SDS (Students for a Democratic Society) had
found organizing difficult and interest almost impossible
to arouse in the majority of students. He wistfully described the mixture of fear and exhilaration of past confrontations with the police. As the interviews progressed,
the Panther trial in New York and the conspiracy trial in
Chicago had revived the movement on campus and he became part of a group * that disrupted a meeting of the
faculty senate and took over the platform to demand that
Columbia provide bail for the Panthers. The success of
the takeover made him outwardly more optimistic about
the movement and also seemed to make him come alive.

But James had far more conflict over the use of violent

---

* The December 4th Movement, named after the date of the shooting
by police of Fred Hampton, Black Panther leader.

tactics than he realized. He dreamed he was leading some dangerous and violent political confrontation that he managed to pull off successfully. He began to run. He was caught in a barbed-wire fence and cut badly. It was gory. He was captured and put in a preventive detention camp. James called this a "political dream" and enjoyed talking about it in political terms. He spoke of the possibility of going to prison for his radical activity and predicted a right-wing reaction in which revolutionary students throughout the country would be placed in preventive detention camps. He believed this would be the only way to stop left-wing violence. He almost seemed to need and want some forceful outside reaction to control his behavior.

In his associations to his "political dream," James came close to the personal origins of the anguish he felt, when there was no preventive detention camp to stop him from doing what he said he wanted to do. He recalled an incident that occurred when he was home visiting his parents over Christmas vacation. A blizzard had left a great deal of snow and ice on the ground. James wanted to drive the car. Both his parents were anxious over his taking it, but his father said nothing and let him have the car, although he had been out and he knew driving was impossible. "Fifteen times," James said furiously, "I nearly killed myself or someone else." He came home and argued with his father over why he let him use the car, knowing the conditions as he did. His father answered that he had not wanted him to take it, but that he felt James would think he was overprotective if he refused and would be angry.

James was certainly indicating here that he needed outside control from his father to prevent his being involved in destructive or self-destructive activity. But emotional withdrawal, not permissiveness, would be a more accurate description of his father's behavior. In this instance, his father wanted to avoid having to deal with James's anger. James was not only furious at his father's withdrawal, but he had learned how to use his father's difficulty in expressing his feelings as a weapon against him. While he began our sessions claiming that his parents supported his aims if not all of his tactics, he eventually admitted with a satisfied smile that he sensed his father was inwardly seething at the things he was doing, but was unable to say anything about them.

These students generally revealed a history of parents with little ability or desire to see their children as they are, or to confront their actual feelings. This kind of emotional abandonment is anything but "permissive."

Amy, a bright, militant, and successful radical leader, was, like most of the radical students, more at ease discussing politics than her personal life. She tried to see her personal feelings in political terms, for example, attributing the loneliness she felt in high school to the fact that all the other kids had more middle-class values than she. She came to Barnard hoping that, as a city school, it would reflect the diversity of social classes in New York. But she soon came to feel that Barnard was insulated from city life. Although politically sympathetic to SDS, in her first year she attended only one meeting and had no real involvement. She tended to be cynical and skeptical as to what could be accomplished by radical action. All this changed when the building occupation and strike of 1968 made her feel she had to take some stand. On the second day of the strike, she went into a building and stayed there until the "bust," when she was arrested. This was a crucial point in her political life; she became increasingly active. At first she was shy and held back at meetings, but she gradually became known and liked and by 1970 she had become part of the hard-core leadership of both SDS and the December 4th Movement.

Amy began by emphasizing the closeness of her family during our early sessions, claiming she discussed her political activities with them, although they are only "creeping socialists" and she is a "violent revolutionary." As our talks progressed she began to suggest that although it was possible to discuss politics with her family, non-political, personal matters were avoided. She then had a rather frightening dream: She was standing by a window with her mother in her parents' apartment on a high floor overlooking the East River. She and her mother were looking at the water. As Amy looked closely at the river, she saw waves growing bigger and bigger, until she realized that they were going to rise up to engulf the highest floors of their apartment building. The building began to crumble and she felt the waves would go on to destroy them and to destroy the whole world. She was calm in the dream and had the feeling that there was nothing she could do to change the situation.

Amy "makes waves" in her dream by looking at things too closely or too long. She felt this had to do with the fact that in our sessions she was examining her life more closely. She then began to relate "making waves" to conflicts with her family that she had long repressed. It was obvious that the family relationship she first described as close and secure she now represented as being too fragile to withstand any examination. The surface calm with which she and the other radical students initially discussed their parents proved to be a mask for the true state of affairs. The connection between the personal and the political was also suggested by the dream—the waves that will destroy Amy and her family will also destroy the world, that is, society. But in her everyday life she had actually tried to concentrate on society and to leave her family out of it.

Both politically and personally Amy's parents withdrew from her whenever she needed them most. When she called her father for advice before participating in her first occupation of a campus building, he refused to give an opinion other than to say he was sure she would do the right thing. But whenever they disapproved of what she did, her parents would say that it was not really Amy who occupied a building or got arrested. They implied that she was led or influenced by others and would say that if she thought about it, or was really "herself," she would see things their way. Commenting that they had always behaved like this, she told of buying a bedspread for her room when she lived with her parents. Her mother said she did not think it was good for her room and insisted that if Amy thought about it, she would see that it was not really her taste.

Amy's parents repeatedly tried to avoid direct conflict by insisting that it was not really Amy who was seeing, or feeling, or behaving whenever she saw, felt, or did anything they did not like. The means they chose for avoiding conflict with her maintained the illusion of closeness without much of the content; they preserved the outward form of discussion without any acceptance of Amy's tastes or character. The only Amy who existed for them was the non-Amy they wished to see.

Nonrecognition or intolerance of her feelings enabled Amy's family to create an illusion of harmony, but left Amy with the problem of coping with the very tastes, feelings, and character her parents denied she had. She had partly adopted her parents' way of dealing with her and was not in touch with her feelings, particularly toward them. She spoke of them in a detached, objective way as being well meaning, but as having a life-style that she would not choose for herself. Kenneth Keniston writes that radical students have achieved a detached, objective view of their parents. But as with Amy, the use of psycho-analytic interviewing techniques makes clear that such detachment usually conceals pain too difficult for the students to face. Their acute ability to see and feel the flaws of society is in striking contrast to their need not to see or know the often devastating effects their family life has had on them.

If Amy was pained by not being seen, Carl's experience with an even more painful family situation had made him want to be invisible. At twenty-two he had been "busted" six times and convicted twice for his political activity and was increasingly attracted to the revolutionary underground. He came to his first interview in shorts and sneakers and wore large, dark sunglasses throughout the session. He sank so deeply into his chair that he seemed to be lying rather than sitting. He spoke in a soft, almost faint voice and seemed generally quite depressed. He began the hour by talking about a conflict he felt over leaving the group he was involved with, a conflict that illustrated the degree to which he concealed his feelings from others.

Carl said he had felt more and more "fucked over" by the group and had had the urge to leave them to join a group of activists who are not college educated and who lived and worked in a working-class neighborhood where he grew up. He felt they had taught him about people and life and that he was more comfortable with them than with the affluent kids in his commune, whom he envied and resented. His bitterest complaints centered around Kenny, whom he called his closest friend. He had been hurt by Kenny's possessiveness toward Ellie, a young woman in the commune, and by how intensely he resented any interest she showed in him. The situation became worse since Arlene, a young woman Carl fell in love with some time ago, returned from Cuba and joined their group. She told Carl she did not want a serious sexual involvement with anyone and he consequently tried to control or hide his sexual feeling for her. Kenny, however, did become sexually involved with Arlene. He came to Carl for sympathy, help, and advice because he felt caught between the two women. When Carl, suppressing his anger, merely replied that he did not want to be bothered with his problem, Kenny acted hurt and had even cried. Carl tried to hide his rage from him much as he tried to conceal his sexual desire for Arlene.

Carl found it far easier to express his anger with the establishment than with Kenny. The night of his most intense frustration and rage with Kenny, he dreamed of having a gun battle with the police. His passivity with Kenny and Arlene went hand in hand with his extreme political activism, a commitment that included becoming skillful with firearms in preparation for guerrilla warfare. He said he was very turned on by Weathermen and he believed he would become part of the revolutionary underground. When I asked whether he felt he would be able to kill anyone, he answered, "Yes." He thought it might be difficult for him at first, but he expected that some of his friends would be killed and that their deaths would make it easier for him to kill.

Carl's need to hide his anger and his retreat from competition had operated to give him a peculiar role in his political life. While not himself a leader (his old friends jokingly ask him why he had not made the big time like Mark Rudd or Bernardine Dohrn), he was often a catalyst for more violent political protest than the actual leaders had planned. When a friend who had become prominent in SDS was leading an outdoor protest (permitted by college rules) against recruiting on campus by a company involved in military production, Carl took over the group and succeeded in getting them to forcibly occupy the building. Once inside, however, he turned to his friend and said, "It's your group. Now it's your baby."

Carl related his difficulties in competition and his retreat from the limelight to a lifelong problem in showing his emotions. "If you show your feelings, you get your legs cut off," was his way of putting it. He came from one of the few families in which there was an actual physical breakup: his mother and father were divorced when he was eight. His father, whom he saw occasionally through the years, belittled any feelings Carl expressed. Forced to support the family, his mother was bitter at her situation and exhausted from work. Carl described her as withdrawn and unaffectionate.

Carl learned to keep his feelings to himself and to stay out of his mother's sight. That he somehow knew the degree to which he was supposed to be neither seen nor heard was rather movingly suggested by his behavior as a child: he slept under his bed. He recalled a recurring nightmare during this period in which he came home from school and rang the bell to his house. He was told by his mother that she did not know him and that he did not belong there. He went to his cousin's house and they told him the same thing. Finally he walked across the

country to his father's house in California and was told
by his father that he did not know him and that he did
not belong there. The dream ended with him disappear-
ing into the Pacific Ocean.

If Carl was able to conceal his feelings in silence,
Nancy, an attractive, witty radical leader, concealed them
in vivacity. "I was a nice girl from a nice family and everything in my life moved a certain way until a year and a
half ago (the time she had been in college) when everything changed," she said. Her current life, which was a
series of encounters with the authorities, would seem to
have changed from the outwardly tranquil high school
life in her home town.

While she was away from school during Easter recess,
the FBI came twice to search her room and she was really
"freaked out" about it. She described being in trouble with
the "pigs" almost every day because she would not pay
her subway fare (in protest against a fare increase),
which resulted in her being chased through subway sta-
tions. She had been in trouble for taking food from the
larger chain stores. She felt there was nothing wrong in
taking food from the large, impersonal supermarkets
since her stealing was less of a crime against society than
they were committing.

When she came to Barnard, Nancy explained, she realized that there was nothing worthwhile in this society
to be part of and the only worthwhile thing was to be
opposed to everything in society. She was active in SDS,
was one of the organizers of the December 4th Movement, and when I saw her she was under indictment and
awaiting trial for her political activities.

Nancy believed that people "aren't interested in your
feelings," and that "really, you should take care of these

things yourself." "These things" seemed to refer to some inner turmoil. Her accounts of her childhood suggested how she came to think that people were not interested in what she felt.

Nancy's parents were both professional people with active careers. As the oldest of the children, she had to care for her two younger siblings. She seemed to have been disturbed not so much by her duties as by the feeling that she was forced to be independent at too early an age and was deprived of a childhood. She described her parents as "nice, pleasure-loving people" who are "sort of like camp counselors." She added that she "sort of liked" some of her counselors, even though she was miserable at camp. She said, "My parents aren't the sort who feel the family has to do something on a Sunday, so if they are together they get along fine because they are doing things that independently they want to do. If it happens that two of them want to do something at the same time, then it's OK. If they all had to go to the zoo together, they'd probably kill each other. They're better than families who feel they have to be together. My parents aren't the type who sacrifice themselves for their children. I don't think parents should."

Nancy defended her family's lack of contact by contrasting it with a constricting family in which everyone was bound together through some overwhelming sense of obligation. She talked as though these were the only possible alternatives. She adopted a tragicomic, humorous tone in describing her frustrations with her parents. For example, while she had dropped out of college, was devoting all her time to her political activities, and was scheduled for trial in a few weeks, her last letter from her mother suggested that she take a course in marine biology that her mother enjoyed some twenty years ago. Needless to say, Nancy had no interest in marine biology. In a light, ironic way, that did not conceal the sadness in her eyes, she told me that her parents were persuaded that her brother stayed home from school to study with his friends when actually he spent all his time with them "tripping acid."

Although she alternated between irony and defensiveness in describing her parents' lack of contact with her, it was clear she had experienced it as a profound rejection. That "lack of contact" was her euphemism for emotional abandonment was most movingly suggested in an event she related that occurred after a tonsillectomy when she was eleven. She was left alone in the house. She developed a severe hemorrhage and became panicky. Her mother had gone out for several hours and told her to call a neighbor if something like that happened. But she knew that the neighbor was a hysterical woman who would be of no help. Nancy recalls standing by the screen window for two hours choking on the blood in her throat, waiting for her mother to come home, feeling that she had no right to expect her to take care of herself in that kind of situation. She was still figuratively drowning in her own juices and unable to trust anyone enough to ask for help.

In 1971 members of the various Marxist revolutionary groups considered SDS and other radical groups without a formal program merely dilettantes, not serious revolutionaries, and implied that their lack of coherent political beliefs explained their personal "confusion." Now radical politics has virtually shrunk to disputes between dogmatic political factions. But John, who was recently arrested for forcibly disrupting a municipal meeting, is typical of to-day's revolutionaries and has problems quite similar to those of Carl, Amy, James, and Nancy.

John sees his willingness to participate in political violence as a kind of redemption from what bothers him about himself. After a recent bloody fight with a "defense squad" of another radical group, John was elated. But that night he dreamed a friend who was in the fight and who was arrested was being beaten by a whole group of people in a line and John was one of those doing it. His friend asked him why. He had no answer and felt like an idiot.

John identified with the friend and spoke of the beating he himself takes as self-administered. Like James, he pursues violent action and punishment simultaneously. His politics are a form of self-flagellation in which he returns from each nightly meeting depressed at his own failure to be more effective—a word he usually equates with violence. Similarly in the recent confrontation where he fought with policemen he knew he would be beaten up. Even in his many fights with other revolutionary groups, his defeat is usual, since the more hopeless the odds the more he is attracted to the fight.

John has confined his life to his political violence. He dropped out of college just a few credits short of graduation, and has made success as a revolutionary the main focus of his life. Although he is always bothered by doubts over whether he has been violent enough in politics, outside of the political sphere he complains of a pervasive passivity. He feels unable to assert himself directly with coworkers or with the superintendent of his building, but is in his political violence able to assert himself on behalf of others he feels are being pushed around. He tries to appear tactful at work, but says if people really knew how angry he is, he would be fired.

John insists that anyone who cares for him take his anger seriously. He is literally determined to be humorless about his politics. At a political meeting where the chairman was particularly inept and amusingly so, his girlfriend made a joke about how comic the scene was. Although he himself had thought it was funny, he became furious with her because he had kept his impulse to laugh in check and was enraged that she had not.

John feels that all his life his parents, and his mother in particular, did not take him seriously or consider his wishes important. He complained of her coldness on the phone in discouraging him from coming home for Christmas. He retaliated against her by giving her a detailed account of a planned illegal political activity. He told me that as a child he got back at her by hiding while they thought he was lost. He still enjoys their worry over the trouble he gets into.

Revolutionary students then and now are plagued by a lifetime of emotional invisibility. Like John, they have been able to reach their parents only through their parents' anxiety for them, or like Nancy, not at all. All described parents who withdrew from them when they needed them most or were simply not available. While I showed this study in advance of publication to the students involved partly to insure that their lives had been sufficiently disguised, most of the students were more interested in seeing to it that their parents would see the material and in making sure that their parents did recognize them.

Most of their parents had a left-wing, or at least liberal background. But their ideology proved to be less important than the fact that political discussions were the closest thing to personal exchanges that took place in the family—a fact that may have some bearing on the use of politics to express feelings that are personal. An atmosphere of polite estrangement seemed to prevail between these parents, who got along well with each other on the surface, but who were not deeply involved with each other. All the students saw their parents as failures as parents. Although they felt their parents were capable of compassion and pity for the weak, the oppressed, or the handicapped, they did not see them as able to experience genuine passion.

Most of the students felt that they too would have difficulty in sustaining personal passion in the intense and powerful way they can experience their political commitment. Their feelings of abandonment and parental withdrawal have left them with a pervasive depression and a diminished self-confidence. They have an unusually great fear of losing out to other men or women in competition for the opposite sex and in competition for various kinds of achievement. Considering their vulnerability and despair, it is not surprising that they feared both closeness and loneliness.

The inner turmoil of these revolutionary students in no way invalidates their critique of society. Since this turmoil is so much a part of youth in this culture today, their very lives are probably a deeper and subtler indictment of American life. Nor can psychological forces alone explain why students become revolutionaries or cease to become so at a particular time and place in history. But to see the rise and fall of the recent student revolutionary movement purely in terms of the withdrawal of troops from Vietnam, the diminution in America's affluence, or the greater unwillingness of society to tolerate violent protest is to fail to see these students as badly as their families have failed to see them.

Identification with the poor and the oppressed permits the radical students to react to poverty and oppression without having to face how personally impoverished and victimized they feel. Their acute sense of injustice derives from the personal, if often unrecognized experience of being victims. To insist that they are products of over-privilege, the spoiled sons and daughters of the affluent, is to insist that the only hunger is for food and the only deprivation is economic. The fervor with which they attack property, the intensity with which they scorn America's concern for money must be understood in the context of their lives. They themselves have suffered in families who more than provided for their material needs, but frustrated their personal needs, and continue to be blind to them as people. In rejecting the life-style of their parents as too concerned with property, wealth, and economic security, what they do not readily say but clearly feel is that their parents were too unconcerned in any meaningful way with them.

In the revolutionary culture many of the students have also found a family that gratifies their emotional needs better than their own families ever did. Since the movement discourages exclusive, monogamous relationships, it does much to soften their anxiety over not being able to form such deep attachments. Many young men like John and Carl who complain of passivity in their personal relations find that they can be forceful and aggressive in behalf of the radical cause. Danger from outside—from police, college, and federal authorities—cements the closeness that comes from shared values and beliefs and tightens the bonds within the revolutionary family. While their own parents, like Amy's or Nancy's, refuse to realize that their daughters are young revolutionaries, not marine biologists, these students find in the reaction of the authorities some adequate response to themselves. They have a need for enemies that transcends their realistic suspicions that their phones have been tapped, their ranks infiltrated, or their rooms searched by federal authorities. Why the craving for violence or violent retaliation?

Revolutionaries then and now are drawn to violent protest as the means of their emotional liberation. Then and now politics plays a key role in their relations with their families, often becoming the only vehicle for their rage. Through the turmoil of their political careers these students and parents often stick together to present a surface picture of harmony. Yet the students have learned their parents' weapons. They now refuse to acknowledge their parents' true feelings at all. It is now the parents who feel obliged to go along with a situation they hate but cannot control. Inwardly furious, they often continue to support the radicals in or out of college. These students seldom hesitate to accept this support and at times seem pleased at so effectively coercing it from their parents. Whether or not the students directly attack their parents, they do say they are "irrelevant." But it is the power of irrelevance, the pain that can be inflicted by treating someone's needs and character as having no *raison d'être* that they have learned so effectively at the feet of their parents.

The active release of rage in violent protest is at the core of the appeal of "revolution" to the student. Such release was enormously attractive to large masses of students who then and now share the radical students' sense of depression, apathy, and resentment. But revolutionary students are not currently able to politicize and tap that anger. The end of the war, the more difficult economic future facing students in the seventies, the unwillingness of society to continue to tolerate violent protest only partly explain the loss of the appeal of violent political action to students.

While the expression of anger or release of rage in political violence can bring students temporarily out of apathy, passivity, or depression, it does not alter the more pervasive despair they have about their lives. More importantly, such anger is not an emotional state most students care to maintain. Even those, like John, who do sustain such a mood are inwardly ambivalent and frightened by their own violence. Turmoil is heightened by the pressure of the movement to prove yourself by committing violence or being arrested. Many who left the movement did so because they felt they were becoming "hate freaks."

The pressure toward violence is not the only pressure that turned students away from the radical movement. Equally distasteful for many is the movement's intolerance of individual expression that is not oriented toward group aims. One young man who wanted to spend the summer studying music knew his group frowned on this and felt too guilty to do it. One young woman who had formed a relatively long relationship with another radical had been denounced by Weathermen friends for being too monogamous.

It was inevitable that students would turn the sense of the absurd that they apply to establishment institutions on to the radical movement. John's outrage at his girl-friend for laughing at what was funny in their group is an accurate recognition that absurdity is a powerful weapon.

One student who was actively involved in radical politics and was beginning a commitment to political violence when he came to college was very conscious of the injustices to the poor and the blacks and the "accident" of his own privileged childhood in suburbia. Four years later, he is still interested in helping the disadvantaged, but has contempt for the radical movement: "They want to control every aspect of their members' lives while preaching that when they come to power everyone will be free."

Student revolutionaries were accused of not providing any alternative plans for a future society. Today's more doctrinaire revolutionaries even try to attribute the inner turmoil of earlier radical students to their very lack of a program. But John and those of his contemporaries that I have seen are more similar to the earlier leaders than they realize. Certainly the emotional lives of students in both groups are far more bound up with immediate violence than with plans for the future. But these students are hardly interested in their own future, let alone in the future of the rest of us. The future will "take care of itself" and the "future as an idea is vastly overrated" are typical comments. They predict they will die young either in the revolution or in some nuclear or ecological disaster that will end the world. The prediction of cataclysm for the world must be seen partly as a projection of their inner world since the inner revolution that consumes them is already in progress, their personal environment has already been poisoned, and the bombs that have destroyed some of them have been of their own making.

Student revolutionaries are not so different than other students. Feelings of never having been seen, of estrangement, of depression and smoldering rage are sufficiently widespread on campus that it is no wonder revolutionaries aroused the empathy of so many students. What is unique to revolutionaries is their adaptation to their conflicts. They are drawn to political violence as the means of transforming themselves. Through politicizing their rage they hope to sever themselves from the personal origins of their frustration and despair. Hemingway, writing of war almost forty years ago, believed that war brought home the sense of individual, personal suffering, that the bell that tolled out death always "tolls for thee." Today's student revolutionaries use their own self-made wars to depersonalize their suffering, to convince themselves that bells can only toll for the impoverished masses in which they disappear.

Emotionally unseen, passed over as people, when revolutionaries go underground they are only giving concrete expression to the emotional state they have long been forced to endure. The political violence practiced by student revolutionaries is an index of a more subtle, ruthless violence. This is the destruction of feeling between parents and children who do not want to know each other, between students who fear getting too close to each other, between people whose common bond is rage at their lives. In this American war for impersonality even revolutionary attacks on social injustice conceal a burial of self.

PART FIVE | The Age of Sensation

13 | Diminishing Expectations

NOTHING SAYS MORE about the American family than how painful a subject it has become. People are often simply annoyed by anything that sharpens, rather than alleviates, their sense of responsibility for the difficulties of their marriages or their children. "They're OK, I'm OK" is the message many Americans want to hear—many will hear no other about their children. Young people who do not collaborate with what is often the sham of family equanimity often inspire more resentment than guilt.

Joseph Heller's devastating account in *Something Happened* of a man's relation to his wife and children captures in an extreme way how angry parents can be when a child's unhappiness challenges their need to see themselves as blameless. Her unhappiness "is infuriating to us," says Slocum about his daughter. "I have been so enraged with her . . . that I have wanted to seize her fiercely by the shoulders, my darling little girl, and shake her, pummel her frenziedly on the face and shoulders with the sides of both my fists and scream, "Be happy—God dammit! You selfish little bitch! Can't you see our lives depend on it?"

In the flight from guilt and blame parents often join their children in blaming society exclusively for their unhappiness. Certainly students have even more reason to bury the pain and anguish of their family situation and blame "the system." Left to their own devices, most of them do, although often such repression leaves them more locked into their painful past. But an exploration of their inner lives quickly reveals how much the students feel they have been the victims of the war in their families— the war between their parents or the war between their parents and them.

Carl dramatized the feelings of many students in his dream of his childhood as an underground combat area in which he and his brother were caught in the crossfire between the Mafia and the blacks. Marion spoke of learning to talk very late because both her parents were so involved in their rage and withdrawal from each other that no one spoke to her. Yet such students do not usually remain innocent victims of the war between their parents. More frequently with daughters than with their sons, mothers made their children their allies. This intense closeness, often following an initial rejection, had devastating effects on children who came to feel enslaved and devoured by their mothers. Daughters of such women invariably learn their mothers' defensive system against men and become detached, managerial appraisers of the men they may intend to marry, seeing them as replaceable as a pet dog. The pattern of initial maternal rejection and subsequent closeness through alliance against a father was a significant and repetitive pattern among homosexual men.

Situations of unidentified, unnamed family tension

were among the most devastating for the students. In such families parents would express no discontent with their marriage, but the student felt he had somehow had a miserable childhood that continued to plague his life. Sometimes the parents appeared to get along by not incorporating the child into their lives. Diana saw her parents as content with each other, but their constantly boarding her out had resulted in her feeling unloved and unlovable as in her image of herself as a drowned rat. Jules, whose parents' pursuit of their respective careers resulted in his being raised by a grandmother and several maids, remained bitter that they had never committed themselves to their children as they had to their work or each other.

In some cases parental discontent is focused on the children. In this process the parents' discontent with each other and with their lives can be buried. The child is judged bad, but the marriage is good. A deep-rooted and often unconscious sense of having been sacrificed to their parents' lives pervades such students. George saw his situation as being in an underwater world where the adults were cannibals mutilating and devouring the children they were supposed to be caring for. He wrote a story about people who survive by draining the life out of others. Both his dream and his story underline his sense that his parents' marriage has survived through their mutual destruction of their children.

Many students had been profoundly damaged by mothers who had tried to control them in ways they could not control their husbands or their lives. Such women had often seen their husbands escape them and the children by burying themselves in work. They proceed to make their children the people who will not escape them.

Women students from such families had a lack of confidence in themselves that was reflected in Rachel's conception of herself as fat, clumsy, the inevitable embarrassment of a mother who demanded she weigh herself daily and report her weight to her. She saw her mother as slim, chic, "perfect." Such mothers invariably left their daughters feeling hopelessly inferior to them and unable to make decisions. And these young women are among the most vulnerable, the most unable to protect themselves from the anger or control of other people.

Alan was typical of male students from such backgrounds. He dramatized his perception that he had never been allowed to develop and satisfy appetites of his own in his dream of being forced to eat an apple pie as big as a house, or his fantasy of a happy world as one in which he could feel hungry. Such students had been fed literally and figuratively according to their mother's needs and not their own. Such mothers invariably attempt to control the career choices of their sons and daughters with a lack of regard for their children's actual interests and enthusiasms that serves to spoil their children's pride and pleasure in work.

How much fathers who withdrew into work inflicted a painful wound on their wives and children was expressed vividly in Ellen's dream of having been numbed or crippled by her father's inattention. When fathers were more involved, often they were so in a controlling way with the entire family and in a belittling, competitive way with their sons. Sons from such backgrounds saw their fathers as simultaneously urging their achievement while undermining their confidence in their ability to succeed. They found themselves behaving similarly with their friends or girlfriends or caught up in a struggle to avoid doing so.

"No one should stay alive for anyone else's sake," said Larry after his severe suicide attempt. Young people with increasing frequency feel their lives consist of fulfilling parental demands made without regard for their interests. They believe their parents want them to look nice, do well, and achieve in ways their parents and their parents' friends can measure. At the same time they think their parents do not care about what they feel or what kind of people they really are. It is not surprising that student rebelliousness takes the form of getting back at their parents through their clothes, their hair, and their marks. They will not look like their parents want them to, they have difficulty in pursuing goals they feel are their parents' and not theirs. They frustrate their parents in the one open language of communication there has been. Their sense of pride and pleasure in themselves is lost in the process.

Pleasure and enjoyment are abilities that frequently seem to have been wounded in the modern war of the family. Children who have grown up feeling that their parents did not regard them as sources of pleasure have suffered a profound narcissistic injury that either numbs them or drives them toward the perpetual pursuit of pleasure detached from emotion.

For most children who have inspired little pleasure, the hurt to pride, the pain and the anger of their early experience is underground—too primal an injury to be anything but buried. They are conscious only of a mistrust of involvement. Several students dreamed of their childhood as the Civil War. They wish the family strife were something that happened long, long ago, but the attempt to treat the family experience as remote and irrelevant to their present lives barely conceals the pain, hurt, and anger beneath. In addition, if one has been dismissed as irrelevant, one learns to use irrelevancy as a weapon to dismiss others. But the attempt to see the war with parents as ancient history, and to dismiss the self-hatred that flows from feeling vanquished in that battle, is ultimately the way of treating oneself as irrelevant, and one's feelings as of little importance.

The burial of frustration and pain, the emphasis on function over feeling, the wish to flee from feeling entirely into pleasurable sensation or emotionless performance fill many students' lives and might seem to be designed for a society which stresses the technological virtues and consumer appetites. Certainly, social thinking since Marx has held that the character traits predominant in most individuals in a society are the product of what the economic system needs to function. Erich Fromm described "consumer-oriented modern capitalism" as needing and producing people able to manipulate each other—people who saw their personality as a salable commodity. Riesman's "other directed" man, as befitted the product of a consumer society, took his cues from others who had become more significant in his working and social life. Whether society was described as consumer-oriented capitalism or as a corporate state, the principle was the same. We were producing the sort of people we needed to make the system work. The family was sometimes seen as a refuge from the marketplace but more often as the molder of the social character our system needed.

But the family has a dynamic of its own; it is not merely an economic institution nor one that has so rigid a relation to the larger world. To see the family as passively reflecting society's economic needs and supplying the demanded product ignores a social revolution as profound as our technological one, a revolution in the status of women, of children, and of human aspiration itself.

Permissiveness, for example, was said by Riesman in his stimulating and provocative *The Lonely Crowd* to reflect parental realization that peers were more essential than parents for the socialization of the child because the rapid rate of change in this society had rendered the parents' values and ways obsolete. Parents cannot decide what is best for their children or even what best means since in this "other directed" culture one's "contemporaries are the source of direction" and judges of values. Parents can only "equip the child to do his best whatever that might turn out to be" or at most help make the child aware of and sensitive to the vibrations of the playmates from whom he was to receive his guidelines. Talcott Parsons spoke of "greater permissiveness to children, more concern with them as persons" as if permissiveness and concern were the same. But they are not.

The upsurge of parental permissiveness and the parental wish to let peers become more decisive in the child's life had another source so obvious that it was easily overlooked. This was the desire of many parents over the last twenty years to use the peer group as a surrogate for their own involvement with their children. More obviously permissiveness was a way of acceding to children or granting them material things when parents did not want or were not able to be emotionally involved and available. What children were given presumably might distract them from demanding that the parents give more of themselves. How little this necessarily reflects concern for a child's welfare was dramatized by James's father, who gave his son the car when he asked for it even though a blizzard was raging outside and the streets were coated with ice. It is not surprising that James, skidding through the streets, was not grateful to his father for the car. This incident was typical of the many stories students told of families who had satisfied all their material demands but few of their emotional needs.

The popular myth of fifties togetherness is exploded by the lives of both the activists of the late sixties and the so-called politically apathetic, materialistic students of today. Both the rejection and the pursuit of affluence reflect the sense many students have that, whether you despise or cherish them, all you can be sure of is your possessions. Despite the affluence there was a profound emotional impoverishment in the lives of the children of many such families. The talk of togetherness and abundance seems to have risen to the extent that neither of those things existed in emotional fact.

The mothers and fathers of today's students were themselves products of a psychological revolution which had transformed their expectations from life. One aspect of this was particularly apparent in attitudes toward marriage. Psychoanalysis itself contributed to a conception of life as perfectible and human relations as the main arena for satisfaction. For people who married in the early fifties marriage was to be the locus of self-fulfillment, of sexual, intellectual, and social growth. Whatever the Oedipus complex in Victorian Vienna, the psychological revolution begun by Freud helped modify the Oedipal situation that would develop after his work had stimulated expectations. In America by the fifties no one would have been satisfied with merely the equivalent of his mother or father. The marriage one's parents had made would not have matched the extraordinary hopes people had of each other.

The romanticization of love and marriage, the belief that the two would coincide reached its peak in the generation of these students' parents. Delmore Schwartz's shattering story "In Dreams Begin Responsibilities" deals with a son whose life has been pure misery. He is watching a film of his parents' first meeting, their deepening love, the excitement and anticipation of each other rises toward the wedding scene. The son rises screaming at the screen, "Don't do it. . . . Nothing good will come of it, only remorse, hatred, . . . and two children whose characters are monstrous." It is no accident that students today continue to be moved by this story.

More than any generation before them, the mothers of these children had great hopes for personal fulfillment and growth that were likely to conflict with the needs and demands of small children. These well-educated, middle-class women were also more aware than any generation of mothers before them of the importance of infancy and early childhood in the formation of character and personality. Being good, psychologically sophisticated mothers was another expectation they had of themselves. These two expectations placed them in an unavoidable existential conflict where they were torn by concern for their children's welfare and their own happiness. Women who had given up or postponed career aspirations sometimes felt engulfed in resentment of their children and self-hatred for letting themselves down as well. At the same time they often found their husbands without much sympathy or understanding for their position and escaping from them and the problems at home by burying themselves in work. Women in the past had been able to bury their frustration with their husbands and with their own lives in devotion to their children. But this was virtually impossible for women who felt they had had other, larger alternatives and had hopes for personal fulfillment.

Faced with unhappy wives in a seemingly unalterable situation who needed great emotional support and children who wanted a father, many men withdrew. The often-mentioned passivity of American men in relation to their wives and children sometimes reflects the father's abandonment of his children to his wife as a way of keeping her occupied so that he can retain his freedom. Having paid the price of his children for his emotional freedom, the father escapes into work or the company of his friends. Society has been easier on bad fathers who are good providers than on bad mothers with successful careers because the American model of masculinity has not until now included being comfortable with feelings, particularly with those of children. Nor has the culture shown a realistic appraisal of the importance of fathers in the lives of young children. If society in the fifties forgave men who defaulted emotionally, their wives did not. Nor were they unaware of how necessary—and how unavailable—their husbands were to them and their children during this period.

When these men withdrew from their wives it was often because they too had been painfully disappointed. These men also expected more emotional understanding from their wives and children than had fathers before them. They were bitter about having been denied understanding, support, and empathy for their emotional limitations. Even men who were not in flight from their families but merely had a traditional vision of their role as men as limited to their work performance could not soften wives who were bitter about their husbands' discomfort with their emotion.

Whether they mean to or not, unhappy mothers and distant fathers have a negative effect on their children. Few women students felt close to their fathers. Many young men were only drawn into empathy with their fathers' situation as it grew to be their own—as the pressure on them to achieve, to escape their mothers made them sympathetic to their fathers' problems at work and their need to escape their wives.

Parents who attempted to live through their children did so in an unhappy and driven way. The message they gave was that their children's achievement must be sufficiently great to justify the parents' unhappiness. Often children were pushed into work one parent might have liked, regardless of their own talents. Some mothers had made their daughters their allies in denigration of motherhood and geared them to see men through their own disillusioned eyes. Fathers had too often given their sons a model of a man who found little pleasure in his wife, was uninvolved with his son, or both encouraged and disparaged the son in ways that give little satisfaction to both of them. From the bitter unhappiness of such family extremes come children who sense that their parents had use for them in so far as they reflected well on them or did not challenge the view they held of what life offered.

Much of family life over the past twenty years has become a paradigm of discontent. Escalating hope for satisfaction is stifled by the reduced capacity of men and women to give, to be with children, to feel protective and loving toward each other. Nothing more thoroughly belies the real concept of the family than the portrait of home life as a factory for producing people who fit into the economic system. The families of many of these students reflected the opposite: built-in discontent, disruption, abrasiveness, and egocentrism. Such families are the breeding ground for depression, impotence, work failure, murderous anger, drug abuse, and people in flight from emotion. No economic system benefits from forces like these which disrupt society. The frequent absence of intimacy, affection, warmth, or shared concern, the prevalence of families in which no one had gotten what he needed or wanted, has had a profound impact on this generation.

Out of this disaffection has come a generation of young people who are trying to stop their own romantic impulses in the suspicion that intimacy may end in disaster. Where the parents of this generation may have expected too much from each other, young people today have gone the length toward becoming a generation of no expectations. This is a generation characterized by a belief that intimacy is dangerous, that the way to live safely is to reduce your vulnerability or combativeness to the low level survival requires. Expect nothing, they seem to suggest. You cannot get less.

14 | The Age of Sensation

WAR IS THE contemporary image for the experience of young people today in work, in friendship, or in sex. The sense of life as war is far more than the residue of injuries suffered in growing up. It is crucial to see the role of the family in reflecting and producing our current difficulties, but as crucial to realize that our difficulties are not merely a snarled family story. Personal discontent is far easier to resolve when the culture provides what Erik Erikson has called "content for the ready loyalty of youth and worthy objects for its need to repudiate." But today the conflicts of family life are echoed a thousand times by the sense of combat that reverberates through American life. Some of our novelists have defined our condition in parables of actual war.

In 1955, when *Catch 22* was published Joseph Heller used World War II to project a vision of life in the fifties: a system that killed body and spirit not through malice, but through selfishness, stupidity, and corruption. Yet the hero, Yossarian, actively resists in an effort to maintain his personal emotional intactness. By Vonnegut's

Slaughterhouse-Five the war is again the image for mindless destructiveness, but escape is possible only through the uncaring detachment of the "So it goes" attitude or the fragmentation and spaciness of Billy Pilgrim. War is used again to portray the impersonal destructiveness of society in *MASH*. But the heroes there are clear products of the system who use their detachment, their pursuit of the pleasurable moment, and their greater cool to outwit the system. In Pynchon's *Gravity's Rainbow,* 1973, we have a nightmare vision of a world after war in which evil and death are triumphant, the Devil rules on Earth, and the best one can do is join in the celebration of his victory, a triumph shown in the devouring relationships of people who are nothing but rapacious appetites.

You cannot be killed if you are already dead (numbness). You cannot be hurt if you withdraw (detachment). You cannot be completely wiped out of you divide your forces (fragmentation). Young people are looking for escape from the war at work and between the sexes. Their personal defenses provide it. But we are a society which is bolstering the withdrawal of men and women from each other and providing social defenses against facing sexual war.

Because women are demanding less protectiveness from men and offering less protectiveness themselves, many young men feel justified in abusing them. The women's movement reflects not merely the demand for greater control of social, personal, and political life, but is partly a banding together of women for support in a climate of male hostility, male refusal of tenderness, friendship, and involvement. For many women, the way of handling their personal difficulties is through objectifying their problems and focusing on the social pressures against them or the social sources of their vulnerability. For some young men relaxing with other men in sports or at bars is the only relaxation they experience with another human being. It is not that men are brothers to each other—the competitiveness that marks their lives often prevents that. Men are, however, brothers in mistrust of women, as women are sisters in their fear of their own vulnerability. What unites men to men and women to women are shared problems, the anger and fear they find incommunicable across the gulf of sex.

Some trends in popular culture attempt to deny the gulf. Unisex is the myth of eliminating the angry differences that cause so much trouble and of bridging the gap between the sexes by denying there is one. Nevertheless, beyond the unisex clothes and haircuts are the personalities that remain distinct and distinctively engrossed in separate problems.

What does unite men and women is the bitterness that drives each toward finding weapons and defenses against the other. "Psychokarate" is now taught at a New York college, a course in the art of psychological weaponry against the assault of feeling. What many young people wish for is the power to take and not be hurt, to advance into human encounters with the best possible armor. While men may exploit women, women may barricade themselves behind a defiant independence and often outdo men in their coolness. Both are creating the contemporary androgyne as the asexual figure of the hater, the exploiter, the lonely, the perpetually angry.

The social defense against rage is now an accessible way of escaping the personal sources of feeling. The late sixties saw the burgeoning of an attempt to live in and through anger while covering up its personal sources. Student revolutionaries won widespread support even among apolitical students because they tapped the rage of people who were unable to find solace or tenderness or protectiveness in each other and who were caught in their own encapsulated wars. The revolution provided an outlet for the expression of anger as well as the experience of closeness between young people protesting social and political outrages. It virtually made anger into a positive bond. The Vietnam war gave a legitimate political sanction to the students' sense of being at war at home, murdered by their daily lives. Political violence also concealed that the sources of rage were far deeper and more personal. For many it was easier to fight for victims who were poor, black, or Vietnamese than to see that they were victims themselves. Most students, however, could not take that pitch of open anger for long.

Society is now moving further toward the politicization of feeling, the objectification of anger into an extended social drama. What were once personal choices are now causes proselytized and offered as the wave of the future. Drug abusers did not simply make a personal choice for drugs, they advertised themselves as cultists. Timothy Leary is only the best-known example of the many who made drugs a cause. Gay liberation is the attempt to shift homosexuality into a problem solely of social persecution. Some people who are confused about their sexual preference claim their fragmentation is liberation and call for the institutionalization of bisexuality as a life-style. People who do not want to have children form the National Organization of Non-Parents, elect a nonmother of the year, and claim they have been persecuted by the dominant culture that stresses marriage and parenthood. What is involved is more than the freedom to be "childfree," take LSD, or be homosexual, or the comfort of being with people who believe as you do. Treating feeling as a political issue permits one to make the enemy external, to turn pain into open anger and avoid the conflicts within.

The politicization of feeling, the open rage of the social defense against pain does not work for the many people who wish to get away from rage entirely. Through different ways and in many forms people seek out fragmented sensory experience as a way of avoiding the tragedy of inner war and outward protest and escaping completely the involvement with feeling.

Sensation is king in a nation in which it seems the best antidote to pleasurelessness and deadness. How widespread is our joylessness is suggested by the number of products whose advertising appeal is "you only go around once in life, so you have to search for all the gusto you can." Or "If I have only one life, let me live it as a blonde!" The appeal of such slogans is as an antidote to present deadness, not future death.

The cultural trend is toward greater and greater stimulation of appetites. Everyone wants what the other person has. Once the most distinctive form of American envy was the desire for material possessions. But now the most rapacious greed is for experience. Openness about sexual life, articles on bisexual chic, group sex, or swinging singles bars provide glimpses into experiences other people are having and describing in glowing terms. Magazines are directed at the burgeoning interest in other people's lives. The growing confessional tendency in fiction and in life in this culture is moving people toward unquestioning belief in the unquestioned good of trying everything.

While the pressure to experiment may move some people to become happy samplers of each other, it has the effect of turning many more into rapacious consumers of people and often dissatisfied customers. The tendency to envy those who seem freer, the wish not to want to miss out on anything are bound to create difficulty between people each demanding of the other "I want what they have!"

Given the demand for more and more experience, it is not surprising that attitudes toward forming a family have changed. In the nineteen forties and fifties the family was seen as a refuge from the harshness of the world outside; today a husband or wife is all right as long as he or she contributes to the need to grab all possible pleasures. The family increasingly reflects the larger social need to replace commitment, involvement, and tenderness with self-aggrandizement, exploitiveness, and titillation. The state of the family expresses how much the demand for pleasure can become bound up with the desire to hurt and become merely another weapon in sexual war.

The cultural trend toward a preference for the meaningless, disconnected sensory episode reflects a hope that by seeing all experience as casual and meaningless, it might be possible to drain the anger and pain from life. Our fascination for the broken and episodic nature of reality is reflected in the increasing numbers of young people for whom life is at best a series of sensory experiences, of momentary pleasures. Many students described themselves as wandering Odysseuses with no Ithaca to return to and no desire for any road map of what they might encounter along the way. What they knew of life was often so unhappy that they preferred to live in a perpetual unknown. As Odysseus told the Cyclops he was Noman, put out the giant's eye, and escaped unharmed, so increasing numbers of young people today hope to blind themselves to the monster they feel is within them and to escape unharmed by denying who they are.

Students embrace irony and are ironic about themselves. Their attempt to treat life as an absurd joke, to bury the past, to treat it as irrelevant is more than a philosophic perception or a sophomoric attitude. If one's early life has been empty, if one's parents have merely gone through the motions of love belaboredly, if one's culture provides no adequate content, one is being prepared for a life that lacks a sense of connection with feeling, value, and point. The sense of the absurdity of one's life, however, that develops in such a situation, becomes an active defensive operation.

Hugh was the most dramatic example of a student who loved to tell stories of life's absurdity—of towns disrupted because a garter snake was thought to be a cobra, a woman killed out of suspicion that she was a witch, the wrong man executed for the killing. The sense that people live and die in a meaningless, absurd way is a reflection that no matter what they did nor how much they pleased their parents, they were annihilated anyway. As Vonnegut would say, So it goes.

Many students try to detach themselves from the experience of pain, anger, and emptiness by believing in the meaninglessness of life as a positive value. In a perceptive article praising the best of rock music for its celebration of random events, Richard Meltzer compliments a performer on his "attempt to free man by rescuing him from meaning rather than freeing man through meaning." Fragmentation is the attempt to create a personality that is never the sum of its parts and never whole. Young people today cultivate fragmentation in their attempt to bury their past disappointments with their family and to reach a sense of disconnection that will protect them against present disillusionment. By avoiding becoming a whole, these students hope to avoid the pain of recognizing what they feel, what they are, what emotional possibilities they have. George, who becomes in his dream a disassembled jigsaw puzzle in order to avoid being slaughtered, makes dramatically clear what an effective defensive operation disassembly can be.

The random or indiscriminate use of many drugs and of psychedelics in particular is expressive of the craving for fragmentation. Such drug use would not be important as a cultural phenomenon if the fragmentation it encouraged was not a defense being used by increasing numbers of young people who achieve it without drugs.

Taking drugs is an American pastime that reflects this culture's growing flight from feeling or preference for the experiential solution to all problems. Psychiatrists are as caught up in these trends as everyone else. The drugs prescribed for students aim at diminishing the subjective experience of rage, fear, or depression so the student can deal with his life better. Reduction of anxiety, anger, and depression is regarded as inherently good, although the drug that detaches a student from such feelings usually puts him out of touch with himself and his life. He becomes less trouble for everyone concerned, but no less troubled. His experience of actual turmoil has merely been replaced by numbness, a kind of mock serenity.

The drugs some students take contain more contradictory elements. If some drugs students abuse aim at detachment, others produce pleasurable sensory changes that can give a feeling of being alive that provides a temporary antidote to pervasive lifelessness. But it may be as effective to try to alter mood through affecting pleasurable sensation as it is to alter the subjective experience of rage or fear. If the students' cure for the lifelessness that plagues so many of them is brief and illusory, it is certainly no more so than the detached functioning that is the goal of psychiatric drugs. Neither solution provides more than the illusion of a cure. Certainly, all the drugs Americans use and abuse are clear indices of what forces most threaten our lives, of the sensations we hope will overpower our deadness or turmoil.

Americans are supposed to believe in the unbridled goodness of success. Yet competition in this culture is now so intensely violent and combative it arouses guilt, humiliation, and profound conflict. Marijuana is the drug of a culture that needs help in subduing its competitiveness and its rage. The drug virtually took over the country, spreading from the youth culture to the adult world with a wildfire rapidity that suggests how united we are in our problems. Abused most by those who are determined to constantly subdue their combativeness, it is needed by many more who are riveted in a life of vicious competitiveness, but need at least a temporary respite. Its popularity is not surprising in a society in which everyone feels the wounds of daily combat and many find release in a drug that makes them feel humane.

We are supposed to be a culture whose young people are convinced of the dangers of technology. Yet the envy many young people have for machines is evident in the degree to which they strive to be like them. Amphetamines are the symbol of a culture in which feeling counts less than smooth functioning. Increasingly people try to resist their depression with a simulated high, they try to hone themselves into efficient automatons able to perform at school or with friends by behaving according to someone else's standard.

The many young college women who drive themselves to act against their feelings, to push themselves toward men they do not want to marry, toward careers that are not interesting to them reflect the flight from feeling whether they take amphetamines or not. What is significant is the replacement of actual emotion by the sensation of the operator who gets things done, who wheels and deals despite all odds.

Young people today are supposed to be open to life, experience, and each other. Heroin is only the radical symbol of the trip many young people want to take to the state of total self-containment. What student heroin users derived from the drug, what they were willing to risk everything for was heroin's power to render them impervious to other people, to be the pleasure source that makes sex irrelevant, that made the taker invulnerable to being left, disappointed, or needed. What student heroin users also dramatized was quite literally the junkie mentality rampant in this culture. The "rip him off before he rips you off" law of the heroin world, the sense of everyone being out for himself, determined to get his particular fix for a lifetime is an extreme and pessimistic statement of the quality of relationships in this culture. Heroin's power to confer total imperviousness to people is a growing dream of escape among many young people who do not take the drug.

The need to resolve problems over intimacy and commitment has long been described as part of the task of the developing young adult. Rudolph Wittenberg in a sensitive and thoughtful book described the recognition of time, including an awareness that life goes on whether or not you exist, that must be dealt with in this period. But the desire to postpone time, to prolong adolescence appeared with increasing frequency in the case histories reported by Peter Blos and others in the 1960s. Commitments to work or to someone loved are often viewed as confining and restricting the subsequent variety of experiences available, as reducing one's options. The delay of such commitments once seen as the natural wish of many and a problem for only a few is turning out to be a widespread cultural change. The affluence of the sixties made careers and work seem less urgent; the economic anxiety of today makes them seem more crucial. But an increasingly high percentage of young adults even in challenging professions regard work as merely the means to money for leisure. Comparably, most go on to acquire greater adeptness in relations with the opposite sex with little change in affective tone. This is not simply a matter of young people prolonging the time they take before making commitments. Instead increasing numbers are trying to work out life-styles in which there are only tentative commitments, all options remain open, and nothing in the way of sensation or experience is sacrificed.

Some hope that such life-styles will augur a new and creative openness. Robert Lifton in an interesting essay draws on the myth of Proteus, who could transform himself constantly, to propose a positive vision of contemporary protean man. But just as the mythological Proteus uses his transformations as a defense in a wrestling match against being forced to give his questioners self-knowledge, so do young people today use a shifting self-image, a sense of playing different roles as a defense against emotional self-knowledge.

Popular psychology reflects the widespread desire to

see life in terms of its multiple possibilities and people as actors who can play all possible parts. Psychodrama, which was once conceived of as therapy for a few, has become a cultural preoccupation. How much role playing is a powerful expression of what we feel we are is brilliantly parodied by John Barth, whose novel *The End of the Road* opens with his hero announcing, "In a sense, I am Jacob Horner." Suffering from a psychic paralysis in which he has long periods of blankness, he encounters a mysterious doctor who prescribes "mythotherapy." Jake is told to see his life as a series of dramas and to cast himself as a suitable character in each. "It's extremely important that you learn to assume these masks wholeheartedly. Don't think there's anything behind them; there isn't. Ego means I and I means ego and the ego by definition is a mask. If you sometimes have the feeling that your mask is insincere—impossible word! it's only because one of your masks is incompatible with another. . . . The more sharply you can dramatize your situation, and define your own role and everybody else's role, the safer you'll be."

People out of touch with their feelings are strongly drawn to the idea that life consists of playing roles. Game playing (transactional analysis) goes even further in providing a model for how to deal with other people without even considering one's feelings toward them. Transactional analysis is predicated on the assumption that since people are incapable of intimacy and spontaneity, their lives consist of a series of games. What people need are strategies that would strip risk (and whatever spontaneity remains) from the games they play. If role playing is a parody of our concern with narcissism, game playing is a parody of our concern with mastery and control.

Shifts in the most serious analyses of the nature of human reality also reflect our changing vision over the last fifty years of what people are like. The emphasis on ego psychology in the nineteen forties, fifties, and sixties reflected a concern with functioning and behavior that epitomized an age of increasing technological sophistication. It was a far cry from the emphasis on sexual repression that characterized the Victorian origins of Freud's first formulations. Freud made us aware that much of the behavior that did not appear sexual was sexually motivated. The psychoanalytic contribution to our understanding of sex in the last forty years has been the realization of how much behavior that appeared sexual was not sexually motivated. But the desire for dependency and power expressed through sex are being reinterpreted today in terms of narcissistic concerns and frustrations that seem so dominant in contemporary patients. A burgeoning concern with narcissism is inevitable in a culture drifting toward a sense of people as actors and relationships as the stage for eliciting applause if your role is well played or derision if it is not.

From the suicidal students who are willing to jump off a building to be noticed, to the young woman who would like to be so famous an actress she could have a public temper tantrum and be applauded for it, to the young man who wants to be successful enough—it does not matter at what—to flash a card and move to the head of the ticket line, the need for special recognition and attention is pervasive. While his or her family may frustrate a child's need for recognition and stimulate an obsessive need for it, it takes a particular kind of culture to reinforce the feeling that recognition and attention are bigger than life.

However much we ridicule Evel Knievel's attempt to leap over a canyon with his motorcycle, we are a society that will pay the money to encourage the big jump.

Increasingly Americans find that although they have many of the sensations they want, they, like the hero of Heller's *Something Happened*, "don't enjoy anything anymore." Twenty years ago detachment, impaired ability to feel pleasure, and fragmentation were considered signs of schizophrenia. That adaptive measures that were considered extreme twenty years ago are now found necessary by vast numbers of people is a measure of our social difficulties. People increasingly see life in terms of emotionless behavior. More and more people are coming to believe that human problems are insoluble in traditional human terms.

Increasingly what unites people in this culture is a sense of shared misfortune and depression, a feeling of impotence in the face of forces they feel they cannot shape or control. Erikson put it sensitively when he wrote that "any span of the [life] cycle lived without vigorous meaning, at the beginning, at the middle, or at the end, endangers the sense of life and the meaning of death in all whose life stages are involved." Erikson pulls back from confronting the forces today which endanger meaning. But we are a culture in which the elderly are treated as refuse, the middle-aged in their discontent turn to the young for salvation and in so doing undermine youth by expecting the impossible from them.

The lessening of open conflict between the generations has led some people to assume things have significantly improved. But this is not the case. What had the effect of bringing the generations closer together toward the end of our involvement in the Vietnam war was the students'

sense that their parents' generation finally shared their bitterness toward society. Watergate did not split the generations, but rather united them in greater mistrust of
governmental institutions. Similarly, the economic anxiety of today further dramatizes the doubts of both generations about the ability of our institutions to manage
fairly or at all the distribution of wealth and resources.
While such harmony in despair may come to serve as a
collective stimulus, at present it is a sign of our collective difficulty.

Some of the new social options that serve to relieve the
strain between the sexes have led some to assume that our
problems will correct themselves. Greater freedom to remain single or marry but not have children has possible
benefits for everyone. It not only results in many people
who would be happier single not marrying, and many who
would be happier without children not having them, but
also will give everyone greater freedom to make these
choices for themselves and to make them in their own
time. The option to marry when one is ready, to decide
when and if to have children could only benefit a society
in which so many children are unwanted.

The discontent of women with children and of men
with work, the sexual war that ensues when each sex
imagines the other has it easier have led many people to
seek a coalescence of opportunities, responsibilities, and
experiences between men and women. As women are accepted into business, the academy, and the professions as
equal competitors, many are becoming aware of the pressures that men confront and the limitations there can be
on a career. As men become more involved with young
children, some begin to understand the intense emotional
demands children make on women. But finding a balance

between a child's needs and a woman's aspirations is a dilemma to which neither psychoanalysts nor feminists have yet found adequate solutions.

The possibilities for the future depend on recognizing the present cataclysm for what it is, and on not leaving to chance that the forces for greater accord between the sexes will win out. How much contempt for love and tenderness is becoming institutionalized is only suggested by the new entertainments we are devising for young children. The frog, the toad, the troll who turns into a prince when kissed by a generous woman was the mainstay of the fairy tale, taught to little boys and girls for centuries. But in the modern Sesame Street version of Beauty and the Beast when the princess kisses the beast she turns into one. Similarly when the prince comes to kiss Sleeping Beauty, the touch of her lips puts him to sleep too. We are teaching our children that intimacy brings out the worst in everyone, a theme rife in contemporary adult fiction. Certainly the sexual revolution begun in the fifties as a protest against the work and ambition ethic has become a revolution against intimacy.

American society is virtually encouraging the forces that lock men and women out of passionate sexual and intellectual commitment. No matter what her experience in growing up, the young woman today is subject more and more to the social and cultural pressure of peers who regard vulnerability with contempt and romanticizing a man as a weakness. Young men today seem more frequently than young women to be romantic about the opposite sex; but the romance is usually for the far-off, unavailable woman. Students today have no difficulty appreciating the Inamorati Anonymous, Thomas Pynchon's fantasy in *The Crying of Lot Forty-Nine* of an organization dedicated to helping people kick the love habit.

Young people in our culture are creating new ideal men and women who can resist each other's impact. The emotion-free, the controlled, the impenetrable, the invulnerable are praised as having characters geared for survival in the modern emotional jungle. Students who had achieved maximal detachment from feeling are, in the new youth culture, admired as unshakable. One contemporary hero is Hugh, who had fixed his life like a chess game he could never lose. His primary involvement was with his writing, he kept his fiancée at a distance, remained detached from his friends, and carved from his withdrawal a small arena in which he could always be in control of what happened. One contemporary heroine is Marion, who felt she had escaped the trap of female vulnerability. Her most powerful commitment was to her work. She had contempt for women who "got slaughtered" in relations with men and prided herself on her coolness. She saw her fiancé as easily replaceable.

There are young people who do make a deep commitment to work they genuinely enjoy. Despite the difficulty virtually all had in caring for someone of the opposite sex, some are able to do so. But even those best able to be involved with work or another person are subject to what now amounts to a cultural pressure to experience all, to exploit others, and to evaluate what they do, think, and feel according to a standard of quantifiable, solitary gratification. In a culture that institutionalizes lack of commitment, it is very hard to be committed; in a nation that seems determined to strip sex of romance and tenderness, it is very hard to be a tender and faithful lover. We subject even young people who are most apt for life to an extraordinary pressure to be less than they are by idealizing the forces which are pulling us apart.

Psychoanalysis has traditionally aimed at putting people in touch with their feelings and effecting a harmony between inner and outer life. It has been condemned by Philip Rieff and others for not providing transcendental values, but for aiming to make "man happy in his own grim and gay little Vienna." Most young people today would find the goals that Rieff condemned as too limiting, too expansively optimistic. The reaction of some graduate students who read this book was to agree with the portrait of life it presented, to say that relations between the sexes were terrible, but to affirm that the momentary experience was all there was to live for and that the fragmentation and burial of feeling described were necessary and inevitable. Such frankness about one's own life, such lack of sham and hypocrisy and indeed the lack of self-pity that accompanies their resignation are appealing qualities of this generation. Can any society, however, want to institutionalize this pessimism? Will the transmission of culture be an indoctrination into the need for self-protection?

Efforts to institutionalize adaptations that work against sexual harmony work against society as well. The pessimism and lack of confidence people feel in each other have led them to feel that "anything goes" that reduces unhappiness for the moment. A laissez-faire attitude, which is appropriate and humane toward individuals who find life works for them in a homosexual marriage, or an acid commune, is no longer appropriate with regard to the development of political movements lobbying to embed them in the social fabric. "Anything goes" is a legitimate attitude for consenting adults toward each other or the neighbors they like, but for a culture to declare it as a credo is to miss entirely the stake all of us have in the harmony between the sexes and in the family as the irreplaceable necessity of society, whether we as individuals want to form one or not.

Winston Churchill said democracy is the worst form of government except for all other forms. Something similar might be said of the family. The only students who are able to escape the dreariness of the endless competitiveness of society described by Riesman, Fromm, and others, who can resist the cultural pressures toward cool self-interest or the junkie mentality that dictates that anyone or anything ought to be ripped off are those who have the self-confidence and love and capacity for pleasure that were initially given them by their parents and are now theirs to give. Students who have experienced such despair in their families that they feel required to eliminate their family from their emotional lives are forever tied to their parents by the love they never got, by numbness, depression, and inability to feel pleasure and love for a person, a cause, a career.

The flight from emotion seems the only available way out in a culture where people are increasingly adrift in their discontent. Belief in society, in institutions, or even in social change once enabled people to repress their personal unhappiness and to find purpose in their adult lives. But disaffection with the possibilities of happiness between men and women now finds little surcease in religious, political, or social institutions. Social distress and private unhappiness have coincided, political and social movements now reflect and reinforce private disbelief and disaffection. As a nation we are plagued by, but do little to reverse, the erosion of our confidence, stability, and even our home on this planet.

If our physical environment is worth saving, our emotional environment is equally so, perhaps more so since the one provides us with means to sustain life and the other is our humanity; the one offers the necessities of survival, the other a life worth living. There is no government agency to protect our emotional environment and speak for its primacy in our lives. Yet the equivalent of air and water is the source of the ability to feel, to love, to endure. And the most endangered of our vital resources is people.

References

Barth, John. *The End of the Road*. New York: Avon, 1960.

Becker, Ernest. *The Denial of Death*. New York: Free Press, 1973.

Bettelheim, Bruno. "The Problem of Generations." In *The Challenge of Youth*, edited by Erik H. Erikson, pp. 76–109. New York: Doubleday, Anchor Books, 1965.

Bibring, Edward. "The Mechanism of Depression." In *Affective Disorders: Psychoanalytic Contributions to Their Study*, edited by Phyllis Greenacre, pp. 7–48. New York: International Universities Press, 1953.

Bieber, Irving. *Homosexuality: A Psychoanalytic Study*. New York: Basic Books, 1962.

Blos, Peter. *On Adolescence: A Psychoanalytic Interpretation*. New York: Free Press, 1962.

Brown, Norman O. *Life Against Death: The Psychoanalytical Meaning of History*. New York: Random House, Vintage Books, 1959.

Erikson, Erik H. *Childhood and Society*. New York: W. W. Norton, 1950.

——. "Identity and the Life Cycle." *Psychological Issues* 1 (1959): 1.

——. *Insight and Responsibility*. New York: W. W. Norton, 1964.

——. *Young Man Luther*. New York: W. W. Norton, 1958.

——, ed. Preface to *The Challenge of Youth*, pp. vii–xvi. New York: Doubleday, Anchor Books, 1965.

Freud, Sigmund. *Civilization and Its Discontents.* Translated and edited by James Strachey. New York: W. W. Norton, 1962.
——. "Mourning and Melancholia," (1916). In *Collected Papers.* Vol. 4, pp. 152–170. London: Hogarth Press, 1949.
——. *Totem and Taboo.* New York: W. W. Norton, 1962.
Fromm, Erich. *Escape from Freedom.* New York: Farrar & Rinehart, 1941.
——. *Man for Himself.* New York: Rinehart, 1947.
——. *The Sane Society.* New York: Holt, Rinehart and Winston, 1965.
Grinspoon, Lester. *Marijuana Reconsidered.* New York: Bantam Books, 1971.
Hartmann, Heinz. "The Application of Psychoanalytic Concepts to Social Science." In *Psychoanalysis and Social Science,* edited by Hendrik M. Ruitenbeek, pp. 63–72. New York: E. P. Dutton, 1962.
Heller, Joseph. *Catch 22.* New York: Simon & Schuster, 1955.
——. *Something Happened.* New York: Alfred A. Knopf, 1974.
Hemingway, Ernest. *For Whom the Bell Tolls.* New York: Charles Scribner's Sons, 1940.
Hendin, Herbert. *Black Suicide.* New York: Basic Books, 1969.
——. *Suicide and Scandinavia.* New York: Grune & Stratton, 1964.
Hendin, Herbert; Gaylin, Willard; and Carr, Arthur. *Psychoanalysis and Social Research.* New York: Doubleday, Anchor Books, 1965.
Kardiner, Abram. *The Individual and His Society.* New York: Columbia University Press, 1939.
——. *The Psychological Frontiers of Society.* New York: Columbia University Press, 1945.
Kardiner, Abram, and Ovesey, Lionel. *The Mark of Oppression: Explorations in the Personality of the American Negro.* New York: W. W. Norton, 1951.
Keniston, Kenneth. *The Uncommitted: Alienated Youth in American Society.* New York: Dell, Delta Books, 1960.
——. *Young Radicals: Notes on Committed Youth.* New York: Harcourt Brace Jovanovich, Harvest Books, 1968.
Leary, Timothy. *The Politics of Ecstasy.* New York: College Notes & Texts, 1965.

Lifton, Robert J. *Death in Life: Survivors of Hiroshima.* New York: Random House, Vintage Books, 1969.

——. *History and Human Survival.* Edited by John Simon. New York: Random House, 1969.

Lowell, Robert. *Life Studies* and *For the Union Dead.* New York: Farrar, Straus & Giroux, Noonday Press, 1956.

McGlothlin, William H., and West, Louis J. "The Marijuana Problem: An Overview." *American Journal of Psychiatry* 125 (1968): 126–134.

Marcuse, Herbert. *Eros and Civilization: A Philosophical Inquiry into Freud.* New York: Random House, Vintage Books, 1962.

Marx, Karl. *Economic and Philosophical Manuscripts of 1844.* Edited by Dirk J. Struik. Translated by Martin Milligan. New York: International Publishing, 1959.

Meltzer, Richard. "The Aesthetics of Rock." In *The Age of Rock: Sounds of the American Cultural Revolution,* edited by Jonathan Eisen, pp. 244–253. New York: Random House, Vintage Books, 1969.

Mconikoff, Alvin; Rainer, John; Kolb, Lawrence; and Carr, Arthur. "Intrafamilial Determinants of Divergent Sexual Behavior in Twins." *American Journal of Psychiatry* 119 (1963): 732–738.

Parsons, Talcott. *Social Structure and Personality.* New York: Free Press, 1964.

Pynchon, Thomas. *The Crying of Lot Forty-Nine.* New York: Bantam Books, 1967.

——. *Gravity's Rainbow.* New York: Viking Press, 1973.

——. *V.* New York: Bantam Books, 1964.

Reich, Charles. *The Greening of America: How the Youth Revolution Is Trying to Make America Liveable.* New York: Random House, 1970.

Rieff, Philip. *The Triumph of the Therapeutic: Uses of Faith after Freud.* New York: Harper and Row, 1966.

Riesman, David; with Glazer, Nathan; and Denney, Reuel. *The Lonely Crowd: A Study of the Changing American Character.* New Haven, Conn.: Yale University Press, 1950.

Roheim, Geza. *Psychoanalysis and Anthropology.* New York: International Universities Press, 1950.

Schafer, Roy. "Talent as Danger: Psychological Observations on

Academic Difficulty." In *The College Dropout and the Utilization of Talent*, edited by Lawrence A. Pervin, L. Reik, and W. Dalrymple, pp. 207–222. Princeton, N.J.: Princeton University Press, 1966.

Schwartz, Delmore. "In Dreams Begin Responsibilities." In *The World Is a Wedding*, pp. 188–196. New York: New Directions, 1948.

Skinner, B. F. *Beyond Freedom and Dignity*. New York: Alfred A. Knopf, 1971.

——. *Walden Two*. New York: Macmillan, 1948.

Vonnegut, Kurt. *Sirens of Titan*. New York: Dell, 1959.

——. *Slaughterhouse-Five*. New York: Delacorte Press, 1969.

Weiss, Edoardo. "Clinical Aspects of Depression." *Psychoanalytic Quarterly* 3 (1944): 445–461.

Wittenberg, Rudolph. *Postadolescence: Theoretical and Clinical Aspects of Psychoanalytic Therapy*. New York: Grune & Stratton, 1968.

Zilboorg, Gregory. "Differential Diagnostic Types of Suicide." *Archives of General Psychiatry* 35 (1936): 270–291.

Index